MICHAEL COLLINS

THE MAN WHO WON THE WAR

T. RYLE DWYER

MICHAEL COLLINS

THE MAN WHO WON THE WAR

MERCIER PRESS

WHAT YOU NEED TO READ

MERCIER PRESS

Cork

www. mercierpress.ie

Trade enquiries to CMD,

55A Spruce Avenue, Stillorgan Industrial Park,

Blackrock, County Dublin

© revised edition: T. Ryle Dwyer, 2009

ISBN: 978 1 85635 625 1

10 9 8 7 6 5 4 3 2 1

A CIP record for this title is available from the British Library

 Mercier Press receives financial assistance from the Arts
Council/An Chomhairle Ealaíon

Printed and bound in the EU.

Contents

To Anne Maria, Bob, Kevin and Jack MacSweeney

Preface

In formally proposing the adoption of the Anglo-Irish Treaty on 19 December 1921 Arthur Griffith referred to Michael Collins as 'the man who won the war', much to the annoyance of Defence Minister Cathal Brugha, who questioned whether Collins 'had ever fired a shot at any enemy of Ireland.'[1]

Amid cries of 'Shame' and 'Get on with the Treaty', Brugha complained that Collins had originated the story that there was a price on his head and had personally sought the press publicity which built him into 'a romantic figure' and 'a mystical character' that he was not.[2] Most of those present sat through the tirade in stunned silence, because there was no real substance to his wrath, just spite.

Even Brugha's strongest critics – those who disagreed with what they believed was a grossly distorted assessment – accepted that he was telling the truth as he saw it. Collins has since been the subject of numerous books, but nobody has ever documented a single instance in which he fired a shot at the British.

Yet when Griffith rose to wind up the debate he had begun three weeks earlier, he made no apologies for the remark to which Brugha had taken such exception. 'He referred to what I said about Michael Collins – that he was the man who won the war,' Griffith explained. 'I said it, and I say it again; he was the man that made the situation; he was the man, and nobody knows better than I do how, during a year and a half he worked from six in the morning until two next morning. He was the man whose matchless energy, whose indomitable will carried Ireland through the terrible crisis; and though I have not now, and never had, an ambition about either political affairs or history, if my name is to go down in history I want it associated with the name of Michael Collins. Michael Collins was the man who fought the Black and Tan terror for twelve months, until England was forced to offer terms.'[3]

The assembly erupted with a roar of approval and thunderous

applause. It was the most emotional response of the whole debate. Those who had listened to Brugha's invective in embarrassed silence jumped at the opportunity to disassociate themselves from the earlier embittered remarks.

Who was this Michael Collins, the man who could engender such passion, and what was his real role in the War of Independence? How was it that two unquestionably sincere, selfless individuals like Griffith and Brugha could differ so strongly about this man?

Unfortunately the papers of Michael Collins have been scattered to the four winds. His nephew, the late Liam Collins, had Michael's papers for many years. In the 1950s he lent them to the writer Rex Taylor, who returned them in the same condition he received them. When another English writer subsequently approached Liam Collins, he lent him five diaries and never saw them again. The writer denied ever receiving them and the five diaries have vanished.

In the 1950s some of the Big Fellow's earlier papers were sold, such as records that he kept as secretary of the Geraldine GAA club in London and essays that he wrote while attending night school at King's College, London. They were purchased by Marquette University in Wisconsin. The man in charge of the archives told me that the university gave the Geraldine material to the GAA for its museum, and was planning to give the other material to UCD.

Knowing the story of what had happened to the diaries I approached Liam Collins for access to the Collins papers in 1980. Figuring that people were always looking for things but never giving him anything in return, I enclosed copies of some letters that Michael Collins had written to Austin Stack. I had been allowed to copy them by the late Nannette Barrett, a niece of Austin Stack.

Liam Collins promptly invited me to meet him. Before responding to my request for access to the papers, he had one question – what did I think of Eamon de Valera? I had already written a short biography of de Valera for the *Gill's Irish Lives* series, so I told him that while critical of de Valera's role regarding the Anglo-Irish Treaty, I felt he did a magnificent job in handling Irish neutrality during the Second World War. Liam immediately announced he would give me the metal trunk of papers, and went on to explain that he was sick of people denouncing de Valera. Growing up, he said he was friendly with de Valera's youngest son, Terry, and was often in the de Valera home, where Sinéad de Valera frequently told him of her admiration for Michael Collins and what he had done for their family while Eamon de Valera was in the United States in 1919 and 1920.

All too often it seemed that people were expected to argue that if Collins was good, then de Valera was an ogre, or the other way around. Following the initial publication of my book *Michael Collins: The Man Who Won the War*, I was invited to take part in an RTÉ discussion programme chaired by Joe Duffy. The programme included Tim Pat Coogan, Mary Banotti and the late Brendan O'Reilly. It was like a Michael Collins love-in.

It became so obsequious that as an historian I felt distinctly uncomfortable. At one point I complained the programme sounded like an argument for his canonisation, but that he was no saint. Joe Duffy joked that Mary Banotti – a grandniece of Michael Collins' – had just fallen off her stool.

Some weeks later I received a letter from Liam Collins, mentioning that he had heard the radio programme. 'I was very taken aback at the time by your contribution,' he wrote. 'Since then I have decided to read your publication *The Man Who Won the War*. And quite frankly I am very glad I did so. As I see your book, it recognises in quite a fair and honest way the pluses and minuses of the man.'[4]

'I am sorry that the stance as taken by Tim Pat Coogan only allowed you to develop and argue the more or less "downsides" of my uncle,' he continued. 'I know from others to whom I have spoken that the view I took of you that day, of being a definite anti-Michael Collins person, was shared by them. Naturally I now accept that I was at fault in my "reading" of you in the radio programme.'[5] Over the years I received a number of other kind letters from Liam Collins that I have treasured.

There has been too much distortion on all sides in relation to this period of Irish history, and there should be no room in a book for polemics, distorting leading figures into either gods or devils. De Valera made an invaluable contribution to the history of the period covered in this book by his promotion of the Bureau of Military History, which conducted interviews in the 1940s and 1950s with hundreds of survivors of the War of Independence.

After any war those involved frequently do not like to talk about it. This was especially true in the wake of the bitterness of the Irish Civil War, when men who had struggled side by side during the War of Independence took opposite sides in the Civil War. Those most involved in the War of Independence seemed to talk least, with a few exceptions. Having remained silent while the soapbox patriots sounded off, many of those who had been active were only prepared to talk to the Bureau of Military History, as they did not consider this bragging, because their statements would only be released after their deaths.

Michael Collins: The Man Who Won the War has been reprinted ten times since it was first published in 1990. The current edition has been expanded with a considerable amount of material that was not available earlier, especially the insights afforded by the witness statements at the Bureau of Military History. I would like to commend Mercier Press for keeping the book in print throughout this whole period. I have since written three other books in relation to other aspect of Collins' life: *Big Fellow, Long Fellow: A Joint Biography of Michael Collins and Eamon de Valera* in 1999, *The Squad and the Intelligence Operation of Michael Collins* in 2005, and *'I Signed My Death Warrant': Michael Collins and the Treaty* in 2007.

TRD
Tralee

1

'Mind that Child'

Michael Collins was born on 16 October 1890 near the tiny County Cork hamlet of Sam's Cross, where his father had a sixty-acre farm. He was the youngest of eight children.

'Well do I remember the night,' his sister Helena wrote some eighty years later. She was seven years old at the time. 'Mother came round to the three youngest, Pat (6), Katie (4) and myself, to see us safely landed in bed. Next morning we were thrilled to hear we had a baby brother found under the proverbial head of cabbage.'[1]

It was a closely-knit family. 'We were a very happy family even though we lived under very primitive conditions in the old house, where we all were born,' Helena remembered. Michael had a normal childhood, though being the youngest of such a large family he tended to be rather spoiled.[2]

Michael's father was generally somewhat aloof with his children – Mary Anne was charged with looking after their needs – but he had a particularly soft spot for Michael as the youngest. He would frequently bring him on his rounds of the farm. At other times the boy's older sisters were charged with looking after him – a duty they relished. 'We thought he had been invented for our own special edification,' Hannie said years later.[3]

In addition to the eight children, there were usually a number of aunts and uncles about the house. Michael's father, Michael John Collins, was born in 1815, the youngest of six boys. He lived at Woodfield, the farm where he was born, all his life. He believed his children were the sixth generation of the family born there. In 1875, at the age of fifty-nine, he married his goddaughter, Mary Anne O'Brien.

It was a made match. Michael John was living with his three

older bachelor brothers, Maurice, Tom and Paddy, and they needed a housekeeper. Mary Anne O'Brien was twenty-three at the time. She was the eldest daughter of a family of ten. Her father, James O'Brien from Sam's Cross, was killed when his horse shied. Mary Anne's mother was seriously injured in the accident. As a result, Mary Anne and her older brother, Danny, had to take responsibility for the large family at an early age. Mary Anne became a second mother to the younger members of her family. After she married, her younger brothers and sisters were frequently to be found in the Collins home. The last of Michael's paternal uncles died some four months before he was born.

The family would usually gather in the kitchen at night. This was before the age of rural electricity, radio or television, so they had to make their own entertainment. Discussions would invariably take on a patriotic slant, with nationalistic songs or poems figuring prominently. Mary Anne's brother, Danny, would sing rebel ballads and her mother, Johanna O'Brien, who lived until 1899, would recount watching victims of the Great Famine die by the roadside half a century earlier. West Cork was one of the areas most severely hit by the famine.

These evenings would have formed some of Michael's earliest memories. At the age of four and a half he began his formal education at Lisavaird National School. 'The boys were on one side, and the girls on the other side of a semi-detached building,' according to Helena. 'Both heads were strict disciplinarians. Miss Ellen Collins, a cousin of ours, was head of the girls' school and Mr Denis Lyons of the boys'. We had no intercourse with each other; we might have been miles apart.'[4]

In later life people would remember Michael taking a particular delight in listening to old people reminiscing. 'Great age held something for me that was awesome,' he later told Hayden Talbot, an American journalist. 'I was much fonder of old people in the darkness than of young people in the daylight.'[5] This attachment to old people may have had something to do with his early memories of the family gatherings in the dimly lit kitchen and the fact that his father was already seventy-five years old when Michael was born. In terms of age he was much more like the boy's grandfather.

Michael never forgot an incident that occurred when he was with his father on the farm one day. They were out in the fields and his father was standing on a stone wall from which he dislodged a stone accidentally. Michael remembered looking at the stone as it came towards him, but he figured that it would not hurt him because his father had dislodged it.

'Would you believe it?' his father would say. 'There he was, barefooted, and the stone rolling down on him, and him never so much as looking at it! And when I got the thing off his foot and asked him why he had stood there and let it hit him, what do you think he replied? He told me 'twas I who sent it down! It's a true Collins he is.'[6]

In December 1896, when Michael was six, his father had a heart attack from which he never really recovered. He lingered for a couple of months, but never went out again. 'Our darling Papa died on March 7th 1997,' Helena recalled. 'Mama called us all at about 10 p.m. and we all got round the bed. Papa who was quite conscious spoke.'[7]

'Mind that child,' he said, pointing to Michael. 'He'll be a great man yet, and will do great things for Ireland.' He added that Nellie (his pet name for Helena) 'will be a nun'.[8]

One can easily imagine the kind of influence this incident would have on children at such an impressionable age, especially as the family revered their dying father. Helena duly entered a Mercy Convent and spent the rest of her life as a nun.

Having helped to rear her own brothers and sisters from an early age, Mary Anne Collins was almost trained to cope with the trials of being widowed with a young family. Michael's eldest brother, John, was eighteen at the time and he took over the running of the farm.

The local headmaster, Denis Lyons, was a member of the secret oath-bound Irish Republican Brotherhood (IRB). He had a formative influence on Michael's developing nationalism. Lyons and the local blacksmith James Santry, whose forge was across the road from the school, regaled young Collins with stories of past Irish rebellions. In his mid twenties Michael would recall what a seminal influence they were.

'In Denis Lyons and James Santry I had my first tutors capable of – because of their personalities alone – infusing into me a pride of the

Irish as a race,' he wrote to a cousin. 'Other men may have helped me along the searching path to a political goal, I may have worked hard myself in the long search, nevertheless, Denis Lyons and James Santry remain to me as my first stalwarts. In Denis Lyons especially, his manner,. although seemingly hiding what meant most to him, had this pride of Irishness which has always meant most to me.'[9]

When Lyons or Santry talked of the events of the nineteenth century, the Great Famine, the Young Ireland Rebellion and the trauma of the 1870s and 1880s, they were talking about times through which Michael's father and uncles had lived. His paternal grandparents' lives went back well into the eighteenth century. Indeed, one of his father's brothers had been old enough to remember the Rebellion of 1798. Michael's paternal grandmother's brother, Tadgh O'Sullivan, had been a Professor of Greek at the University of Louvain and had acted as an emissary for Wolfe Tone, who was regarded as the father of Irish republicanism. It was therefore understandable that young Michael Collins showed a great interest in the history of the past century.

Lyons detected 'a certain restlessness in temperament' in young Michael, whom he described at the time as 'exceptionally intelligent in observation and at figures'. Collins was 'a good reader' with a striking concern for political matters and 'more than a normal interest in things appertaining to the welfare of his country'. His political idol at the time was the man who would later credit him with winning the war. 'In Arthur Griffith there is a mighty force afoot in Ireland,' Collins wrote in one of his school essays in 1902.[10]

In spite of the above-mentioned 'restlessness in temperament', his teacher still described him as 'able and willing to adjust himself to all circumstances.'[11] Having finished National School, Michael went on to school in Clonakilty to prepare for the civil service entrance examination. During the school-week he lived with his eldest sister, Margaret O'Driscoll. Her husband owned a local newspaper and Michael helped with the reporting, usually on hurling or football matches. While there, he learned to type.

His best friend in those early days was Jack Hurley, whose sister married Michael's brother, John, and so became an in-law of the Collins family. The two boys were inseparable and often stayed the night at each other's homes.

In July 1906 Collins went to London to take up a job with the Post Office Savings Bank. It was a natural move for an ambitious boy of his age, because there were few prospects for him in west Cork. His second oldest sister, Johanna (or Hannie, as he called her) was already in the civil service in London, and they lived together at 5 Netherwood Place, West Kensington.

'There were no loose ends about Michael, physically or mentally, and he was very impatient of loose statements and vague information, holding that no one had any business speaking on a subject which he had not studied,' Hannie recalled. 'He was an omnivorous reader: like the other members of his family, he had got through a good course of the English classics before he was sixteen: Scott, Dickens and Thackeray, Swift, Addison, Burke, Sheridan, Dryden, Pope and Shakespeare and Milton, as well as Moore, Byron, Shelly and Keats. Later he read Hardy and Meredith Wessels, Arnold Bennett and Conrad, also Swinburne and Oscar Wilde, as well as contemporary writers like W.B. Yeats, Pádraig Colum and James Stephens.[12]

'No one appreciated Bernard Shaw more than he,' Hannie continued, 'and he felt his influence, as all among the younger generation who think at all have come under the same salutary influence. How we discussed literature together and how often have we sat up long after midnight discussing the merits and demerits of the English and Irish and French writers who happened to be our idols at the time. He was thoroughly modern and liked realism and the plays of the younger dramatists who wrote for the Abbey Theatre.'[13] A number of people later expressed surprise at the range of his reading.

Michael appeared to have no problems fitting in. 'I had Irish friends in London before I arrived, and in the intervening years I had made many more friends among Irish residents in London,' he recalled later. 'For the most part we lived lives apart. We chose to consider ourselves outposts of our nation.'[14] One of those friends was his boyhood pal Jack Hurley, who had emigrated some months earlier. Hurley's presence undoubtedly eased the transition to life in London, but even so Collins retained and developed a rather romantic view of Ireland, given how much he missed his home.

'I stand for an Irish civilisation based on the people and embodying and maintaining the things – their habits, ways of thought, customs – that make them different – the sort of life I was brought up in,' he wrote. As a result he and his friends never really integrated into British society, and never wanted to. 'We were proud of isolation,' he said, 'and we maintained it to the end.'[15]

'Once,' he explained some years later, 'a crowd of us were going along the Shepherd's Bush Road when out of a lane came a chap with a donkey – just the sort of donkey and just the sort of cart they have at home. He came out quite suddenly and abruptly and we all cheered him. Nobody who has not been an exile will understand me, but I stand for that.'[16]

During the nine and a half formative years that Collins spent in London he took a very active part in the Irish life of the city. In 1907 he helped raise money when Arthur Griffith's new party, Sinn Féin, ran a candidate in a parliamentary by-election. The candidate, who had resigned his seat in order to re-contest it on a Sinn Féin ticket, was defeated. Party supporters tried to put the gloss of moral victory on what was really a devastating defeat from which the party did not recover for many years.

Those years had a profound influence on Michael. 'He kept his interests exclusively Irish, and his holidays were always spent at home in Woodfield,' according to Hannie. 'He cultivated the society of old people who knew Irish, and never tired of drawing them out and listening to the tales and traditions of the past. He was popular with both old and young all his life. His tastes and inclinations were for a country life – and he chafed against the restrains and restrictions of London existence.'[17]

Like many other Irish immigrants, he probably became more acutely aware of his Irishness while in exile, and this reinforced his sense of nationalism. Although his parents had both been native Irish speakers, they associated the Irish language with the economic backwardness of

Gaeltacht areas, so while they spoke to each other in Irish when they did not want the children to understand, they only spoke English to their children. Michael started to learn Irish on a number of occasions, but other events inevitably took precedence.

His work – together with his educational, political and sporting activities – all combined to take up a lot of time. He continued his education by attending night classes at King's College, London, from the autumn of 1907 to the spring of 1909. Many of the essays that he wrote there have survived and give an insight into his adolescent mind. On reflection, they may well provide an explanation for his actions in later years, when he became the prototype of the modern urban terrorist.

Ironically, those writings suggested he was critical of urban life, especially the overcrowding. 'Families of four or five each, all living in one room, can hardly be healthy or moral,' he wrote. Last year there were '122,000 underfed children in London. These children will grow up to be unemployables – unfit for almost everything save crime – made characterless by the sordid conditions under which they were reared.' He was equally critical of the death rate in cities, especially infant mortality, which he believed was double the rate of rural areas.[18]

'Do not we, as Englishmen, understand that it is our sacred duty to Christianise and civilise the savage lands all over the world,' Michael Collins wrote in a letter dated 10 January 1908. 'The more territory we hold, the more self-supporting will our empire become, and the more advantageous fields for emigration will it offer to the surplus population of the mother country, as well as providing a more extensive market for our manufactured goods.'[19]

'Your disgust at our withholding self-government from some colonies is ridiculous,' he continued. 'Did we not give it freely to those that were able to make laws for themselves; and as soon as the others reach that responsible stage we will undoubtedly also grant it to them.'[20]

Collins never thought of himself as an Englishman. This letter was written as part of an academic exercise at King's College. He had been assigned to write two letters, one to 'a friend who thinks that the British Empire is expanding too rapidly and his reply.' It was not the first letter, which had '14 Idiot's Row' as it return address, but the second letter from '11 Wiseman's Alley' that reflected his real views. 'The strongest link of your argument on the advantages of expansion is the honour of christianising. Do you not think that it would be well if we first christianised ourselves?' he wrote in the reply. 'But it is not for this laudable purpose that England goes abroad; it is for the acquisition of territory. An English missionary gets killed, his country bemoaning his fate shrieks loudly for *revenge*, an army in red coats is sent out, and the country is coloured red on the map.[21]

'The expansion of the already large British Empire means,' he argued, 'a greater responsibility to the mother country, and an increased force to keep the colonies in subjection – as they cannot be expected to be very loyal, because every country has a right to work out is own destiny in accordance with the laws of its being, which eventually may mean conscription.'[22] Ironically, eight years later it was to avoid being conscripted into the British army during the First World War that Collins left London and returned to live in Ireland.

Presence of mind was probably the single characteristic that most distinguished him when under pressure in the coming years. As a teenager he actually wrote a college essay on the subject. Quick thinking was 'one of the most valuable qualities as well as one of the least common,' he wrote. 'To know what to do at a crisis we must, if we have an opportunity to learn up thoroughly the matter before-hand, and by practising this in trivial things we will beget a habit of ready resource in untried or unforeseen circumstances.[23]

'History and tradition are rich in instances demonstrating the values of presence of mind,' Collins continued. 'All great commanders have been famed for their coolness in the hour of danger, which perhaps contributed more largely to their success than their actual courage ... Real valour consists not in being insensible to danger, but in being prompt to confront and disarm it.[24]

'Of course, this excellent quality is largely constitutional, but it also is largely cultivatable,' he added. 'As Socrates, who had at one time a most violent temper, by long training and constant practice, acquired a mild and equable one, so can people who are not naturally born to it, achieve the rare gift of presence of mind.' Even at this early stage it seemed that he was preparing for the future.

'No great and noteworthy achievement was ever attained without exertion and ambition,' Collins wrote in another essay on 24 April 1908. 'We have only to look around us and see how many of the failures in life that are due to the fault of blindly and fatuously trusting in "luck". To wait passively for good fortune to smile on us is like waiting for the stream to run dry.[25]

'Good luck knocks at least once at each man's door but the tide must be taken at the flood and in a lively and vigorous manner,' Collins added. 'In the history [of] the world's famous men we find that all of them were ready to venture even their existence on the attainment of their ends. Washington played for a large stake, and it was only by venturing everything he was master of, that he won it. The same was true of Garibaldi in Italy, and in England Richard III unfeelingly sacrificed his nephews because they were in his way to the throne.[26]

'We must not however be too rash. It has been truthfully said that "vaulting ambition o'erleaps itself" and history is rich in stances.' He went on to cite Napoleon and Cromwell as examples: 'Fire, when kept under restraint, is a useful servant, but when it gets the upper hand it is a merciless tyrant. The same holds good of ambition. If we take it to mean an unquenchable desire to advance by honest methods towards perfection, it is one of the best qualities a man can be endowed with.'[27]

In an essay on contentment, written a couple of weeks before his eighteenth birthday in October 1908, he foreshadowed his own determination to make the best of his lot during his internment in Frongoch, Wales, following the Easter Rising. 'Fretting never does any good, but often much harm, as no amount of grumbling and peevish ill-humour can change our lot, but only serve to make others dislike us,' he wrote. 'If we look into the pages of history we find that nearly all great leaders were funny hearted men. The hopefulness of Columbus cheered on his men, and the genial kindness of Washington contributed largely to his success.' Some would later remember Collins as 'the laughing boy', while others would be appalled by his apparent desire to make light of matters, even in the most inappropriate conditions. 'Happiness consists in the fewness of our wants, and we must remember that we want but little here below, nor want that little long,' he wrote. 'This being the case we must take care that our wishes are also few. If abundance comes let us enjoy it, but if it does not, we must cease wishing for it …'[28]

He held particularly strong views on charity when he wrote on the subject in the first week of November 1908:

> Charity cannot be tested by the magnitude of its gifts, but by the feelings that prompt them. To be poor and in distress is only too common a condition of men around us, and surely we can all find some little work to do, whereby a struggling comrade may be encouraged and comforted.
>
> But on the other hand, we must be careful not to do mischief by giving our alms promiscuously. It is a melancholy but indisputable fact that a very large percentage of ordinary beggars are rogues and impostors. Many with good show of reason maintain that we should never give to any beggar without knowing his history or being prepared to follow it up.
>
> There is no doubt whatever, that to give open assistance to any person is in a great measure to spoil his independence, as it deprives him of the spirit of self-reliance and causes him to fall into idleness and open beggary. In many cases begging becomes a disgusting trade, practised by skulks too lazy to work. The most infamous means are taken for moving our feelings. Sores, often wilfully produced, are paraded before us. Infants with bare feet and scanty clothing appeal to our sympathy … The really deserving are, as a rule, too proud to expose their misery before the world, and must be sought out in their homes and kindly persuaded to receive our help.
>
> We should be careful about giving to charitable institutions without first satisfying ourselves as to their worth. Many of them are mere shams got up to exhort money from the generous-minded.[29]

Piaras Béaslaí, who was active in Irish circles in London at the same time, wrote that Collins was active in Sinn Féin as a teenager in London. He gave prepared speeches on 'The Catholic Church in Ireland' and 'The Great Famine of 1847' at Sinn Féin meetings in London during 1908.

The address on the church was violently anti-clerical and 'full of all the intemperance and exaggeration of a boy'.[30] Desmond Ryan noted in his book *Remembering Sion* that Collins actually called for the extermination of the clergy. The draft of his paper on the famine has actually survived in a school exercise book at Marquette University in the United States. As far as Collins was concerned, the Great Famine was a 'manufactured' catastrophe. 'Though the inexorable laws of nature caused the potato blight,' he wrote, 'England and English muddling caused the famine.'[31]

There had been plenty of warning of the blight in 1845, but the government did nothing about it because, he argued, the English politicians welcomed the catastrophe as a way 'to get rid of the surplus Irish' to ensure that a strong Ireland could not become 'a menace to the Empire.' Moreover, he wrote, 'a depopulated Ireland could export more food to England, than an industrial Ireland could.[32]

'It is not my intention to go into the horrors which characterised the famine years,' Collins continued. 'You know only too well of the frightful miseries which the people suffered hunger. And how hunger was followed close by a nauseating fever. You have also heard of the hinged coffins so largely used in Skibbereen. In that town people will still point you out two large pits where hundreds of corpses found a coffinless grave.' As a result of his research, based largely on the books of John O'Rourke and John Mitchel, Collins was scathing in his condemnation of British famine relief efforts. He was scornful of Queen Victoria's supposed £5 contribution. In fact, she gave £1,000, which was a small fortune in those days, but generations of Irish school children were told she just gave the fiver. 'Didn't the English get subscriptions for us amounting to over £200,000 and was not one of these subscriptions headed by Queen Vic with a donation of £5,' Collins wrote in indignation. 'We may forgive and forget many things but it would pass even Irish ingratitude to forget this £5.'[33]

When he was about twelve years old, he wrote approvingly of Arthur Griffith and Sinn Féin. 'He has none of the wildness of some I could name,' Collins wrote. 'Instead there is an abundance of wisdom and awareness of the things that ARE Ireland.'[34] In 1908, however, the teenage Collins was moving towards wildness himself, as he looked to violence as a means of achieving Irish independence. In his exercise book, immediately before the draft of the famine article, there was another draft entitled, 'Finland and Ireland', in which he argued that Ireland should follow the example of Finland in its quest for self-government.

The revolutionary Eugen Schauman had assassinated Nicholai Bobrikov, the Russian governor general of Finland in 1904. With the help of Russian dissidents who were on the brink of revolution in the aftermath of the loss of the Russo-Japanese War, the Finns gained a significant measure of autonomy from Tsar Nicholas II.

Collins clearly admired the Finns. They are a quiet race and do not specialise in talk. 'Their object,' he said, 'is not to make people cheer, but to make them think. Finland, I am sorry to say, is, with the exception of Russian Revolutionaries, fighting single-handed. Freedom-loving England is friendly with the Tsar.' In fact all of the main countries of Europe were taking a similar line in order not to offend the Tsar.

'France another glorious upholder of freedom is similarly disposed towards him,' Collins continued. 'What is true of France and England is even more forcibly true of Italy, Austria and Germany. The diplomats of all these countries are seeking a Russian alliance and so Finland can scarce[ly] expect much sympathy from them.'

'I have headed my remarks Finland and Ireland,' he went on. 'You will perhaps be impatient to see what all this has to do with Ireland. Let me paint the moral. As a rule I hate morals and hate moralists still more, but in the present case I think it excusable, even desirable.' He saw a parallel between the murder of Bobrikov and the assassinations of Chief Secretary Frederick Cavendish and the much-hated under-secretary for Ireland, T.H. Burke, in the Phoenix Park on 6 May 1882, but 'the results were not so gratifying in Ireland as they were in Finland', because some foolish Irish people denounced the Phoenix Park killers but ignored a horrific incident in Connemara on the same day.

'A little Irish child of 11 or 12 years was bludgeoned to death for shouting for Michael Davitt,' Collins reproached. 'His murderers were not denounced', nor were they 'stigmatised as savages.' Thus he felt that a moral line should be drawn between what happened in Ireland and the way the Finns exploited the Bobrikov murder for their own advantage.

'I do not defend the murder simply as such,' Collins said. 'I merely applaud it on the grounds of expediency.'[35]

He described what happened in Finland in terms of a 'fairy tale'. The Tsar agreed to free elections and the establishment of a national parliament, based on proportional representation and universal adult suffrage. Women were given the vote for the first time in Europe. It did not last long, but the fact that it happened at all was enough to encourage Collins. 'We have seen how the Finns found it advantageous to ally with the Russian revolutionists – may not we also find it beneficial to allow our best to be helped by the English revolutionists,' he explained. 'The Swedes and Finns also united in the face of the common enemy – here then is a lesson for Irishmen all the world over. I maintain that the analogy between Finland and Ireland is almost perfect.[36]

'The Finns are almost less homogenous than the Irish,' he argued. 'Altogether there are 2,000,000 of them and they won against the might of Russia. Cannot we go and do likewise?'[37]

2

Collins and the GAA

The struggle for Irish independence was taking separate but converging paths in Collins' view. 'Irish history will recognise in the birth of the Gaelic League in 1893 the most important event of the nineteenth century,' he later wrote. 'It checked the peaceful penetration and once and for all turned the minds of the Irish people back to their own country. It did more than any other movement to restore national pride, honour and self-respect.'[1]

Collins joined the Gaelic League in London with the aim of learning Irish. Particularly prominent among his contemporaries from Cork were Joe O'Reilly, whom he met for the first time in London, and his long-time friend Jack Hurley, with whom he remained particularly close. 'We think the same way in Irish matters,' Collins wrote. 'At worst he is a boon companion, at best there is no one else I would have as a friend.'[2] Unlike most of his young contemporaries, Collins reportedly showed little interest in the opposite sex at this stage of his life.

'The society of girls had apparently no attraction for him,' according to Piaras Béaslaí, the only biographer who could claim to have been more than a passing acquaintance of Collins. 'The usual philanderings and flirtations of young men of his age had little interest or attraction for him, though he sometimes amused himself by chaffing his young friends over their weaknesses in that direction,' Béaslaí added. 'He preferred the company of young men, and never paid any attention to the girls belonging to the Branch, not even to the sisters and friends of his male companions.'[3]

Maybe this teasing actually prompted him to cover up a relationship he had been conducting across the water with Susan Killeen, a girl he had met in London. His frequent correspondence with her after her return to Dublin certainly bespoke an affectionate relationship, as he described his loneliness in London. Of course, it would be many years before the letters of that discreet relationship would come to light. In the interim, the image of Mick the misogynist would take root.

In the following years, Collins became particularly close to Batt O'Connor, a builder who constructed hiding places for him. He would often visit O'Connor's home, which was also frequented by other prominent members of the movement, but O'Connor singled Collins out as the one 'that I knew the least because he was always too engrossed in his important occupation to take part in small talk. But the women who worked for him and with him overlooked that characteristic in him and did not expect anything different from him because they knew how much he had on his mind.'[4]

Some people – who never knew Collins – would later suggest that he might have been homosexual. This was pure speculation, based largely on how Béaslaí and Frank O'Connor depicted him, though neither ever actually suggested it.

O'Connor relied heavily on Joe O'Reilly for background information. His portrait showed Collins as a contradictory conglomeration of various characteristics – a buoyant, warm-hearted, fun-loving individual with a thoughtful, generous nature, but also a thoughtless, selfish, ill-mannered bully. While other young men went looking for sex, he was depicted as more inclined to go looking for 'a bit of ear'.[5] He would burst into a room and jump on a colleague and wrestle him to the floor, and then begin biting the unfortunate friend's ear until the other fellow surrendered, sometimes with blood streaming from his ear. It certainly painted a picture of a rather strange fellow.

During the War of Independence Collins frequently stayed in a room reserved for men 'on the run' at Vaughan's Hotel in Rutland (now Parnell) Square. 'He usually shared a bedroom with Boland and myself,' Béaslaí wrote, 'and frequently shared Boland's bed with him'.[6]

Given the times and the circumstances there was nothing unusual about sharing a bed with a colleague. They were lucky to have a bed to share. When Collins stayed elsewhere, Béaslaí did not know about his sleeping arrangements. For much of the period, especially between 1919 and 1921 Collins had no fixed abode. He was a wanted man and he purposely kept colleagues in the dark about where he stayed. If they could find him, then so could the police. It therefore probably suited him to let people think that he had no time for women, because his safe houses were mostly run by single women like the aunts and widowed mothers of colleagues and, in at least one case, the wife of a confidante of the British prime minister.

Having read those early biographies one grandnephew suspected that Michael Collins must have been gay. He said this one day to his grandfather, Michael's oldest brother Johnny, who burst out laughing and said that if Michael had a problem, that was certainly not it. If anything, Johnny Collins seemed to think that Michael was too fond of too many women. There was no suggestion of a sexual relationship with these women, but this did not stop others from characterising him as a rampant philanderer. This charge was akin to suggesting that any man who shared an apartment with a sister was in an incestuous relationship.

Remember, Collins was only fifteen years old when he first went to London, and it would not have been that unusual for someone so young to show little interest in the opposite sex at that point. He was a young, working man, deeply involved not only in furthering his education but was also very active in sport and politics. Tim Pat Coogan uncovered a cache of letters that confirmed the previously mentioned warm relationship between Collins and Susan Killeen during and after his years in London. This relationship began while she was in London and continued after she returned to Dublin in 1915. As none of the earlier biographers even mentioned her, it would seem that the relationship was quiet and discreet. It would not have been surprising if he were in no hurry to form an attachment. After all, his father was sixty years old before he married, and Michael would not be that age until 1950.

Although Collins gave the main credit for promoting Irish nationalism to the Gaelic League, the Gaelic Athletic Association (GAA), founded in 1884, arguably played an even more important role, because it blazed the trail for the Gaelic League to promote the idea that Irish people 'must look to themselves for economic prosperity, and must turn to national culture as a means to national freedom'.[7] The GAA certainly had a much greater influence on Collins, but both organisations had widespread influence on Irish people.

'They reached out to every phase of the people's lives, educating them to make them free,' Collin argued. 'No means were too slight to use for that purpose. The Gaelic Athletic Association reminded Irish boys that they were Gaels. It provided and restored national games as an alternative to the slavish adoption of English sport.'[8]

A key to Collins' thinking can be found in so many of his own writings, which are quite extensive even though he was killed at the early age of thirty-two. He was an inveterate letter writer. Much of what he wrote may be of little interest from the broad national perspective, but his correspondence provides a wealth of insights, contradictory or otherwise, into his own mind and his personality.

In addition to joining the Gaelic League in London, Collins joined Sinn Féin and became particularly active in the GAA, which led him on to the Irish Republican Brotherhood (IRB) and from that to the Irish Volunteer Force, before it became the Irish Republican Army in which Collins made his name as an organiser and brilliant intelligence strategist. He cut his teeth as an organiser in the GAA, which was very involved in track and field athletics as well as hurling and football at the time.

There were ten GAA clubs in London at the time. They included the Brian Boru, Cusacks, Davis, Geraldines, Hibernians, Irish Athletic Club, Milesians, Kickhams, Raparees, Rooneys and later Young Ireland, all under the aegis of what was called the London County Board. Collins enjoyed playing hurling with the Geraldines Club, or 'the Gers' as they were called. He usually played at either wing back or centre field. Opponents remembered him as more effective than accomplished. 'He was not a polished hurler – more like a Clareman in this respect than a Corkman,' Pat Brennan recalled.[9]

Whether on the hurling field or elsewhere, Collins seemed to have an exaggerated sense of his own importance, which did not endear him to some people. Many enjoyed provoking him into losing his temper both on the field and off. He was 'inclined to lose his temper at anything,' one colleague recalled. 'When I was playing against him, I'd play for his toes, and that would make him mad,' said Dinny Daly. 'It was always easy to vex Collins.'[10]

Within the Geraldines, Paddy Belton, the club president, was an active member of the IRB. He recognised the potential of Collins and took him under his wing. He had him appointed as a club delegate to the London County Board, then under the chairmanship of another IRB man, Sam Maguire, a native of Dunmanway. One of those with whom Maguire had a close relationship was Liam McCarthy, the London-born son of Cork parents. He also served as chairman of the London County Board. Those two names are iconic within the GAA, as the premier All-Ireland football and hurling trophies – the Sam Maguire Cup and the Liam McCarthy Cup – were named after them.

In 1907 there was a split in athletics in the London Irish clubs. There were a number of parallel athletic bodies, some of which had links to the Olympic games, but the GAA decried these links because Irish athletes would have to compete under the British flag. The Brian Boru club defected and tried to operate under the Amateur Athletic Association. The London County Board of the GAA denounced the move and threatened to suspend any athlete who competed in the Brian Boru sports meeting. Collins was too young to have had much influence, but he did support his club president, Paddy Belton.

This loyal support was rewarded with advancement. In January 1908 Collins was elected auditor, a minor post in the club. At the next general meeting in January 1909 he voiced strong disapproval of the GAA's handling of the athletic split in London. It was not enough that the club should have nothing to do with the Olympic association; Collins felt that they should have nothing to do with any Irish clubs that competed against such people. At the January 1909 meeting, for instance, Collins denounced the lenient attitude adopted by the London County Board towards those who had competed at the Brian Boru sports meeting. His resolution, which was adopted unanimously by the Gers, read:

That we the members of the Geraldine GAA Club view with dis-
satisfaction, the recent action of the County Board of London in asking
back into the GAA of London (after 5 months) men who had been
previously suspended from said section for a term of 15 months in consequence of having competed at the Sports of the Brian Boru Club in
direct opposition to the ruling of the Board.

We believe this action is likely to lower the prestige of the Board, as
it is a breach of principle and a mean and unnecessary change of policy
detrimental to the best interest of Gaelic Athleticism in London.[11]

Although the club adopted the resolution, this obviously carried little
weight with the London County Board, because it re-admitted four people
who had competed as part of the British team in the 1908 Olympics in
London. Collins protested against the re-admission. One of those re-
admitted was actually named Michael Collins, who had competed in
throwing the discus. Because the London County Board had warned the
athletes in advance that they would be expelled from the association if
they competed for Britain, the Gers protested against the County Board's
decision and decided: 'That no man who competed for England at the
Olympic Games be ever allowed to enter the Geraldine Club.'[12]

That there was such a fuss over the four people who were allowed
to rejoin the GAA having competed in the 1908 Olympics Game in
London would seem suggest that many others did not bother to apply.
Con Leahy, for instance, won the silver medal in the high jump in 1908
while competing for Britain, and Ed Barrett of Ballyduff, County Kerry,
won a bronze medal in wrestling and a gold medal in the tug-of-war,
which was won by the a team made up of London policemen. Barrett
had won an All-Ireland senior hurling medal with London in the 1901
championship, in which London beat Cork in the final. Neither Leahy
nor Barrett were among the four mentioned.

Collins was elected to the influential post of club secretary in July
1909, which was the same year in which Sam Maguire swore him into the
IRB. Collins was only eighteen years old at the time and he retained the
post for the next six years. The club minutes make for interesting reading.
They show him to have been a committed and enthusiastic member, with

a strong nationalistic outlook. He took over as secretary at a particularly good time for the club. The outgoing secretary was especially optimistic in his final semi-annual report.

'We have made greater progress during that time than in any period in our history,' he wrote. 'It is now over six years since the Geraldine Club was started.' In the previous six months the club had attracted fifteen new members. This had helped them to fulfil the ambition of renting a field for Sunday games. 'There always seemed to be an idea in the club that, given a Sunday field, we would do wonders,' wrote his predecessor, whose minutes often gave details of matches and listed the club teams that took the field for various games. Collins very rarely mentioned such matters and never listed the teams in his minutes. He paid more attention to sports days, dances and the club's money problems.[13]

The meeting at which he was first elected secretary was a contentious affair. Paddy Belton – who later became better known in Dublin as a politician and the owner of a number of local pubs – was re-elected president of the club after a tied vote of eleven each. Belton, who was proposed by Collins, used a casting vote to break the tie. This led to 'a scene of excitement,' according to Collins. There were objections, and there was a further proposal that Belton should remove himself on the grounds that he was not entitled to a casting vote as he had presumably already voted for himself. The vote on this motion also ended in a tie, and Belton broke the tie by voting in his own favour. 'He means very well but is a very difficult man to get on with,' Collins later wrote. 'He is obstinate and headstrong and I have never yet known him to have any respect for any point of view but his own.'[14]

The ensuing months as secretary were a baptism of fire for the teenage Collins. The club remained badly split. Its sports day had to be postponed and then cancelled, because the club treasurer failed to pay for the field for the day. 'His protracted retention of the club money and his brazen falsehoods in connection therewith forced the sports committee to abandon the sports day and very nearly lost us our Saturday pitch,' Collins told the next general meeting. 'Eventually we got him to disgorge.'[15]

The club semi-annual meeting on 8 January 1910 'was most disheart-ening,' as only fourteen members turned up, compared with twenty-four the previous time. But then this should hardly have been surprising when they seemed more intent on keeping people out than attracting members.[16] The controversy over those who took part at the London Olympics was followed by another controversy demanding the expulsion of those who took part in so-called foreign games. They lived in England and some considered it natural to play the popular local games like soccer and rugby. Collins took a hard-line view against such people participating in the GAA, but he never seemed to see the incongruity of his own behaviour in working for the British government at the post office. Others were naturally appalled by such inconsistencies and the Geraldines were seriously fractured.

'Our internal troubles were saddening, but our efforts in football and hurling were perfectly heartbreaking,' Collins explained in his report of 8 January 1910. 'In no single contest have our colours been crowned with success,' he wrote. 'In hurling we haven't even the consolation of a credible performance.' The club only fielded a full team for one of its five hurling matches. Only eight players turned up for the one game and nine for another. 'The record is as discreditable to us as it is detrimental to the association,' Collins noted. 'If the members are not prepared to take up hurling more enthusiastically for the coming year than they did last year – then the abandonment of the hurling section is the only sensible course. It will save us looking ridiculous, and save other clubs disappointment.[17]

'I can only say that our record of the past half-year leaves no scope for self-congratulation,' he continued. 'Signs of decay are unmistakable, and if members are not prepared in the future to act more harmoniously together and more self-sacrificingly generally – the club will soon have faded into an inglorious and well-deserved oblivion.'[18]

Belton and Collins were re-elected without opposition, but conditions did not improve. Attendance at the next semi-annual meeting in July 1910 was 'very meagre, in fact, most disheartening,' Collins noted. He suggested that the club 'disband as it had been unable to field a team for more than 6 months'. This apparently energised some of the members present. They rejected his suggestion, but 'there was difficulty experienced in getting members to act as officers,' according to Collins.[19] Belton was re-elected president, but he did not see out the term, as he returned home to Dublin. The club seemed to be disintegrating.

A committee meeting was held on 18 September 'to see if we could not restart the club on a new basis'. This led to an extraordinary general meeting with 'a small but very enthusiastic' attendance, according to Collins, who was re-elected as secretary, with P.J. Barrett as club president. The two of them were elected as the club's representatives on the London County Board, where storm clouds were gathering over the banning of foreign games.[20]

Collins and Barrett walked out of the County Board convention in protest against the decision not to implement Rule 13, which related to the ban on garrison games such as soccer, rugby and cricket. The decision to ignore the rule was passed by twenty-five votes to twenty. Rule 13 stipulated: 'That County Committees shall suspend any member of the association who plays, or encourages in any way, rugby, or association football, hockey, or any other imported game calculated to injuriously affect our national pastimes. County Committees shall, however, be empowered to admit at any time into the association persons who have played foreign games, but who have never been member of the GAA, provided they have not participated in such games for six months previous to the date of admission.'[21]

At the club committee meeting on 30 March 1911, Collins and the president persuaded the club to carry a resolution denouncing the rescission of Rule 13. Some of those who had voted for the changes should not have been eligible for membership of the GAA, according to Barrett and Collins, who got the club's approval to appeal at the annual GAA convention in Dublin.

The club intended to appeal to the convention to stand by those who wished to preserve the Gaelic spirit of the associations unimpaired. It also decided that Collins should appeal to the secretaries of the Rooney and the Hibernian clubs to send a similar motion to Dublin, and decided unanimously 'that we refuse to play the newly formed Young Ireland club on the grounds that we are not satisfied with the said club's bona fides'.[22]

Members of the IRB had long controlled the Geraldines, Rooneys and Hibernians. P.S. O'Hegarty had been the strongman of the Hibernians and Sam Maguire of the Rooneys. The GAA convention in Dublin on Easter Sunday rejected the London County Board's proposal to drop Rule 13. The vote was sixty-six to four.

The London County Board acknowledged its defeat but decided not to enforce Rule 13. As a result the three clubs – Hibernians, Rooneys and Geraldines – broke away and set up their own County Board under the presidency of Sam Maguire, with P.S. O'Hegarty as vice-president.

The Central Council recognised the new County Board, but O'Hegarty later admitted that with the break from the Brian Borus and the Milesians, the GAA lost eighty per cent of its best London hurlers. Thereafter the Geraldines began winning in the association, which had been pared down to just three clubs, until they were joined by Young Ireland. The championship of 1911 was amalgamated into the championship of 1912, which was won by the Geraldines. Collins proposed they should purchase medals in Dublin. As the players were going to have to pay for those themselves, however, the whole thing was scrapped.

At the semi-annual general meeting on 1 July 1912, Collins noted that the president of the club blamed the crisis on the old County Board for refusing to implement Rule 13 of the association. Collins was essentially fighting to preserve a separate identity in Britain by resisting integration, just as the GAA was seeking to ensure that the Irish avoided assimilation within the British Empire.

Of course, Collins seemed to carry that concept further by proposing that club's sports meetings be confined to club members. Peter Hart has gone through copies of the *Irishman* newspaper to find the results of the sports meetings. In a 1911 sports meeting Collins won the 100-yard dash, the mile, the triple jump and was on the winning team in the relay. The only event that he entered and did not win was apparently the 880-yard race. There are many references in the club minutes to Collins urging that the events should be confined to members.

This would certainly fit with Frank O'Connor's depiction of the Big Fellow as a strutting individual who wanted to win every contest and would restrict the opposition to achieve that aim. This was essentially how he got the nickname 'The Big Fellow', which was initially a term of derision – he was not a particularly big man.

Collins stood less than six feet tall and photographs show him as having a wiry athletic frame at the time. His nickname reflected his self-importance, because as a young man he was – people would say – big-headed and full of himself.

At the Whitsun sports meeting for the various Irish clubs, Collins was first in the mile and the long jump, second in the 100 yards and the 16 pound shot, and the Geraldines won the team event.

Hart goes back to the sports results in London before the ruckus over competing in the Olympics. 'If we go back to July 1906 and look at his record in the years preceding August 1911,' he notes, 'there is not one mention of Collins winning or being placed in – or entering – any athletic contest at all! Where were his remarkable ambitions and compulsion then?' Collins used the split in athletics for his own purposes. 'He seized that opportunity to make his name as an athlete,' according to Hart. 'It would not have been possible otherwise.'[23]

Did Collins help to drive off competitors so that he could dominate himself? The standard of Irish athletics at the time was extraordinarily high. In 1906 intercalated Olympic Games were held in Athens. Martin Sheridan from Mayo won three gold medals in field events competing for the United States. Peter O'Connor, the holder of the world record in the long jump, would not compete for Britain, so he had to confine himself to the 1906 games. He won the silver medal in his speciality, the long jump, and took the gold medal in the triple jump in which his colleague Con Leahy won the silver medal, while Leahy won the gold in the high jump. The third member of the Irish team, John McGough, won a silver medal in the 1,500 metres.

Whether those people normally competed under the auspices of the GAA or not, all of them would initially have had their start in athletics in Ireland at sports meetings organised by the GAA. It was utterly absurd to question the athletic prowess of Collins by noting that he did not shine as an athlete in the summer of 1906. With the standard so high, one could hardly have expected him to feature, especially when he was only fifteen years old at the time.

'Loyalty and industry' had brought Collins so far. 'But he was never president or vice-president of anything, ever team captain either, and only briefly vice-captain,' Hart continued. 'He was a valuable foot soldier, but still not officer material.'[24]

It should be stressed, of course, that Collins never sought the presidency or vice-presidency. He was always more interested in influence than position, because he wanted the power to get things done. He was quite prepared to work with others. Even during the final months of his life, for instance, he backed Arthur Griffith as president of Dáil Éireann and stood down for W.T. Cosgrave to take over as chairman of the Provisional Government.

But this is getting ahead of ourselves. Collins was a dedicated member of the GAA. He repeatedly called for jerseys and medals to be purchased in Dublin. When the London County Board got into a financial bind, Collins advocated that the practice of paying expenses to delegates should be discontinued. 'In view of the present unstable condition of the London County Board,' he proposed at the semi-annual general meeting of the Geraldines in the summer of 1912, 'that we do not accept the set of hurleys which we have won.' This was agreed unanimously.[25]

He also proposed testimonials for members who were down on their luck. Others appeared to want to carry the cost-saving a little too far. One of the rare issues mentioned in the minutes in connection with games was whether they would purchase proper Gaelic posts for the summer of 1912. After a discussion, however, Collins was instructed to secure rugby posts instead.

By 1913 Collins was becoming more involved in the IRB into which Sam Maguire had sworn him in 1909. Collins only recorded five meetings of the Geraldines from the beginning of 1913 to the end of 1915, after which he returned to Ireland.

The IRB called it cells in Britain 'sections' rather than circles. Collins was promoted to section master in 1912 and became the treasurer of the IRB in the London area in 1914. His good friend Jack Hurley became a member of the supreme council for Britain. In either the summer of 1914 or 1915 Collins accompanied Sam Maguire to Ballybunion, County Kerry, on IRB business. It was there that he first set up links with Tomas Ashe and Austin Stack.

Joining the IRB marked a moving away from the non-violence advocated by Sinn Féin to a forceful approach to the solution of the Irish question for Collins, who argued that lack of organisation 'was chiefly responsible for the failure of several risings'. It was as an organiser that he would make his name in the coming years. 'A force organised on practical lines and headed by realists,' Collins wrote, 'would be of great consequence. Whereas a force organised on theoretical lines, and headed by idealists, would, I think be a very doubtful factor.'[26] His own organisational ability was recognised with his appointment as treasurer of the south of England district of the IRB.

In 1910 Collins quit the Post Office Savings Bank to work in stock-brokerage, but after the outbreak of the First World War in 1914 he moved back into the civil service to work as a labour exchange clerk in Whitehall. He did not want to fight in the British army, but neither did he want 'the murky honour of being a conscientious objector', so he considered emigrating to the United States and in particular to Chicago, where his brother Patrick had already settled. Patrick wrote from his home at 7708 Oglesby Avenue on the south side of Chicago, encouraging him to move to America.[27] 'Regarding your coming to Chicago I have no doubt but you will be able to land some thing here even if it comes slow you will be sure to have a place to sleep and eat; besides business is getting good all through the country now.'[28] In April 1915 Michael actually secured a job with an American firm, the Guarantee Trust Company of New York, as a prelude to eventual emigration to the United States.

When his personal conscription crisis came to a head in early 1916, however, he decided to return to Ireland, where the IRB was planning to stage a rebellion using the Irish Volunteer Force (IVF), in which his friend Jack Hurley had enrolled him, in April 1914. On handing in his notice he told his employers he was going to join up. They naturally assumed he was joining the British army to fight on the continent, but he was going home to fight the British army in Ireland.

Hannie later said that she tried to persuade him to have nothing to do with the planned rising. 'They'll let you down, Michael,' she warned. 'They'll let you down.' But, of course, he would not be deterred. He left London for Ireland on 15 January 1916.[29]

3

Preparing for the Rebellion

In Dublin he lost little time in contacting two of the IRB leaders, Tom Clarke and Seán MacDermott, who were the driving force behind the planned rebellion. At the outbreak of the First World War, the supreme council of the IRB decided to exploit Britain's difficulties by staging a rebellion, and Clarke and MacDermott were selected to look into the situation. They were authorised to co-opt anyone they wished on to their little committee, which eventually became known as the military council.

The first person they enlisted was Patrick Pearse, a shy, self-contained individual who was probably the most effective public speaker in the country. A poet, playwright, lawyer and educator, the leadership of the military council was turned over to him. Others later added to the council included Joseph Mary Plunkett and James Connolly, the militant labour organiser, who was included to prevent his Irish Citizen Army from embarking on a separate rebellion.

Collins was assigned as an aide to Joseph Mary Plunkett, the chief military strategist of the rebellion. A slender, pale, sickly young man with absolutely no military experience, he had gleaned all of what he knew about military strategy from books, or from his own fertile imagination. He was a poet with a romantic vision and a desperate need to leave his mark on a world in which he was not destined to stay long. He was already dying of tuberculosis.

'This place has many advantages over London,' Collins wrote to Hannie after little over a week. 'It's just lovely to see the mountains of a morning. My present job is at Kimmage far out – seems to be as remote as Woodfield but it's only a short walk and a penny tram from the emerald pasture of College Green.' He was 'working three days a week 10 to 4 as a financial adviser to Count Plunkett for which I get lunch each day and £1 a week.[1]

'There are quite a few of my old associates here,' he added. Some fifty of the Irish Volunteers from Britain were staying on the grounds owned by the Plunketts, making up what Pearse would call a standing army. George Plunkett was their captain and they were nicknamed 'George's lambs' by the Plunkett family. The men were housed in an obsolete mill on the property. They spent a considerable amount of time making shells and grenades. Collins, as usual, was full of self-importance and somewhat aloof from the others, according to Joe Good, one of the London group at the mill. They knew he worked in the Plunkett household, but did not know if he stayed there at night. In fact, he initially stayed with an aunt, one of his mother's sisters. 'As Easter Week approached he was busy making something that I felt was ominous,' stated Good. 'He was hurried and unusually discourteous. But his attitude, his urgency, was never a bore.[2]

'He came into our quarters at the mill on one occasion when a good deal of fun was going on; we were industrious making grenades,' Good recalled. 'Mick spoke roughly to one of the "lambs" who was slotting screws, suggesting he was not working hard enough, and passed generally abusive remarks. I suggested Mick should show us how to work faster, put a three-cornered file in his hand and gave him a bolt-head to slot. He proceeded to show us and a crowd gathered about him. Of course the file slipped on the round bolt head.' Collins did not realise he was being set up.

'Do you think this way might be right, Mick?' Good asked, having put half-a-dozen bolts in a vice.

'I ran my hacksaw over the half dozen bolts and "heigh-presto" six were slotted,' Good added. 'The "lambs" roared with laughter and, Mick swearing at us, went up the stairs to George Plunkett, followed by a gibing chorus of "The birds of the air fell a-sighing and a-sobbing when the heard of the death of poor Mick Collins".'[3]

At night many of the men would gather at Constance Markievicz's nearby home in Surrey House. It was not a mansion as the name suggested, but a small red-brick building in a little row of suburban houses at 49B

Surrey Road, Raheny. 'Crowds used to gather into it at night,' Frank Kelly recalled. They had tea in the kitchen at a long table with Madame cutting the bread and handing around the slices, which was eaten as fast as she could cut them. 'She had lovely furniture and splendid pictures,' he added. 'We used to go into the sitting-room and someone would sit at the piano and there would be great singing and cheering and rough amusements. She had lifted her lovely drawing-room carpet, but left the pictures on the walls and on the bare boards there was stamping of feet. In one corner James Connolly would sit at the fire and take no part in the pranks of the juniors.[4]

'I remember him one night,' Kelly added. 'He sat at the fire, looking into it, hour after hour, and never saying a word. Then he got up and went home. That same night Collins was reciting at the top of his voice Emmet's Speech from the Dock.'[5]

Robert Emmet was one of the great patriots of Irish history who had tried to stage a rebellion in 1803 but the whole thing went disastrously awry and ended in mere mob violence. He was arrested and tried. He entered no defence at his trial and was convicted without the jury even leaving the box. He was then asked if he had anything to say before the judge passed sentence and he responded with a long eloquent speech from the Dock. 'I have but one request to make at my departure from this world – it is the charity of its silence,' Emmet said. One can easily imagine Collins as he delivered the famous concluding words of the speech: 'Let my memory rest in oblivion and my grave remain uninscribed until other times and other men can do justice to my character. When my country takes her place among the nations of the earth, then and not till then, let my epitaph be written.'[6]

The aim of the military council was to proclaim an Irish Republic and set up a Provisional Government on Easter Sunday, 23 April 1916. Using the combined forces of the Irish Volunteers, Citizen Army, and Hibernian Rifles, they would seize prominent buildings throughout Dublin and hold them for as long as possible. A consignment of German arms was due to land that same day near Tralee, so volunteers in the rest of the country could rise in conjunction with the rebellion in Dublin.

Much of the negotiation with Germany had been conducted through John Devoy of Clan na Gael, the IRB's sister organisation in the United States, but the British admiralty had broken the German codes and was reading the messages between New York and Berlin, so British naval intelligence knew well in advance of the rebellion on Easter Sunday and of the plan to land arms in Tralee Bay.

Michael Collins was not very influential at this stage, but he was to form a strong relationship, which would eventually turn particularly sour, with Austin Stack, so it is important to understand the role that Stack played in order to understand the vicissitudes of his relations with Collins.

At this stage Stack, or Augustine Mary Moore Stack, to give him his full name, was a law clerk and a prominent member of the IRB. It was he who called a public meeting at the County Hall, Tralee, on 10 December 1913. He was the first secretary of the John Mitchel's Football Club, and he was secretary of the Kerry County Board of the GAA from 1904 to 1908. At the time he played on the club team that won eight consecutive county championships, and he captained the Kerry team that won the All-Ireland football final of 1904. Cathal Brugha swore Stack into the IRB in 1908 and he quickly became the centre, or head, of the movement in Kerry.

As one of eight children, Stack had seen some difficult times. There was never much money at home, as his father – Moore Stack – was overly fond of drink. Austin's biographer, Fr J. Anthony Gaughan noted that when Moore Stack was jailed for his Fenian activities in late 1866, he sang like the proverbial canary. He provided the authorities with details of the movement and requested somebody to help jog his memory so that he could even give further details. Although distrusted by colleagues, who suspected him of betraying information even before he began to talk, Moore Stack emerged from jail as a hero in extreme nationalist circles. Austin Stack was therefore thought of as the son of a Fenian patriot.

Alf Cotton had joined the IRB while still a teenager and had engaged in organisational work for the secret society in the Sligo area before he was transferred to Kerry in June 1914. While working in the Labour Exchange, he was appointed captain of the Tralee Volunteer Cycle Corps. He was dismissed from the civil service as a result of his volunteer activities in early 1915. He then became full-time volunteer instructor and organiser for County Kerry, with the rank of vice-commandant and brigade adjutant of the Tralee Battalion.

Pearse personally told Stack and Cotton of the plans for the rebellion. 'Austin Stack and I visited Pearse at St Enda's,' Cotton recalled. 'Pearse definitely made us promise that we would tell no one the information he had given us.' He told them the rebellion was to begin on Easter Sunday, and that they were to arrange for the arrival of the German arms' ship at Fenit and the distribution of the weapons. They were also to arrange for a message to be sent from the cable station in Valentia to the United States that the Rising had begun.[7]

Cotton began preparing for the arms' landing by holding some weekend camps in the Banna area, which was quite near Fenit. 'These camps were just weekend holiday camps attended by a few unemployed volunteers who would go out on Friday or Saturday morning and members of the Cycle Corps going out from Tralee on Saturday evening or Sunday morning,' Cotton recalled. 'The time was mainly spent in bathing, playing games and generally enjoying themselves. The Volunteers carried arms but there was little display of military activity.[8]

'I intended that on Good Friday a small but effective armed force of Volunteers would be encamped there to deal with any emergency which might arise and to have men on the spot when the arms' ship arrived,' Cotton explained. 'But unfortunately this intention was not carried out, for while on a visit to Belfast in March 1916, I was served with an order under the Defence of the Realm Act forbidding me to return to the counties of Cork and Kerry and confining me strictly to the city of Belfast.'[9]

Cotton said that he had planned to ignore the exclusion order, but Seán MacDermott was afraid that his presence would endanger the arms' landing and Cotton was told to return to Belfast and sever all connections with Kerry until the rising took place. 'I was unaware of what was happening in Kerry but I was confident that the Volunteers would be ready when the time came,' Cotton continued.[10]

Roger Casement, who had distinguished himself in the British foreign service before becoming an ardent Irish nationalist, had been involved in arranging the Howth gun-running in 1914 and he went to Berlin to organise German help for the planned rebellion. He sought arms and men. The Germans allowed him to recruit some fifty-five Irish men from among the British army prisoners of war, but the Germans were not prepared to send any of their own soldiers. They were ready to send Casement and the fifty-five men on a ship along with a consignment of 20,000 rifles and ten machine guns, but Casement realised that the whole thing would be futile and he was not prepared to expose the men. He asked the Germans to send him ahead by U-boat so he could prepare for the landing of the arms, but his real reason was to try to stop the rebellion as he felt it was doomed to fail.[11]

'The one last hope I clung to,' he later told George Gavan Duffy, 'was that I might arrive in Ireland in time to stop the Rising, and then face the fate I knew must be mine.' He felt he would have condemned himself to a life of contempt if he had stayed in Germany and allowed the *Aud* to arrive in Ireland, because he felt the planned Rising would go ahead and it would be a disaster. 'So I saw nothing else but to go to Ireland and still try to get there before the steamer.'[12]

Casement and two colleagues set out for Ireland on the U-20 on 12 April 1916, but from this point on everything seemed to go wrong. The submarine developed engine trouble and had to return to port and transfer to the U-19. They lost five vital days.

On the Tuesday 18 April, the United States secret service raided the office of the German consul in New York and discovered the message from Ireland requesting that the arms not be delivered before Easter Sunday. The Americans promptly passed on the information to the British. Hence London and Berlin knew that the Irish were expecting the arms' ship on 23 April, but the crew of the ship did not know that the date had been changed.

Joseph Plunkett had been vainly endeavouring to make contact with the ship with a homemade radio at Larkfield House, Kimmage. On Thursday Con Collins arrived in Tralee from Dublin with orders to establish a wireless station in Tralee with a transmitter that was to be stolen in Caherciveen the following day by a group sent from Dublin.

That evening the German arms' ship arrived in Tralee Bay. The U-boat arrived in the early hours of the following morning, 21 April 1916 – Good Friday – while the arms' ship was still waiting for a pilot to guide it into Fenit pier. Stack had not been informed that the Germans were still expecting to be met on the Thursday.

Casement arrived without any warning. He was ill, suffering from a recurrence of malaria, and his two colleagues headed for Tralee to get some help, but before help could be arranged the police, roused by finding the boat on which the three men had come ashore, found Casement hiding in a rath near Banna. He was taken to Tralee by a couple of RIC constables. He could easily have been rescued at that stage, but no effort was made to save him.

The RIC head constable in Tralee, John A. Kearney, recognised him and sought to have him rescued. As Casement was ill, Kearney sent for a local doctor Mickey Shanahan, who was a known Sinn Féin sympathiser. Kearney then left the two of them together, hoping that Casement would confide in the doctor. To make doubly sure, before Shanahan left the station, Kearney showed him a newspaper photograph of Casement and mentioned that he was the prisoner. Shanahan dutifully disagreed, but Kearney was just warning him that the RIC knew who they were holding.

Kearney, confidently expecting the local IVF to rescue Casement, told his wife to keep their children upstairs and out of harm's way. Although Austin Stack pretended not to believe Shanahan, he knew the truth, as he had already been talking to Robert Monteith, one of the men who had accompanied Casement on the U-boat. Stack later said that Pearse had told him to let nothing happen in Tralee before the arms were due to land on Sunday. 'Pearse was insistent that there must be the utmost secrecy in all our preparations,' Alf Cotton later explained. 'Only the very minimum of information considered necessary was to be given to men selected for any special work, and these men were to be carefully selected for their particular jobs. That secrecy was to be preserved up to the last minute. Much depended on the element of surprise, both for our local activities and for the larger project.'[13]

In the circumstances Stack felt that he could not attempt to rescue Casement. Maybe this demonstrated that he was a loyal follower, but it did not exhibit any leadership qualities in terms of taking the initiative in unforeseen circumstances. By then, the arms' ship had left Tralee Bay anyway. He sent two messengers to Dublin by separate routes and then announced that the was going to the RIC station, as he had received a message from the head constable asking him to see Con Collins, who had been arrested earlier that day. Why did Kearney send the message – was it to give Stack an excuse to come to the station to rescue Casement?

Paddy J. Cahill, the acting vice-brigadier, suggested Stack ensure he had nothing incriminating on him. Stack duly handed over a revolver, but arrived at the RIC barracks with between eighteen and thirty-three letters on his person from people like Patrick Pearse, Bulmer Hobson of the IRB and Eoin MacNeill, the president of the Irish Volunteers. When he was searched at the barracks, these were found and he was arrested, which was possibly why he went to the barracks with the letters. Did he conclude that the planned rebellion was falling apart and therefore deliberately get himself arrested to ensure that he would be in custody when the rebellion began?

Meanwhile, Casement asked for a priest. Even though Kearney knew that Casement was a Protestant, he sent for a Catholic priest from the nearby Dominican priory and left them together. Casement identified himself and asked Fr Francis Ryan to get a message to the IVF leadership in Dublin. 'He told me that he had come to Ireland to stop the rebellion then impending,' the priest later recalled. 'Tell them I am a prisoner,' Casement said, 'and that the rebellion will be a dismal hopeless failure, as the help they expect will not arrive.'[14]

Fr Ryan was taken aback. He had come on a spiritual mission and had no desire to get involved in this kind of politics. 'Do what I ask,'

Casement pleaded, 'and you will bring God's blessing on the country and on everyone concerned.'[15]

'I saw the leader of the Volunteers in Tralee and gave him the message. He assured me he would do his best to keep the Volunteers quiet.'[16] It was assumed that Fr Ryan had spoken to Stack, which would have reinforced the appearance that plans for the Rising were disintegrating, but, in fact, the priest did not pass the warning on to Stack at all. It was not until Monday morning that Fr Ryan actually informed Paddy Cahill of the meeting with Casement at the RIC barracks.

'Casement definitely came to prevent the rising and gave a message to that effect to Fr Frank Ryan, O.P. of Tralee, and I was present when Father Ryan delivered that message to Paddy Cahill in his office at John Donovan & Sons Ltd., The Square, Tralee, and I knew that Cahill had that message conveyed to Headquarters in Dublin,' his friend Tadhg Kennedy later recalled.[17]

'I also told the head constable of the steps I had taken, and my reasons for it,' Fr Ryan later explained. 'He agreed with me the that it was perhaps the wisest course to follow.'[18]

Although Cahill had been chosen as Stack's deputy, he was clearly unprepared for the position following Stack's arrest. Cahill pleaded that he did not know what to do and insisted Robert Monteith should take charge, even though Monteith had only just returned from Germany that morning and did not know any of the men he was supposed to lead. Events were spinning out of control. That Friday night, the men sent from Dublin to seize the radio transmitter in Caherciveen took a wrong turn outside Killorglin and drove off the short pier at Ballykissane; the radio operator Con Keating and two others were drowned. Of course, even if they had obtained the transmitter it would have made no difference, because the arms' ship had no radio and had already left Tralee Bay.

Shortly afterwards the *Aud* was intercepted by the Royal Navy and ordered to put into Queenstown for inspection. The crew changed into their uniforms and scuttled the boat off Queenstown on Saturday while Casement was being transferred to London. That day the *Kerry*

Evening Post reported that 'a stranger of unknown nationality' had been arrested not far from where a collapsible boat was found between Banna and Barrow. 'A rumour is around that he is no less a personage than Sir Roger Casement,' according to the report. 'The captured man was taken under a strong armed escort to Dublin by the 10.30 train this morning.'[19]

Casement asked to be allowed to appeal to his colleagues to call operations off, but Admiral William 'Blinker' Hall, the chief of naval intelligence, wanted the rebellion to go ahead. He had already been withholding information about the planned uprising from the Dublin Castle authorities so the rebellion would take place. The British government could then easily be manipulated into introducing the repressive measures that Hall thought desirable in Ireland. 'It is better that a cankering sore like this should be cut out,' he told Casement in London on Easter Sunday.[20]

Casement told Basil Thompson, the head of intelligence at Scotland Yard, that when he realised the Germans were not going to send proper help, he felt 'it his duty to come and warn the rebels a rising would be hopeless.[21]

'I have done nothing treacherous to my country,' Casement insisted. 'In this last act of mine in going back to Ireland, I came with my eyes wide open.' He knew that the British would consider his behaviour treasonous. 'Some Irishmen are afraid to act, but I was not afraid to commit high treason. I am not endeavouring to shield myself at all. I face all the consequences.

'I came,' he said, 'knowing that you were bound to catch me.'[22]

Although the rebels would be drawn mainly from the IVF, Eoin MacNeill, the leader, had not been told of the planned rebellion by the IRB, which secretly controlled his organisation. It was they who had initially decided to set up the IVF in the first place and had merely turned to him because – as a professor of early Irish history and president of the Gaelic League – he provided a cover of academic respectability. They thought they would always be able to manipulate him to further their aims. Whereas he looked on the Irish Volunteers essentially as a means of counteracting the influence of the Ulster Volunteer Force in order to maintain pressure on Westminster to grant Home Rule to Ireland, the IRB leaders were looking for much more than a devolved parliament within the United Kingdom framework. They wanted a sovereign, independent Irish republic, and they saw the Irish Volunteers as a potential army to drive the British out of Ireland.

For months the Irish Volunteers had been drilling and marching publicly, with the result that little notice was taken when the organisation called for nationwide parades on Easter Sunday. Only when the men gathered together on that day would they be told of the rebellion.

MacNeill learned of the plans on the Wednesday beforehand and threatened to call the whole thing off, but Pearse managed to persuade him to go along with the military council by assuring him that arrangements had been made to secure German help. But then one disaster after another occurred – the men going to seize the radio transmitter had drowned, the arms' ship had been scuttled and Casement had been arrested. In the face of those setbacks, MacNeill decided to call off the rebellion. He sent out messengers with orders to suspend all manoeuvres planned for Sunday and he put a notice to the same effect in the *Sunday Independent*.

Some, like Seán McGarry of the IRB, thought MacNeill's actions the most damaging. McGarry had spent Saturday night at a hotel with Tom Clarke, one of the leaders of the planned rebellion, and was appalled when he read the papers the next morning. 'On my way home I got the paper and read the order countermanding the mobilisation,' McGarry recalled. 'I walked home in a daze to find Mick Collins who had been staying with Plunkett and who came after Mass to breakfast in my house. I showed him the paper. He became dumb. We breakfasted in silence and left for Liberty Hall where we found the Military Council in session.' Clarke 'seemed crushed,' according to McGarry. 'He regarded MacNeill's action was of the blackest and greatest treachery.'[23]

The rebellion had been called off, and Sunday passed without incident, but the IRB leaders were now desperate. With the capture of Casement, it was obviously only a matter of time before they would be rounded up. They therefore quietly sent word to the Dublin battalions that the postponed manoeuvres would take place at noon the following day, Monday 24 April. The British were caught totally by surprise, which was understandable because so were MacNeill and the vast majority of those the IRB had hoped would take part.

Plunkett spent Easter Sunday night in a Dublin nursing home in Mountjoy Square. He was so weak that Collins had to help him dress in the morning. When Commandant W.J. Brennan-Whitmore arrived, Plunkett introduced him to Collins.

'I can't say that, at the time, I was much impressed with Collins,' Brennan-Whitmore noted. 'He appeared to be silent to the point of surliness, and he gave my hand a bone-cracking squeeze without saying a single word.'[24]

Collins helped to deliver Plunkett to Liberty Hall. Dressed in his staff captain's uniform he looked smart, especially in comparison to others of the Kimmage garrison who arrived in high spirits, clad in ill-fitting military outfits, which were an assortment of different shades of green that were anything but uniform. He was not impressed with them and flushed with anger when they – irritated by his smug air of self-importance – retaliated by sniggering at his appearance.

Fifty-seven men boarded a tram for the city centre at Harold's Cross around 11 a.m. They were a rather motley group, some with bandoliers, laden with rifles, pistols, as well as pick-axes, sledge-hammers and shovels. A woman passenger was upset at being prodded by the rifle of one heavily-laden man who insisted in sitting down beside her without removing any of his equipment.

'Fifty-seven two-penny fares, and don't stop until we reach O'Connell Bridge', the officer in charge told the conductor as he handed over the exact money.[25] One of the volunteers sat down with his rifle nonchalantly pointed at the head of the driver, who ignored the pleas of passengers wishing to alight as he raced by their stops on the way to the city centre.

There was a farcical air about proceedings as the men lined up outside Liberty Hall. Pearse was about to take his place at the head of the group when he was embarrassed by one of his sisters. 'Come home, Patrick, and leave all this foolishness!' she pleaded.[26]

Pearse blushed with embarrassment, and the men around him shuffled nervously.

'Form Four,' Connolly shouted and ordered the men to march off, giving Pearse the excuse to brush past his sister to the head of the group marching off towards Sackville Street.[27]

Plunkett, Connolly and Pearse formed the first line, with more than 300 men marching four abreast behind them. Brennan-Whitmore was on the extreme left with Collins on his immediate inside. Clarke and MacDermott did not consider themselves soldiers so they followed on the pavement.

It was a holiday and the streets were relatively quiet. Onlookers, now used to such parades, did not realise anything unusual was happening until the men reached the General Post Office (GPO) and Connolly gave the order to charge the building.

4

'We Lost, Didn't We!'

Collins and Brennan-Whitmore linked arms with Plunkett to help him into the building. Connolly ordered the staff and customers out.

'Everyone outside,' he barked.[1]

Some left reluctantly, muttering in resentment as they were hustled out the door. Lieutenant Chambers of the Royal Fusiliers was sending a telegram to his wife when the men charged in, and Plunkett ordered that he be taken prisoner. Collins went into a telephone booth and yanked out the flex, which he used to tie up the unfortunate officer whom he lifted bodily and dumped in the telephone booth with a laugh.

'Please don't shoot me,' pleaded Constable Dunphy of the Dublin Metropolitan Police (DMP) as he was taken prisoner, 'I done no harm.'[2]

'We don't shoot prisoners,' replied Collins, who ordered two volunteers to bring the man upstairs and lock him in a room.[3]

When Connolly ordered the ground floor windows to be knocked out, Collins took a boyish delight in smashing the glass.

'Glory be to God!' cried a startled woman outside. Huddled in a black shawl, she looked on in amazement. 'Would you look at them smashing all the lovely windows!' Collins laughed boisterously and the men around him joined in his laughter.[4]

Pearse went outside and, as a small group looked on indifferently, proclaimed the Irish Republic 'in the name of God and of the dead generations'. Inside the men continued with their task of fortifying the building for the expected counter-attack. Collins and Brennan-Whitmore were detailed to ensure all windows were properly barricaded.

When Collins went to the canteen he poured two tierces of porter down the drain. 'They said we were drunk in '98,' he remarked, 'they won't be able to say it now.'[5]

There were unfounded reports that the Germans had landed, that German submarines were blockading Dublin Bay to ensure the British could not bring in reinforcement, that the Turks had landed in Waterford, and that Big Jim Larkin was returning from the United States with a force of 50,000 Irish-Americans. One of Connolly's men rushed into the GPO to announce that King George and Lord Kitchener had been captured. 'In the Henry Street Waxworks!' he added after a calculated pause.[6]

The only real engagement that those in the GPO had with the enemy on the first day was when a company of British Lancers rode down Sackville Street in formation on horseback, apparently hoping that their appearance would frighten the rebels. It was an absurd gesture. When the firing began three of the horsemen and two of their horses were shot dead and another man fell mortally wounded, while the remainder bolted for safety.

'If that's the way they attack a fortified building,' one of the rebels cried, 'there's some hope for us yet.'[7]

The Lancers had not even fired a shot, but the insurgents suffered a number of casualties anyway. A volunteer in a building across the street was killed in the cross fire, and another was injured on the GPO side, while a third shot himself in the stomach accidentally. The British officer dumped by Collins in the telephone booth had a narrow escape when a stray bullet lodged in the timber inches from his head. His bonds were cut and he was sent to join the other prisoners upstairs.

The second day was largely one of anticipation as the rebels waited for the British to attack, while an orgy of looting was taking place outside throughout Sackville Street. Realising that the police would not dare enter the street, people from the nearby slums broke display windows and helped themselves to whatever they desired in the shops. Pearse went out to the foot of Nelson's Pillar in front of the GPO and denounced the looters as 'hangers-on of the British army'.[8]

'The country is rising in answer to Dublin's call, and the final achievement of Ireland's freedom is now, with God's help, only a matter of days,' he declared in this address to the citizens of Dublin. 'The valour, self-sacrifice, and discipline of Irish men and women are about to win our country a glorious place among the nations.'[9]

Wednesday dawned with still no sign of the expected British assault, but as the morning progressed there were sounds of shelling when the gunship *Helga* opened fire on Liberty Hall. The men had not expected the shelling. Connolly, a dedicated Marxist, had confidently predicted the forces of British capitalism would be so anxious to avoid damaging property that they would not use artillery on an expensive building, but storm it with troops instead.

The men in the Eden Quay area were ordered to abandon their positions and move to the GPO, only to find that the messenger who had brought the order had been confused: Connolly had not wanted them to retreat at all. They therefore had to make their perilous way back across Sackville Street amid heavy British sniper fire. The incident was indicative of the confusion that reigned in republican ranks throughout the week.

There were unfounded rumours the British were preparing to attack the GPO with gas, so one of the men with some chemical training was assigned to prepare an antidote. He put together a concoction and distributed it in the building in buckets.

'What the hell good will that do?' Collins asked him.[10]

'None,' the man conceded and that put an end to the idiotic scheme.

Collins was much too practical to waste time on such matters. He was actually singled out as 'the most active and efficient officer in the place' by Desmond Fitzgerald, who had been placed in charge of the GPO canteen.[11]

Having been ordered to economise rigidly to ensure that the food supply would last for three weeks, Fitzgerald irritated many of the men by providing only meagre portions. Collins baulked at such petty restrictions. He came in one morning with some men who had been working hard on demolishing walls and building barricades. He told Fitzgerald the men were to be fed properly, even if meant that they took all the remaining food.

'I did not attempt to argue with them,' Fitzgerald related. 'The men sat down openly rejoicing that I had been crushed. Apparently some of them had already been the victims of my rigid economy.'[12]

The most difficult time for soldiers is invariably while waiting for a battle to begin, and those in the GPO had to wait for the best part of four days. Every so often someone brought news of British troops massing for an attack, but each time the report turned out to be a false alarm and this inevitably began to affect morale. At one point on the Wednesday night Connolly tried to raise the men's spirits with a song. He began:

> We'll sing a song, a soldier's song
> With cheering, rousing chorus,
> As round the blazing fires we throng,
> The starry heavens o'er us.
> Impatient for the coming fight,
> And as we wait the morning's light,
> Here in the silence of the night
> We'll chant a soldier's song.[13]

Others joined in the chorus as it built to a crescendo, with some fifty voices belting out what would one day become the country's national anthem:

> Soldiers are we, whose lives are pledged to Ireland;
> Some have come from a land beyond the wave;
> Sworn to be free, no more our ancient sireland
> Shall shelter the despot, or the slave.
> Tonight we man the *bearna boaghail*
> In Erin's cause, come woe or weal;
> 'Mid cannon's roar and rifle's peal
> We'll chant a soldier's song.

Collins, who had been sleeping when the singing began, awoke looking decidedly perturbed. 'If this is supposed to be a concert,' he said factitiously to Connolly's secretary Winifred Carney, 'they'll want the piano in the back room.'[14]

The weather the next day was glorious, with a slight breeze from the east blowing over the putrefying carcasses of the two dead horses outside on the street. Having knocked out all the glass in the windows the men had to endure the nauseating stench while the interminable waiting for an assault continued. The British never did attack as Plunkett and Connolly had anticipated; instead they began shelling Sackville Street with heavy artillery placed a short distance away in Rutland Square. Before long the east side of the street was in flames.

Connolly led some men out of the GPO on a raid, but was wounded in the process. Pearse, meanwhile, was busy preparing an address that he delivered to all available men in the main hall of the GPO that evening. Although it was supposedly a pep talk for the troops, it was really addressed to posterity, over the heads of the gathered men, to whom he referred in the third person throughout.

'Let me, who have led them into this, speak in my own name, and in my fellow commandants' names, and in the name of Ireland present and to come, their praise, and ask those who come after them to remember them,' he said. 'They have held out for four days against the might of the British Empire. They have established Ireland's right to be called a Republic, and they have established this government's right to sit at the peace table at the end of the European war.'[15]

Collins had little time for Pearse, an impractical dreamer, politically inexperienced, militarily innocent and obsessed with mystical visions of blood sacrifice. Writing in December 1915, Pearse had described the first sixteen months of the First World War as 'the most glorious' period in European history.[16]

'Heroism has come back to the earth,' he wrote. 'The old heart of the earth needed to be warmed with the red wine of the battlefields. Such august homage was never before offered to God as this, the homage of millions of lives gladly given for love of country.'[17] He wrote this blasphemous drivel as if he were experiencing some kind of spiritual orgasm.

A medium-sized man with a handsome face, marred by a pronounced cast in his right eye (which usually made him have his photograph taken in profile to conceal it), Pearse had a messiah complex. It was more than mere coincidence that he selected Easter Sunday for the rising. Just as Christ had sacrificed himself to save mankind, Pearse believed he was sacrificing himself to save the Irish people's sacred right to nationhood. Just why the son of an Englishman should take such a task upon himself one can only wonder.

Although a general in the rebel army, he had the mentality of a scout master, with some rather strange ideas. Other writings betrayed an extreme attitude when it came to proving manhood. 'Bloodshed is a cleansing and a sanctifying thing,' he wrote, 'and the nation which regards it as the final horror has lost its manhood.' It was as if he wanted to prove his masculinity by shedding his own blood.[18]

Looking back on Easter week some months later, Collins would be quite critical of the way the rebellion was conducted in general and of Pearse's leadership in particular. This was hardly surprising. While in London he had written about the need to have the Irish forces organised on practical grounds and headed by realists. 'Whereas a force organised on theoretical lines, and headed by idealists, would,' he wrote, 'be a very doubtful factor.' Time proved him right, at least in his own opinion.[19]

'I do not think the Rising week was an appropriate time for the issue of memoranda couched in poetic phrase, nor of actions worked out in similar fashion,' he wrote. 'It had the air of a Greek tragedy about it, the illusion being more or less completed with the issue of the before-mentioned memoranda. Of Pearse and Connolly I admire the latter the most.'[20]

While Connolly shared Pearse's enthusiasm for the rebellion, he had a saner view of the horror of war. 'We do not think that the old heart of the earth needs to be warmed with the red wine of millions of lives,' he wrote in response to Pearse's obnoxious drivel about the First World War. 'We think anyone who does is a blithering idiot.'[21]

'Connolly was a realist, Pearse the direct opposite,' according to Collins. 'There was air of earthy directness about Connolly. It impressed me. I would have followed him through hell had such action been necessary. But I honestly doubt very much if I would have followed Pearse – not without some thought anyway.'[22]

Collins also held two of the other leaders, Clarke and MacDermott, in high esteem. Not being soldiers, they went into and remained in the GPO as excited spectators rather than participants. 'Both were built on the best foundations,' according to Collins, who was especially impressed by MacDermott. 'Wherever he walked there went with him all the shades of the great Irishmen of the past. He was God-given. He was humble in the knowledge of his own greatness and in the task that he had chosen to do. He did not seek glory as a personal investment but as a national investment.'[23]

In writing to friends about the rebellion, it was particularly noticeable that Collins never mentioned the fifth and only other member of the military council in the GPO, Joseph Mary Plunkett. Maybe his reticence had something to do with a sense of loyalty to the man to whom he had been an aide. Plunkett, like Pearse, was a poet overly given to a sense of the dramatic, and his jewellery – a bangle and a large antique ring on one of his fingers – seemed incongruous with military masculinity. In addition, he was physically weak and tired very easily. It had only been three weeks since he had had an operation for the glandular tuberculosis that was obviously killing him, so he spent a great deal of time in the GPO resting.

'On the whole I think the Rising was bungled terribly, costing many a good life,' Collins explained. 'It seemed at first to be well organised, but afterwards became subjected to panic decisions and a great lack of very essential organisation and co-operation.'[24]

On Friday, the fifth day of the rebellion, the British began firing incendiary shells at the GPO. Collins and a large detail of men held the fire at bay for as long as possible, putting barriers of sand across doorways and flooding the floors with water, but this was only a delaying measure. 'Although I was never actually scared in the GPO I was – and others also – witless enough to do stupid things,' he wrote some months later. 'As the flames and heat increased so apparently did the shelling. Machine-gun fire made escape more or less impossible. Not that we wished to escape. No man wished to budge. In that building, the defiance of our men, and the gallantry, reached unimaginable proportions.'[25]

The fire gradually took hold and it became necessary to evacuate the building. Pearse called all the available men together to deliver another of his addresses in the main hall.

'If we have accomplished no more than we have accomplished, I am satisfied,' he told them. 'We should have accomplished the task of enthroning as well as proclaiming the Irish Republic as a sovereign state, had our arrangements for a simultaneous Rising of the whole country – with a combined plan as sound as the Dublin plan has proved to be – been allowed to go through on Easter Sunday. Of the fatal countermanding order which prevented those plans being carried out, I shall not speak further. Both Eoin MacNeill and we have acted in the best interests of Ireland.'[26]

With the fire in the GPO out of control, it was decided to move the headquarters to a factory on Great Britain Street, but Pearse took the decision without enquiring about the position of enemy forces in the area. The O'Rahilly and some men went to make preparations and had only just left when one of the volunteers told Pearse that Great Britain Street had been solidly in the hands of the crown forces since Thursday.

'Stop The O'Rahilly,' Pearse shouted. 'He's gone into Moore Street with some men.'[27]

Collins darted out the door and ran up Henry Place, but he was too late. The O'Rahilly had already been cut down. Collins and those who followed him took refuge in the terraced cottages lining Moore Street, where the other survivors of the headquarters staff joined them. Pearse had led them from the burning building with his sword drawn and held aloft in a heroic gesture, symbol of his impracticality.

For a time the volunteers tried to reach the British barricade at the top of the street by breaking a way trough the walls of the terraced houses, but the idea of setting up a new headquarters in the factory in Great Britain Street was clearly no longer feasible. Pearse therefore looked for surrender terms next morning. The British insisted on 'an unconditional surrender', and Pearse decided to concede, though some of the Kimmage contingent wanted to fight on. Clarke tried to convince them but failed, as did Plunkett.[28]

'If you fight on,' Collins pleaded, 'you'll do nothing but seal the death warrants for all our leaders.'

'Sure, they'll all be shot anyway,' someone replied. In desperation, Collins asked MacDermott to talk to them.

'Now what is it you fellows intend to do?' MacDermott asked them. He listened patiently to their arguments and then tried to persuade them to surrender, mentioning some civilians having been shot that morning.

'We're hopelessly beaten,' MacDermott said. 'We haven't a prayer of fighting our way out of here. You've already fought a gallant fight, every one of you. You gain nothing; you lose everything if you try to continue. You think you'll be killed, do you, if you surrender. Not at all.

'Some of the rest of us will be killed, but none of you,' he continued. 'Why should they kill you? And why should they put you in the British army? You'd be no good to them. They'll send you to prison for a few years, that's the worst. But what does it matter, if you survive? The thing you must do, all of you, is survive, come back, carry on the work so nobly begun this week. Those of us who are shot can die happy if we know you'll be living on to finish what we started.'

Nobody else had anything to say. The men who had returned from Britain to take part in the Rising relented. 'I know you wanted to fight on, and I'm proud of you,' MacDermott said. 'I know also that this week of Easter will never be forgotten. Ireland will one day be free because of what you've done here.'

They then ate what was left of their rations and said the rosary, some holding a rifle in one hand and rosary beads in the other.[29]

Collins marched out with the headquarters staff into Sackville Street and turned left up towards the Parnell monument where they downed arms and surrendered. They were joined by men from the Four Courts and then marched up to the green in front of the Rotunda Hospital, where they were herded together, surrounded by a ring of soldiers with bayonets at the ready.

The officer in charge of the crown forces was Captain Lea Wilson, a florid-faced, thick-lipped Englishman, who behaved as if he had had a little too much to drink. He roared at his own men and issued contradictory orders while rushing from one prisoner to another, shouting that he was going to have them shot. He singled Clarke out for particularly harsh treatment.

'That old bastard is the commander-in-chief. He keeps a tobacco shop across the street. Nice general for your fucking army.' He had Clarke stripped naked and prodded him mercilessly, while nurses looked on from the windows of the Rotunda. Collins watched in indignation.[30]

'A dark night, a dark lane, a stout stick – and that fellow!' one volunteer was heard to mutter.[31] Collins never forgave Wilson for what he did to Clarke. Four years later he would take particular delight in having Wilson killed in revenge for what he did that day.

On Sunday morning the prisoners were marched through the streets to Richmond barracks. W.E. Wylie, who was put in charge of the guard, feared that there would be trouble as people tried to rescue the rebels. But his fears proved groundless. 'I might have saved myself the trouble,' Wylie wrote, 'for instead of cheering the prisoners, all of the old women and men in the streets cursed them. The prisoners needed more protection from the crowd than the soldiers did.'[32]

The rebels were pelted with rotten fruit and vegetables by Dublin people, who blamed them for the devastation of the rebellion in which more innocent civilians perished than anybody else. Two hundred and sixty-two civilians were reported killed, while the crown forces suffered 141 deaths and 62 rebels were killed in the fighting. Among the latter was Collins' great friend Jack Hurley.

'Do you think they'll let us go?' a volunteer asked as they were being walked though the hostile crowd of onlookers.

'Bejasus, I hope not,' replied Jim Ryan.[33]

'The citizens of Dublin would have torn us to pieces,' according to Piaras Béaslaí.[34]

The prisoners were taken to the gymnasium at Richmond barracks, where police detectives circulated among them, picking out known activists for special treatment. These were Irishmen singling out other Irishmen for trial and in some cases, execution.

Collins had only been in Dublin for three months, so the detectives did not know him, as he was not one of the recognised leaders. The prisoners were placed in dormitories, where they had to sleep on the hard floor. Joe Good remembers sharing an overcoat with Collins.

'What has you here?' a British sergeant asked Collins.

'England's difficulty,' Collins replied

'England's difficulty!' the bemused sergeant exclaimed. 'What the hell's that?'

'Well, England's difficulty is Ireland's opportunity,' Collins replied, completing the old adage.

'I wonder will they try to force us into the British army?' one young lad asked.

'They wouldn't touch us with a forty foot pole,' Good said.

'Shut your bloody mouth!' the sergeant snapped.

'Mick squeezed my knee delightedly,' Good recalled.[35]

At one point Collins thought he heard his name being called in one corner of the gym, and he walked there to find himself among a group about to be shipped directly to Britain. That evening he and 488 other prisoners were marched to the North Wall.

'Well it was a good fight, Mick,' a colleague said as they were going down the quays.

'What do you mean a good fight?' he snapped in reply. 'We lost, didn't we?'[36]

The men were herded together on a cattle boat and deported. Out of the country, Collins would not learn for some time of how the British over-reacted in Ireland during the following days.

In addition to rounding up the rebels, they arrested and deported hundreds of people who had taken no part in the rebellion, people like Eoin MacNeill and Arthur Griffith, the founder of Sinn Féin. The wholesale arrests and the sixteen executions that followed were a terrible blunder on Britain's part because they generated enormous compassion, which turned to sympathy, for the rebels. In death, Pearse – notwithstanding his own somewhat demented view of the world – became a national hero and his mystical rhetoric coloured the perception of what he had tried to do. Henceforth the rebellion would be seen in terms of a kind of religious experience. The executed were referred to as 'martyrs' and it was said that the executions 'helped to convert' the Irish people to the separatist cause. The rebellion itself came to be known as the Easter Rising, and in the process Pearse's accomplishment would be symbolically equated with the greatest of all of Christ's miracles.

5

'In the End They'll Despair'

Upon arrival in Holyhead, the prisoners found two trains waiting for them on either side of a railway platform. One went to Knutsford, and the other, which Collins boarded, to Stafford.

He and 288 other rebels were marched from the railroad station to Stafford military detention barracks. At one point on the way a couple of bystanders tried to attack one of the prisoners, but were driven off by a burly English sergeant. 'Get back you, bastards,' he shouted at the assailants. 'These men fought for their country, you won't.'[1]

For three weeks the prisoners were kept in solitary confinement, and only allowed out for short periods to walk in single file around a courtyard in total silence. They had no news of the outside world. In the monotony of this daily routine, each man got to know his cell intimately, the stone floor, thirty-five panes of glass and the black iron door. They had a slate to write on, a pencil, a bed board, a stool, a table, a can, a bowl, a glass and endless time to think. They could hear the noise of the town in the distance.

'It was for the most part an unpremeditated solitary confinement,' Desmond Ryan recalled. 'Our khaki guardians came round to give us mugs and mattresses and to examine the cells; it took them the best part of a week to adjust themselves completely to the invasion.'

'What caused the riots?' the British soldiers kept asking.

'We heard early that we must shine tins, until we could see our faces therein, must fold our blankets along certain lines, keep our cells as clean as pins, listen to what the staff had to say to us, preserve the strictest military discipline with silence, not whistle or sing, not attempt to communicate with other prisoners, not to look out the windows under penalties of bread and water and an appearance before the commandant.'[2]

After two weeks they were allowed to write home, and Collins wrote to Hannie. 'Positively you have no idea of what it's like – the dreadful monotony – the heart-scalding eternal brooding on all sorts of things, thoughts of friends dead and living – especially those recently dead – but above all the time – the horror of the way in which it refuses to pass.' He asked her to send him some novels and a French grammar that had been at the flat before he left London. He found it very hard to concentrate and Oscar Wilde's 'Ballad of Reading Gaol' kept running through his mind.[3]

He also had plenty of time to think about 'our little "shemozzle"', as he called the rebellion in a letter to his friend Susan Killeen on 25 May. 'If our performance will only teach the housekeepers of Dublin to have more grub in reserve for the future it will surely not have been in vain.' This was his idea of being funny. 'But seriously,' he added, 'I'm afraid there must have been a lot of hardship and misery which must continue for many a day and which all our sympathy cannot soften.[4]

'Life here has not been so ghastly since communications from the outer world have been allowed, and since we've been allowed reading matter and to write letters,' he continued. 'I saw poor Pearse's last letter in the *Daily Mail* this day and it didn't make me exactly prayerful.'[5]

As the restrictions were relaxed, the authorities became very benign. 'Conditions have improved wonderfully during the last week,' Collins explained in another letter to Susan Killeen four days later.[6]

'We had the life of Riley,' Joe Sweeney wrote afterwards.[7] They revived their spirits with impromptu football games in the courtyard, using a makeshift ball of brown paper and rags wrapped with twine. 'A frenzied mass of swearing, struggling, perspiring men rolled and fought over the ball in the middle of the yard,' Desmond Ryan recalled. 'From the din a tall, wiry, dark-haired man emerged and his Cork accent dominated the battle for a moment. He went under and rose and whooped and swore with tremendous vibrations of his accent and then disappeared again.'

'That's Mick Collins,' someone said.[8]

On 28 June, Collins and more than a hundred others were transferred from Stafford to an internment camp at Frongoch, near Barra in North

Wales. He seemed to have had some regrets about leaving Stafford, because henceforth he would be limited to one letter a week. He was certainly in a reflective mood on the eve of his transfer.

'One gets plenty of time to think here and my thoughts are often self-accusing goodness knows. I can't tell you how small I feel sometimes. 'Tis all very fine for writers to talk about the sublime thoughts which enter into people when they are faced by death – once, when I was in a pretty tight corner, what struck me was how much nicer I might have been to the people who had a regard for me.'[9]

Collins enjoyed the train journey through what he described 'a most engaging country'.[10] At Frongoch they joined internees from Knutsford and other detention centres, and numbers swelled to over 1,800. The camp, which had until recently housed German prisoners-of-war, was divided into two barbed-wire compounds, separated by a road. Collins, internee No. 1320, was put in the north camp, which consisted of a series of thirty-five wooden huts, which were sixty feet long and sixteen feet wide and only ten feet high in the centre. 'Not too much room to spare,' he wrote. Each hut housed thirty internees, so conditions were very cramped.[11]

'It's situated most picturesquely on rising ground amid pretty Welsh hills,' Collins wrote shortly after his arrival in the camp. 'Up to the present it hasn't presented any good points to me, for it rained all the time.' As a result the grass pathways between the huts quickly turned into 'a mass of slippery shifting mud'. The ''uts', as they called them, were cold and drafty even during the summer, which made the men anxious about conditions later in the year. 'I cheer them all up by asking them – what'll they do when the winter comes?'[12] By then he would actually welcome the conditions.

The internees were 'given the control and management' of the camp within the barbed wire. Collins readily adapted himself to the conditions, and made the most of his internment. 'He was full of fun and mischief', remembered Batt O'Connor. 'Wherever he was, there were always ructions and sham fights going on. Mock battles took place between the men of his hut and the adjoining one. We had a football field and whenever there was a game he was sure to be in it. He was all energy and gaiety.'[13]

Each night the men were locked up at 7.30. Between then and lights out at 9.45 they were free to read or play cards. 'They were listening all the time to talk and plans about the continuance of the war as soon as we got home,' according to Batt O'Connor. Many of the men had their own musical instruments, and they frequently staged their own concerts and sing-songs.

Each day finished with rebel songs and recitations. Collins had a poor singing voice; so his party-piece was a forceful rendition of the poem 'The Fighting Race,' by J.I.C. Clarke. It was about three Irishmen – Kelly, Burke, and Shea, who died on the battleship *Maine* at the start of the Spanish-American war. Collins delivered the lines of all five verses with an infectious enthusiasm that made up for his inability to recite properly. The following verse gives a taste of the poem:

'I wish 'twas in Ireland, for there's the place,'
Said Burke, 'That we'd die by right,
In the cradle of our soldier race,
After one good stand-up fight.
My grandfather fell on Vinegar Hill,
And fighting was not his trade;
But his rusty pike's in the cabin still,
With Hessian blood on the blade.'
'Aye, aye,' said Kelly, 'the pikes were great
When the word was 'clear the way!'
We were thick on the roll in ninety-eight –
Kelly and Burke and Shea.'
'Well, here's to the pike and the sword and the like!'
Said Kelly and Burke and Shea.[14]

There was plenty of time to think about what had gone wrong during Easter week. Collins realised the strategy was faulty; it had been foolish to confront the might of Britain head on by concentrating their forces in one area. Henceforth he would learn from the mistake, but he did not believe in dwelling on the past. His attitude was best summarised in an autograph book entry he made in Frongoch: 'Let us be judged by what we attempted rather than what we achieved.'[15]

Each morning the men rose at 6.15. After breakfast about a quarter of the men were assigned to various fatigue groups to clear out fire places, sweep buildings, empty garbage, prepare meals, and tend a vegetable garden, and so on. Those not on fatigue duties would normally go to a playing field until 11 a.m. when all the internees gathered for inspection. The commandant inspected everything in the company of internee officers. The blankets on the bunks had to be folded precisely and placed on the bed boards so that they were in a straight line from one end of the room to the other, and the commandant at times used his stick to determine if the line between any two beds was not exactly straight.

The camp commandant, Colonel F.A. Heygate-Lambert, whom the internees nicknamed 'Buckshot', was a cranky, fussy individual with a lisp, always looking for something or other to complain about. 'It's hard to imagine anything in the shape of a man being more like a tyrannical old woman than the commandant in charge of this place,' Collins complained. 'The practice of confining to cells for trivial things is a thing which the commandant glories in.'[16]

Following inspection the men were free to do as they pleased within the camp. They played football, engaged in athletic contests and set up classes to teach Irish, French German, Spanish, shorthand, telegraphy, and various military skills. They drilled regularly and conducted military lectures, using manuals smuggled into the camp.

'We set up our own university there, both educational and revolutionary,' Sweeney recalled, 'and from that camp came the hard core of the subsequent guerrilla war in Ireland.'[17] Frongoch was indeed a veritable training camp for the rebels, who acquired skills and made contacts that proved invaluable afterwards.

'They could not have come to a better school,' O'Connor wrote. 'They were thrown entirely in the company of men to whom national freedom and the old Irish traditions were the highest things in life.'[18]

Collins and the solicitor Henry Dixon, then in his seventies, were prime movers in organising an IRB cell within the camp, and one of their recruits was Richard Mulcahy. Others in the camp who would work closely with Collins in future years included Joe O'Reilly, Seán Hales, Gearóid O'Sullivan, J.J. 'Ginger' O'Connell, Seán Ó Muirthile, Michael Brennan, Michael Staines, Terence MacSwiney, Tomás MacCurtain and Thomas Gay. Those were only a few of the very valuable people with whom he cemented relationships at Frongoch.

People from the camp were to be found at the forefront of Irish life throughout much of the next half century, especially in the army and police, as well as in the political arena, with a future governor general of the Irish Free State, Domhnall Ó Buachalla, and a future president of the Republic of Ireland, Seán T. O'Kelly, as well as future cabinet ministers Mulcahy, O'Kelly, Oscar Traynor, Tom Derig, Jim Ryan and Gerry Boland.

Collins' bullying tactics and his inability to concede gracefully re-pulsed many colleagues. Being highly competitive, he hated to lose at anything. 'In the camp, if he didn't win all the jumps, he'd break up the match,' Gerry Boland recalled.[19] When Collins had a good hand playing cards, he would concentrate intensely and would resent interruptions, but when the cards were against him, he would look into his neighbours' hands, upset the deck and even jump on the likely winner and wrestle him to the floor. He was fond of wrestling, or looking for 'a bit of ear', but these wrestling bouts often ended in real fights. He was not only a bad loser but also a bad winner. Having forced someone into submission, he would crow with delight in a high-spirited show of exuberance that many found irritating.

Morale was comparatively good considering the circumstances under which many of the men were interned. All of those with whom Collins had been sent to Stafford had taken part in the rebellion, but he was surprised to learn that many of the men in Frongoch had had no part in the fighting. 'By my own count,' he wrote, 'at least a quarter of the men in the north camp know very little about the Rising. One man, a former labourer of my acquaintance, said that he was just forced off the street in the roundup. His only crime appears to be that he was walking the street.'[20]

When Prime Minister Herbert H. Asquith visited Dublin in May following the executions, he talked to some of the people being held at Richmond barracks. 'They were mostly from remote areas of the country and none had taken any part in the Dublin Rising,' he wrote to his wife. He therefore instructed the military to comb out the prisoners properly and 'only send to England those against whom there was a real case'. By then, however, more than 1,900 prisoners had already been deported, so the British government set up a committee to examine the case against each one being held. All of the internees were brought before the committee in London, and a considerable number were freed.[21]

Collins went before the committee in early July. He spent the night in a London prison waiting for the interview. 'This morning I was able to see through the open pane of my window the convicts at exercise,' he wrote. 'It was the most revolting thing I have ever seen. Each convict seems to have cultivated a ghastly expression to match the colour of his turf-ash-grey garb. Broad arrows everywhere. As the men walked round and round the ring – those wretched arrows simply danced before the eyes. That awful convict dress is one horror we're saved at any rate.'[22]

Jim Ryan, who had been in the GPO during the rebellion, was released, but Collins was returned to Frongoch, where the internees held a sports meeting on 8 August. Collins won the 100-yard dash. As he breezed past the leader, he grinned gleefully. 'Ah, you whore,' he said, 'you can't run!'[23] Collins described it as 'a great day'. There was high tea afterwards for the prize-winners. 'It consisted of such stuff as tinned pears, jam and pudding,' he wrote to Jim Ryan. 'We gorged ourselves and ended up with a concert.'[24] His victory was actually mentioned in the House of Commons, much to his own annoyance, because the person who raised it cited his winning time as evidence that the men were being properly fed at the camp, but this had nothing to do with camp food as far as Collins was concerned.

'Actually there isn't a solitary man here of no matter how slender an appetite who could live on the official rations,' Collins wrote. 'There are two or three committees supplying us with additional vegetables and sometimes apples and cocoa.'[25] It was also possible to buy extra food, but most of the men had little money. They could avail of parole to work at a nearby quarry for five-and-a-half pence an hour, but on 1 September the camp commandant announced he was deducting three pence per hour for their upkeep, and they promptly downed tools and refused to do further work. Meals at the camp were therefore important.

There were three meals every day. Both breakfast and the evening meal consisted of eight ounces of bread and almost a pint of tea, and the midday dinner did not show much more imagination. 'With the exception of Friday when we get uneatable herrings, the food never varies,' he wrote. 'Frozen meat, quite frequently bad, and dried beans, are the staple diets. The potato ration is so small that one hardly notices it.'[26]

By mid August after some 600 men had been released, those remaining in the north camp were transferred to the south camp, and the north camp was retained as a punishment centre. Collins' own reaction to the move was rather mixed. 'Most of us do not appreciate the change as much as we ought to,' he wrote. 'But there are many consolations all the same.'

The south camp contained a disused distillery in which an abandoned granary building was converted into five large dormitories, with between 150 and 250 beds in each. The beds consisted of three boards on a frame, four inches off the floor, and each man had two blankets. The low, ninefoot-high ceiling, contributed to the claustrophobic atmosphere in the large rooms, with so many men crammed together, and confined from 7.30 at night until 6.15 the following morning. Long before the morning the air would become quite foul, no doubt aggravated by the renowned flatulent qualities of the men's daily ration of beans.

'In some unfavoured spots, breathing is almost difficult in the mornings,' Collins wrote. His bunk was beside a window and he did not suffer so much in that respect, but when it rained he could get wet, as he could not close the window. To make matters worse the place had been infested with rats ever since it was a granary. 'Had a most exciting experience myself the other night,' he explained in one letter. 'Woke up to find a rat between my blankets – didn't catch the blighter either.'[27]

Although he detested rats, he had an easier time adapting himself to the conditions than many of the men, especially those married with families. He did not have to worry about a wife or children and, in any case, most of his friends were interned with him, with the result that he was never really lonely, unlike many others. 'It is pitiable to see those who have given way to imprisonment now enforcing on themselves the extra burden of loneliness,' he wrote.[28] Of course, it was easier for him, a bachelor, to take a more philosophical outlook.

'I'm here and that's the thing that matters,' he wrote. 'Prating about home, friends and so on doesn't alter the fact that this is Frongoch, an internment camp, and that I'm a member of the camp. There's only one thing to do while the situation is as it is – make what I can of it.'[29]

There was, of course, strict censorship at the camp, but Collins set the groundwork for his future intelligence work by establishing secret channels of communications with the outside. Letters were smuggled out in various ways. Sometimes guards were bribed to post them outside the camp. Another favourite method was to have someone being released take letters out in old envelopes, disguised as letters that had already been censored on entering the camp. The camp staff never bothered to inspect the contents. The freed man would then simply transfer the contents to another envelope and mail it. Another method was to place letters in the wrapping of sandwiches being prepared for men being released.

Messages and letters were smuggled into the camp, on the other hand, by visitors. In addition, a man who worked in the censor's office used to remove mail for Collins before the censor could read it. And so a two-way system of communication with the outside was established.

Collins initially viewed the smuggling as just a contest between the guards and internees. 'The game of smuggling and communication is one for which there is no definite end,' he wrote. 'It gives some spice to the usual monotony.' Collins welcomed the challenge. 'In its present form it could go on forever. Daily the British grow more weary of attempting counteractions to it. As one of them remarked, "If you were bloody Jerries we'd know what to do. But you're not".'[30]

Although the smuggling may have started as a kind of game, it soon proved invaluable for propaganda purposes, as the camp was gradually whittled down to the hardcore activists. Collins found a new thrill in the need to avoid detection, as he was eligible for conscription because he had been living in Britain when the First World War began.

On 3 September Hugh Thornton, one of the internees, was informed that because he had been living in Britain at the outbreak of war he was being drafted into the British army. All told some sixty internees were in the same category. Before the rebellion they had been known as 'refugees' in Dublin and the name stuck.

When the authorities came looking for Thornton two days later, however, he refused to identify himself. All the internees were forced to turn out in the yard and line up in two straight rows, but the guards were unable to recognise Thornton, and he again refused to identify himself. With the internees surrounded by a provocative array of military with loaded rifles and fixed-bayonets, the camp adjutant ordered the roll to be called. As each name was read out the man was to answer, 'Here, Sir', and then march in front of the adjutant to the end of the yard and re-form in numerical order.[31]

'These instructions were promptly and even cheerfully obeyed by all the prisoners,' according to themselves. By the time Thornton, number 1,454, answered to his number, the camp authorities were irate.

'You have hitherto conducted the camp in an excellent manner, but this incident this morning was the worst exhibition of insubordination which I have met so far and I cannot overlook it,' the commandant told the assembled men. As a punishment, he suspended all letters, newspapers and visits for a week.

The internees, according to Collins, resented 'this harsh and unjust punishment'. Many of them did not know Thornton. Michael Staines, their leader, could not have identified him 'even if he had wished to', the prisoners contended.[32]

'Obviously everybody could not have known the particular man,' Collins wrote to Hannie. 'It is not very just to attempt to make prisoners identify a fellow prisoner,' he added. 'On the same day another man was sentenced to cells with bread and water for forgetting to say "sir" to an officer.'[33]

On 9 September another dispute came to a head when internees on fatigue duty refused to clear refuse from the huts of guards. Prior to the beginning of the month this work had been contracted to an outside company, but the camp commandant decided to save money by using internees. When they baulked, he ordered as a punishment that those who refused to carry out the assigned duties should be sent to the north camp and deprived of letters, newspapers, smoking material and visits. Each day thereafter eight more men would be transferred after they refused to do the work.

Although the men had difficulty communicating with the outside, Collins was still very much on top of things, as was evident in a letter that he wrote to Jim Ryan on 2 October 1916: 'Most of my letters have been meeting with accidents,' he wrote. 'Things go on in much the same way here, but there have been some interesting happenings lately, which the Censor's Department forbids us to speak about. Even so the Dublin Corporation meeting tomorrow will give you some idea.'[34]

This was obviously a reference to the refuse strike and, notwithstanding the many 'accidents,' they had managed to smuggle out detailed reports of the refuse strike to Alfie Byrne of Dublin Corporation, who proceeded to publicise the whole affair at a meeting on 4 October. They also smuggled details to Tim Healy, a nationalist member of parliament, who raised the matter in the House of Commons. As a result the refuse strike received extensive coverage, especially in the Irish-American press.

The camp authorities relented on 21 October and moved all the internees to the north camp, where the pathways again quickly turned to mud because of some heavy autumn rains. In spite of the mud, however, Collins welcomed the move back. 'Nothing could be as bad as the horrible stuffiness of the other place,' he wrote to Hannie. 'On the whole, I think the huts are better ... In any case they're more desirable and there's a fire. There are only 29 in each now and we have a nice crowd in ours.' Some of them enjoyed reading like Collins, and they shared their books and magazines. 'Between us we haven't a bad library,' he explained.[35]

Hugh Thornton, the 'refugee' discovered in September, had been sentenced to two years of hard labour for evading conscription, with the result that while Collins was 'very active in the camp', he had to remain inconspicuous and, in order to avoid detection, he never acted as a formal spokesman.[36]

Prisoners were slow about identifying themselves, much to the annoyance of guards. 'Why the fuck don't ye holler out when I call yer fucking names!' exclaimed the Welsh sergeant major.[37] 'For Christ's sake,' another exasperated guard exclaimed, 'answer to the name you go by, if you don't know your real name.'[38] The men naturally took delight in upsetting the guards. One morning while a count was being conducted, an internee started coughing, and the officer of the guard shouted at him to stop, whereupon all the internees began coughing.

In early November the camp authorities tricked one of the refugees, Fintan Murphy, into identifying himself by announcing that he should pick up a package, and they tried to single out Michael Murphy by saying he was to be released as his wife was ill, but that ruse failed because he was not married. The commandant then tried to find him by using the same tactic used to uncover Thornton, but this time 342 men refused to answer to their names. As punishment they were moved back to the south camp, and their privileges were withdrawn. Most of the 204 men who answered the roll call on that occasion did so by agreement in order to keep the two camps opened and thereby maintain contact with the outside world. Fifteen of the hut leaders were court-martialled.

'The court may understand this better if I put it this way,' Richard Mulcahy explained in his defence. 'If a German interned among English soldiers by the Germans were wanted for the German army what would be thought of those English soldiers if they gave the man up and informed on him to the German authorities? There are men here who fought in the insurrection; many are here who did not; but most of them now are very sympathetic with those who did.'[39]

A number of the refugees felt bad about others suffering to protect them. They considered giving themselves up, but Collins – who was generally recognised as the leader of the refugees – would not hear of it.

'Mick burst into the meeting and sat down,' Joe O'Reilly recalled. 'When he heard their proposition he told them to do nothing of the kind but sit tight, and not to mind the cowards.'[40]

The Easter Rising had taught him that Ireland was not capable of beating the British militarily, but in Frongoch he learned it was possible to beat them by wearing down their patience. 'Sit down – refuse to budge – you have the British beaten,' he wrote to a friend. 'For a time they'll raise war – in the end they'll despair.'[41]

He was right. The authorities soon tired of trying to uncover the refugees. But that was not all. With the war on the continent at a stalemate, and the British heavily dependent on American goodwill, the whole internee problem was becoming an embarrassment not only in Ireland but also in the United States.

Because of Alfie Byrne's agitation on the men's behalf, Sir Charles Cameron, a retired medical officer of Dublin Corporation, visited Frongoch on 7 December along with a doctor nominated by the Home Office. The internees tried to create an image of deprivation by dressing in their worst clothes. They also complained bitterly about the food, which was actually upgraded for the occasion.

'Is there anything which you get enough of?' Cameron asked.

'Oh yes,' replied Collins, 'we get enough salt.'[42]

Collins was clearly encouraged by the visit. 'This state of affairs can't last much longer,' he wrote next day. 'While many of the men are looking forward dismally to the prospect of spending Christmas here, I would not be surprised to find myself at home for that event.'[43] No doubt his optimism was encouraged by the recent fall of Asquith and the advent of a coalition government under David Lloyd George.

On 21 December the men were summoned to the dining-hall and told they were being released. The officer on duty said, however, that he needed their names and addresses.

'It's no use,' Collins said. 'You are not going to get any bloody names or addresses.'[44]

'I don't want any bloody names or address,' the adjutant replied.[45]

The officer said that he had no further interest in Michael Murphy, and did not 'give a damn' who was who, but they would have to help him if they wanted to get home by Christmas. 'I will have to telegraph the name and address of every prisoner to the Home Office and Dublin Castle before he leaves the camp,' he said. 'It will be an all night job for me unless you help. I will not be able to get through on time.'[46]

'Take them yourselves and just hand them to me.'[47]

Collins and Brennan-Whitmore drew up the list themselves, which solved the officer's problem. The men were then taken to Holyhead, where Collins got a boat to Kingstown, arriving back in time for Christmas, a free and wiser man.

6

'Being Called Bad Names'

Following his release Collins went home to Clonakilty for a brief holiday. 'From the national point of view,' he wrote to Hannie, 'I'm not too impressed with the people here. Too damn careful and cautious. A few old men aren't too bad, but most of the young ones are the limit. The little bit of material prosperity has ruined them.'[1]

After a brief stay, he returned to Dublin and applied for a job as secretary of the Irish National Aid and Volunteers' Dependents' Fund, an amalgamation of two charitable organisations established following the Rebellion to help rebel prisoners and their families. One had been set up by Dublin Corporation and the other by Tom Clarke's widow, Kathleen, who used gold left over from what Clan na Gael had provided to finance the rebellion. Collins did not realise that some friends from Frongoch pulled strings for him to get the job.

'We worked like hell, though we were careful to keep any knowledge from him of what we were doing,' one of them recalled. 'Mick would have taken a very sour view of our part in the affair.'[2]

Collins realised that there was resistance to his appointment. 'I was regarded with a certain amount of suspicion,' he wrote to a friend. 'I was young and would therefore be almost certain to be irresponsible to the importance of the position.' He thought the committee, especially the ladies, frowned upon his involvement in the rebellion. 'In the end,' he wrote, 'chiefly by good fortune the job became mine.'[3]

In his new position he was in contact with a wide spectrum of people sympathetic to the separatist movement. Kathleen Clarke provided him with the names of IRB contacts throughout the country. As his work was of a charitable nature he was able to travel widely without arousing the slightest suspicion. With the recognised leaders still in jail, he became particularly influential in rebuilding the IRB. He took an active part and 'had a great time' supporting Count Plunkett's campaign for a vacant parliamentary seat in Roscommon.[4]

From the outset Collins was optimistic. 'Consider the situation,' he wrote on 19 January 1917. 'It is ripe for whatever one may wish.' He believed the Irish Parliamentary Party and the crown authorities were now 'in a corner, driven there by what they have done and by the will of the people'.[5]

'The crowds were splendid,' he wrote to Hannie. 'It was really pleasing to see so many old lads coming out in the snow and voting for Plunkett with the greatest enthusiasm. Practically all the very old people were solid for us and on the other end the young ones.'[6] Plunkett won the seat and in the process provided a tremendous boost for the separatist movement.

The work of reorganising the IRB took up a lot of Collins' time because there was so much to be done. 'It is only since being released that I'm feeling to the full all that we have lost in the way of men and workers,' he noted. As a result he was 'kept going from morning till night and usually into the next morning'. He was suspicious of some of the people who were offering help. 'I haven't the prevailing belief in the many conversions to our cause,' he wrote. Indeed, he found that he 'incurred a good deal of unpopularity through telling people so'.[7]

The separatist movement really consisted of a number of different organisations, each with its own leader. Arthur Griffith was the head of Sinn Féin, Count Plunkett of the Liberty League, Eoin MacNeill was still nominally the head of the Irish Volunteers and Thomas Ashe had been elected head of the IRB. In addition, there was Eamon de Valera, the elected spokesman of the prisoners in Lewes jail. He had nominally been a member of the IRB, but had never been really active in the organisation, because he had an orthodox Catholic dislike for oath-bound societies.

De Valera owed his prominence to two factors. One, men fighting under his command had inflicted the heaviest casualties on the British army during the Easter Rising. Two, he was not closely identified with any of the various organisations. He came to prominence at Lewes one morning when – noticing MacNeill coming down the stairs – he called the other rebel prisoners to attention to salute their chief-of-staff. Although many of the men despised MacNeill for countermanding the orders for the rebellion, they heeded de Valera's call rather than show disunity in front of their British jailers. No matter what they thought of MacNeill personally, he was still an Irishman and a fellow prisoner. If only on those grounds alone, they would respect him. De Valera's gesture towards MacNeill was probably more important than anything else in his election to spokesman for the prisoners.

Collins made secret contact with Ashe in Lewes jail, where he was serving a life sentence for his part in the Easter Rising. In April, when a parliamentary by-election was called in Longford, Collins wrote to Ashe about nominating one of the Lewes prisoners, Joe McGuinness from the Longford area, but the response from some IRB prisoners had been critical.

It was only with difficulty that Arthur Griffith had been persuaded not to put forward a Sinn Féin candidate who would split the vote. Consequently Collins resented it when some IRB people were critical of his attempt to run McGuinness. 'If you only knew of the long fights I've had with A. G[riffith] and some of his pals before I could gain the present point,' Collins wrote. 'The difference we had with him in the old school has been continued and grows more intense according as the new school passes into working order.'[8]

Although Griffith had played no part in the Easter Rising, it was nevertheless widely identified with his party in the public mind, because Sinn Féin had been in the vanguard of the separatist movement for more than a decade. Collins found this hard to stomach, notwithstanding Griffith's gesture of not running a candidate.

'It is rather disgusting to be "chalked up" as a follower of his,' Collins wrote to Ashe.

The Big Fellow was anxious that Ashe should not think that he was going soft because he was prepared to deal with Griffith, or Eoin Mac-Neill, who had been released from jail some months earlier. 'For God's sake,' he wrote to Ashe, 'don't think that Master A. G. is going to turn us into eighty-two'ites. Another thing, you ask about Eoin [MacNeill] – well we did not approach him and by the Lord neither shall we.'

The Big Fellow tended to express his views with a harshness that was often unattractive. While Griffith wanted full independence for Ireland, he was not a republican. Instead he advocated an Anglo-Irish dual monarchy on Austro-Hungarian lines, and he believed it could be achieved by non-violent means. Collins, on the other hand, was 'the very incarnation of out-and-out physical force Republicanism'.[9]

'This Sinn Féin stunt is a bloody balderdash!' Collins snapped at one meeting. 'We want a Republic!'

Griffith stared at him and Collins became uneasy. 'Of course,' he added, 'I don't know much about Sinn Féin.'

'Evidently not, Mr Collins, or you wouldn't talk like you do.'[10]

Of course, Collins knew full well what Sinn Féin stood for. As a boy he had admired Griffith and had been active in the party during his early years in London. While he no longer shared Griffith's more moderate views, he still thought enough of him to try to apologise for his rash remark.

A stubborn, opinionated politician with resolute determination, Griffith was a fanatic in his own right, but he was unselfish in his dedication to the separatist cause. He therefore agreed not to put up a Sinn Féin candidate against McGuinness so that the release of all the remaining prisoners who had taken part in the rebellion could be made an election issue. Although Ashe liked the idea, de Valera objected and managed to persuade McGuinness to decline the invitation.

As the by-election was likely to be closely contested, de Valera argued the movement's morale would be irreparably damaged by a defeat at the polls, but Collins was not about to put up with such timidity. Ignoring his instructions from Lewes jail, he had McGuinness' name put forward anyway, much to the annoyance of IRB people in Lewes like Seán McGarry and Con Collins who had sided with de Valera against Ashe on the issue.

'You can tell Con Collins, Seán McGarry and any other highbrows that I have been getting all their scathing messages, and am not a little annoyed, or at least was, but one gets so used to being called bad names and being misunderstood.'[11] He was vindicated when McGuinness was elected on the slogan 'Put him in to get him out'.[12]

The victory helped to increase pressure on the Lloyd George government to release the remaining prisoners. All were freed on 17 June 1917 and returned to a hero's welcome in Dublin the next day. It was little over a year since they had been deported in disgrace, both despised and dispirited.

Collins, who helped organise the welcoming reception, was the model of efficiency. He had worked out the travel costs of all the released prisoners from Dublin to their homes, but his rather abrupt, businesslike manner was a little too officious for some. Robert Brennan, one of those released from Lewes, had already noticed the pale, fast-moving, energetic young man darting here and there. He was all business. He frequently dispensed with formalities like shaking hands or even saying good morning. He came over and, without bothering to introduce himself, said Brennan was to look after those returning to Wexford.

'He had a role of notes in one hand and silver in the other,' Brennan recalled. 'He said that the fares to Enniscorthy amounted to so much, and I found out later the sum was correct to a penny. He added that he was giving me five shillings, in addition, for each man, to cover incidental expenses. As he handed me the money, he looked into my eyes as if appraising me. With a quick smile, he shook my hand and turned to someone else.'[13]

'Who is he?' Brennan asked a colleague.

'Michael Collins,' the friend replied.

'I don't like him,' said Brennan.[14]

As the elected spokesman of the returning prisoners, de Valera immediately gained public prominence. A by-election had been called for East Clare the following month and he was selected to contest the seat.

On making his first appearance on an election platform in Ennis, he was careful to include Eoin MacNeill on the platform, who was practically being ostracised by militants. By associating himself with him, de Valera acquired a reputation as a moderate, as well as a unifying force, because MacNeill was actually representative of a majority of those arrested after the rebellion. Most had not taken part in the fighting, and with someone like him at the forefront they would not feel like second-class supporters. While exploiting the situation with considerable political finesse, de Valera was also careful to appeal to the more militant elements by evoking the spirit of 1916 in his election addresses.

Indeed, he talked so much about the rebellion that some myths gradually grew around his own role in the fighting. It would be said, and widely believed, that he was the last commandant to surrender and the only one to survive the subsequent executions, but neither assertion is true. Two other commandants survived, Thomas Hunter and Thomas Ashe, and the latter had actually been the last to surrender.

De Valera was easily elected in East Clare, as was W.T. Cosgrave in a Kilkenny by-election the following month. Speaking at an election rally in Kilkenny on 5 August, de Valera declared that they would fight England first with ballots, and if that failed, they would fight with rifles.

Later the same month Ashe was arrested and charged with making a seditious speech in Ballinalee, where it so happened that Collins had shared the platform with him. While Ashe was in custody, Collins visited him in the Curragh detention centre and attended his court martial a fortnight later. 'The whole business was extremely entertaining, almost as good a "Gilbert and Sullivan skit Trial by Jury",' Collins wrote to Ashe's sister immediately afterwards. 'The president of the Court was obviously biased against Tom, and, although the charge is very trivial, and the witnesses contradicted each other, it is quite likely that Tom will be sentenced.'[15]

Ashe was convicted and sentenced to a prison term. He demanded prisoner-of-war status and when this was refused, he went on hunger-strike. The authorities decided to feed him forcibly and he died on 25 September as a result of injuries received in the process. His death was to have a tremendous impact on public opinion, especially on young people.

Some people later argued that Ashe's death had a greater effect on the country than even the Easter Rising.

Collins was particularly upset. 'I grieve perhaps as no one else grieves,' he wrote. Dressed in the uniform of a vice-commandant, he delivered the graveside address, which was stirring in its simplicity. 'Nothing additional remains to be said,' he declared following the sounding of the last post and the firing of a volley of shots. 'That volley which we have just heard is the only speech which it is proper to make over the grave of a dead Fenian.'[16]

On 8 October Collins went back to speak in Ballinalee. 'In the circumstances,' he noted, 'I came out on the strong side'. All went well except that there was 'a bit of unpleasantness with a policeman who was taking notes'. When confronted the policeman thought it best to surrender those notes, and there was no further problem.[17]

Without a recognised leader of its own, the IRB supported de Valera when the various separatist organisations came together under the Sinn Féin banner on 25 October 1917. He was the obvious choice because he had been a member of the IRB and was not closely associated with any of the political organisations. In addition his record during the Easter Rising as the commandant whose men inflicted the most casualties on the British made him a symbolic figure for republican militants, and he played on the militancy of people like Collins. 'England pretends it is not here by the naked sword, but by the good will of the people of the country that she is here,' de Valera told the Ard Fheis. 'We will draw the naked sword to make her bare her own naked sword.'[18]

Griffith and Plunkett withdrew their own nominations for the presidency of the newly united party in favour of de Valera, who was duly elected. Griffith was then elected vice-president along with Fr Michael O'Flanagan, while Count Plunkett and Austin Stack were elected joint honorary secretary.

Collins campaigned enthusiastically for de Valera and gave members of the IRB a list of twenty-four people to be supported for the party executive, for which he was standing himself. Most of those on his list were defeated and, to add insult to injury, MacNeill headed the poll with

888 votes, while Collins and his IRB colleague, Ernest Blythe, tied for the last two places with 340 votes each.

The next day de Valera was also elected president of the Irish Volunteers at a separate convention, again with the enthusiastic support of Collins and the IRB. This time Collins was appointed director of organisation of the Volunteers.

A twenty-six-man executive was established, with a small 'resident executive' to oversee the day-to-day running of the Volunteers. Cathal Brugha was put in charge of the executive, but things were a little too loose, so it was decided to set up a headquarters staff. Seven of the most prominent members of the resident executive met at the headquarters of the printer's union at 35 Lower Gardiner Street to select a chief-of-staff in March 1918. Those attending were Collins, Richard Mulcahy, Dick McKee, Gearóid O'Sullivan, Diarmuid O'Hegarty, Rory O'Connor and Seán McMahon.

They discussed the matter and even those close to Collins were 'wary of entrusting him with anything like complete control'. They clearly had doubts because of his volatile temperament, and they looked to Mulcahy instead.[19]

'We agreed among ourselves that I would become chief-of-staff,' Mulcahy wrote.[20] He was a very different character from Collins. A self-composed and impassive individual, he never sought to impress people with the kind of bombast that the Big Fellow used. He could sit patiently and listen or wait, while Collins always had to be on the move. But, in spite of these differences, they still got on very well together because Mulcahy was sure enough of himself not to be upset by what others would have considered meddling. He recognised the tremendous organisational talents of Collins and was prepared to give him full rein without the kind of jealousy that was to mar the Big Fellow's relations with others.

In addition to being director of organisation, Collins was now also appointed adjutant general, which meant that he was in charge of training and inculcating discipline. He therefore travelled around the country re-organising the force and speaking at various meetings, despite harassment by the police. On 2 April 1918 he was arrested in Dublin for a speech that he had made in Longford some days earlier. He was bound over for a further hearing in July. On refusing to post bail, he was transferred to Sligo jail.

'Before me therefore is the prospect of a prolonged holiday and of course July will only be the real commencement of it,' he wrote to Hannie. He had 'hardly anyone to talk to' in Sligo, so he did a good deal of reading and study, especially Irish history and the Irish language.[21] He also tried to follow the political crisis brewing as the British government mulled over the possibility of introducing conscription in Ireland.

'I'm very anxious to know what Lloyd George has done about conscription for this country,' Collins wrote on 10 April. 'If he goes for it – well he's ended.'[22] In fact, the British government had already introduced a bill the previous day to enable it to extend conscription to Ireland. The bill was rushed through parliament, and the Irish Parliamentary Party (IPP) walked out of Westminster in protest.

This was another major turning point for the independence movement. Although separatists had enjoyed four consecutive by-election victories in 1918, they seemed to run out of steam after they came together under the Sinn Féin banner because the party lost the next three by-elections to the IPP in the following months. However, the IPP was damaged irreparably by the conscription crisis; its withdrawal from Westminster in protest against the new act was tantamount to endorsing the abstentionist policy advocated all along by Sinn Féin.

Collins quickly realised the implications of what was happening. 'The conscription proposals are to my liking as I think they will end well for Ireland,' he wrote.[23] The controversy afforded a tremendous opportunity for Sinn Féin to exploit public resentment. He duly posted bail to take part in a massive anti-conscription campaign being orchestrated by Sinn Féin.

A conference of the different Irish nationalist groups was held in Dublin at the Mansion House on 18 April, and it issued a declaration that bore the indelible imprint of separatist thinking by basing the case against conscription on 'Ireland's separate and distinct nationhood' and denying 'the right of the British government, or any external authority, to impose compulsory service in Ireland against the clearly expressed will of the Irish people.'[24]

De Valera persuaded the conference to enlist the support of the Catholic hierarchy, who virtually sanctified the campaign against conscription by ordering that a special mass be said the following Sunday 'in every church in Ireland to avert the scourge of conscription with which Ireland is now threatened'.[25] With the country in uproar, the British dared not implement the bill, but did try to remove Sinn Féin from the scene on the night of 18 May by rounding up the leadership for supposedly being involved in a plot with Germany against Britain.

Joe Kavanagh, a short, dapper sixty-year-old police detective with a waxed moustache, had taken part in identifying leaders of the Easter Rising at Richmond barracks, but he clearly regretted his role and secretly decided to commit himself to Sinn Féin. He gave Thomas Gay, a librarian in the public library in Capel Street, a list of those to be arrested that night. Gay, a former colleague in Frongoch, passed the list on to Collins, who had already received a warning from a different source. Two days earlier a friend had been tipped off by another detective, Ned Broy, a confidential typist in his mid twenties at the detective division headquarters in Great Brunswick Street, Dublin. He came from a farming family in Ballinure near Rathangan, County Kildare. He was assigned to type up lists of Sinn Féin members that the crown police intended to round up. He gave a copy of the list to his cousin Patrick Treacy, a clerk at Kingsbridge railway station. He passed on the complete list to Harry O'Hanrahan, a Sinn Féin sympathiser whose brother Michael was one of the leaders executed following the Easter Rising. On the day of the round up, Broy gave further warning: 'To-night's the night,' Broy said. 'Tell O'Hanrahan to tell the wanted men not to stay in their usual place of abode and to keep their heads.'[26]

It so happened that the Sinn Féin executive was meeting on the evening of 18 May at its headquarters in 6 Harcourt Street. Darrell Figgis, one of the joint national secretaries, arrived at the headquarters to find people busy spiriting away papers in preparation for a raid. There was some discussion at the meeting as to the best course of action. 'It seemed to us that our arrests could not but stiffen the nation's resistance,' Figgis wrote. 'The shock would startle and arouse the country.' Having lost three consecutive by-elections, the Sinn Féin leaders concluded that they could stop the rot by virtually ensuring the victory of Arthur Griffith in a forthcoming by-election in East Cavan, if they allowed the crown authorities arrest them. 'There would be many others to take our places,' Figgis noted.[27]

Afterwards Collins went to warn Seán McGarry, the president of the IRB, but his home was already in the process of being raided, so Collins joined the curious onlookers watching McGarry being taken away. He then spent the night in McGarry's home, as it was unlikely to be raided again that night. As a result he evaded arrest and, with the various leaders out of the way, he and his people soon gained effective control of both the IRB and Sinn Féin itself. He became 'the real master' of the Sinn Féin executive, according to Figgis, who described him as 'a man of ruthless purpose and furious energy, knowing clearly what he wanted and prepared to trample down everybody to get it.'[28]

No convincing evidence of a German plot was produced and certainly the arrested leaders of Sinn Féin, like de Valera, Griffith, Plunkett, McGuinness, Cosgrave and MacNeill were not involved. People inevitably concluded that the arrests were really designed to undermine the Sinn Féin anti-conscription campaign, which was therefore able to gain enormous political capital out of the arrests.

The popular urge to resist conscription was a great impetus for enlistment in the volunteers. Feelings were so strong in Ireland that the Westminster government announced on 3 June that conscription could be postponed until October, at least. As the IPP had been unable to prevent the passage of the bill in the first place, Sinn Féin was given the credit for forcing the government to back down, and Griffith won the by-election easily three weeks later.

With the easing of the crisis there was a distinct decline in the membership of the volunteers, but many new recruits had still been gained.

An even further-reaching consequence of the crisis was the vacuum left at the top of the movement by the arrest of moderates like de Valera, Griffith and MacNeill, who had been exerting a restraining influence. They had designated replacements within the party, but those people lacked the stature to keep militants like Collins and Cathal Brugha in line. The militants suddenly had more influence than ever, and they were gradually able to orchestrate their own ascendancy.

On 5 July the British government banned all public gatherings such as football matches and political rallies without a police permit, and Sinn Féin set about defying the ban. The GAA held football and hurling matches throughout the country in open defiance on 4 August, and on Assumption Thursday, eleven days later, Sinn Féin held some 1,800 public rallies throughout the country in a mass display of defiance against the government.

With so many prominent members of the movement in jail, Collins set about organising a network to smuggle letters in and out of jail. Calling on his own experience from Frongoch, he enlisted the help of certain guards, and visitors to the prisons often carried messages for him.

Although a member of the Sinn Féin executive, Collins concentrated on organisational matters within the Volunteers and was largely contemptuous of politicians. And he felt that Sinn Féin, in particular, lacked direction. Executive meetings were poorly attended, and the discussions 'lacked any great force', according to him. He was particularly critical of Sinn Féin vice-president Fr Michael O'Flanagan for 'hobnobbing' with crown officials, or the 'enemy,' as Collins saw it.[29]

Collins was looking for action, not talk. His views were best expressed in an article written for *An t-Óglách* by Ernest Blythe, a northern Protestant who had adopted the nationalist cause with all the zeal of a radical convert. 'We must recognise,' Blythe wrote, 'that anyone, civilian or soldier, who assists directly or by convenience in this crime against us, merits no more consideration than a wild beast, and should be killed without mercy or hesitation as opportunity offers.'[30]

As director of organisation, Collins was deeply involved in the publication of *An t-Óglách*. He wrote the column, 'Notes on organisation,' and also directed and distributed the publication personally. He was so taken with Blythe's article that he asked for more of the same from him.

With de Valera and Griffith in jail, O'Flanagan was nominally in charge of Sinn Féin, and he presided at meetings of the executive. Collins still had little time for the clergy, and even less so for that political priest and the people around him. They did too much talking and not enough work, while Collins was all action.

When he wanted things done, he wanted them done immediately, with no excuses. 'Have you got it?' he would ask. 'If you haven't got it, don't mind the excuses, but go and get it.'[31]

'There are one hundred copies of the September number of *An t-Óglách* allotted to your brigade, so the amount due is 16/8, please forward this sum without delay,' he wrote to Michael de Lacy in Limerick on 31 August 1918. 'By attending to this at once you will greatly facilitate matters.'[32] In the next ten days he impatiently sent two more reminders, and when he still had not received the money after a fortnight, he dispatched a demand. 'I do not request,' Collins wrote, 'I insist.'[33]

When Ernie O'Malley met him in his office at Bachelor's Walk, he found Collins pacing up and down impatiently. 'He jerked his head to a chair to indicate I should sit,' O'Malley noted. 'He took a chair which he tilted back against the wall. It was an awkward gesture, not an indication of relaxation, because Collins was not relaxed. Instead he projected an image of frustrated restraint, exuding energy with his rapid gestures. A lock of hair would fall down over his forehead, and he would toss it back with a vigorous twist of his head. His tilted chair was an unconscious display of arrogance. This was the Big Fellow showing off. At one point he mentioned a recent raid in which Inspector Bruton of the DMP had found empty packing cases and ammunition wrappers.'[34]

'This looks as if there were brains behind it,' Collins quoted the inspector as supposedly having said. 'I bet it's that fellow from Mountjoy Street.'[35] At the time Collins was living in the Munster Hotel at 44 Mountjoy Street. He was trying to impress O'Malley, but, of course, he was trying too hard. His display of raw vanity had the opposite effect.

O'Malley formed an instinctive dislike that he was never quite able to overcome.

Probably the best insight into Collins' thinking around this time can be gleaned from his correspondence with Stack. The latter had been close to Ashe, a fellow Kerryman, and this probably prompted Collins to hold Stack in extremely high regard, although they could hardly have known each other very well at the time. Collins wrote to him in effusive terms, for instance, informing him of happenings on the outside and seeking his advice. 'I was very glad to get your letter, especially the personal note which I appreciated,' he wrote on 29 August 1918. 'Without insincerity I can say that I do appreciate it more from yourself than from anyone I know.'[36] It was ironic that they would become the most bitter of political enemies in the days ahead.

7

'All Ordinary Peaceful Means are Ended'

Though the signing of the armistice that ended the First World War was warmly welcomed throughout the British Empire, there were some very ugly incidents in Dublin when a large crowd gathered to celebrate. Collins was attending a staff meeting of the Volunteers at the time and so was not involved, but he seemed to take delight in writing about the attacks on soldiers.

'As a result of various encounters there were 125 cases of wounded soldiers treated at Dublin Hospitals that night', he wrote to Austin Stack. 'Before morning three soldiers and one officer had ceased to need any attention and one other died the following day. A policeman too was in a precarious condition up to a few days ago when I ceased to take any further interest in him. He was unlikely to recover.'[1]

This was Collins at his least attractive. While in Frongoch he had asked that those who had taken part in the Easter Rising be judged on what they attempted to do rather than what they achieved, yet he was unwilling to judge the soldiers who had fought in the First World War by the same standard.

Those who had answered John Redmond's call to battle had undoubtedly believed they were acting in Ireland's best interest. Some 200,000 Irishmen fought, most voluntarily, and some 35,000 lost their lives. Against those figures, the number of Irishmen who fought or died in the War of Independence paled into relative insignificance. Some, like Tom Barry and Emmet Dalton, returned from the First World War to fight against the crown in the struggle for independence.

Instead of alienating the war veterans with their thuggery on Armistice Day, separatist supporters would have been better served if they had tried to enlist them in their cause. What the veterans had tried to do was scoffed at by Sinn Féin and then betrayed by Lloyd George and his government, which was prepared to sacrifice everything for short-term political gain. The wily Welshman sought to exploit public feeling by calling a general election in which the government seemed to campaign on a promise to 'squeeze Germany until the pips squeaked'. In the process he and his ilk helped to create the conditions in which Adolf Hitler and the Nazis would later thrive. Britain would pay dearly for the selfish, calculating policies of Lloyd George in the coming years. Indeed she would come perilously close to losing all in the summer of 1940.

Sinn Féin put up candidates throughout Ireland. With so many leaders still in jail because of the so-called German plot, Collins played a large part in the campaign. Together with Harry Boland and Diarmuid O'Hegarty he was responsible for the selection of Sinn Féin candidates, and they resorted to the tried and trusted formula that had proved so successful in the McGuinness campaign in May 1917. They nominated members of the party who were in prison. Many of the candidates did not even know their names were being put forward, such was the extent of backstage management in the party's campaign. Some only learned when prison authorities informed them that they had been elected to parliament.

As far as Collins was concerned the whole thing was a necessary propaganda exercise in which he played a very active, though somewhat reluctant, part. He would obviously have preferred to devote more time to preparations to spring Stack from Belfast jail, where he had recently been transferred. 'Damn these elections,' he exclaimed in a letter to Stack in the midst of the campaign.[2]

His own election address to Cork voters was brief and to the point: 'You are requested by your votes to assert before the nations of the world that Ireland's claim is to the status of an independent nation, and that we shall be satisfied with nothing less than our full claim – that in fact, any scheme of government which does not confer upon the people of Ireland the supreme, absolute, and final control of all this country, external as well as internal, is a mockery and will not be accepted.'[3]

Sinn Féin enjoyed a magnificent victory at the polls, winning seventy-three seats against twenty-six for the Unionist Party and only six for the once powerful IPP. It was a case of almost unparalleled organisational brilliance. The party claimed a clear mandate for its platform to establish an Irish Republic with its own sovereign assembly in Ireland.

Shortly after the election Collins and three others – Robert Barton, Seán T. O'Kelly and George Gavan Duffy – went to England in the hope of explaining the Irish situation to President Woodrow Wilson, who arrived in London on a short visit on 26 December. But the American president was unwilling to meet them. 'We never got any nearer to him than a second secretary in the American Embassy,' according to Barton. 'We had no success at all.'[4]

They held several meetings at the home of Compton Llewellyn Davies in Camden Hill. His wife, Moya, was a daughter of Charles O'Connor, a former Nationalist MP for Wicklow. She was on friendly terms with Collins and Gavan Duffy.

Collins was so annoyed by the unwillingness of the American president to meet them that he suggested kidnapping Wilson to make him listen. 'If necessary,' he said, 'we can buccaneer him'.[5] Fortunately nobody took the suggestion seriously, but the proposal provides insight into why some friends thought Collins was inclined to allow his enthusiasm to get the better of his judgment.

Collins therefore suggested another idea: to have Dublin Corporation pass a resolution on 3 January 1919 to grant the Freedom of the City to President Wilson. The Lord Mayor of Dublin invited the American president to receive the honour, but nothing came of this either, because Wilson said he was too busy to visit Ireland.

On 5 January Collins presided at a Volunteer meeting in Kilnadur, near Dunmanway, County Cork, of the senior officers from the six west Cork battalions in Bandon, Clonakilty, Dunmanway, Skibbereen, Bantry and Castletownbere. They decided to form the Cork No. 3 brigade, which ironically was the brigade that was behind the ambush in which Collins would lose his life little over three and a half years later. Indeed, two of the men elected at this meeting – the new brigade commandant,

Tom Hales, and the adjutant, Liam Deasy – would be the main figures behind the ambush.

An attempt was made to arrest Collins in Dunmanway the morning after the Kilnadur meeting, but he evaded capture and returned to Dublin for a meeting with members of Sinn Féin who had recently been elected to Westminster. Twenty-four of the victorious candidates met to consider their next move on 7 January 1919. At the outset they took the following oath:

> I hereby pledge myself to work for the establishment of an independent Irish Republic; that I will accept nothing less than complete separation from England in settlement of Ireland's claims; and that I will abstain from attending the English Parliament.[6]

The meeting proceeded to discuss arrangements to set up the promised national assembly, Dáil Éireann. Collins wrote that he was 'very much against' this while so many elected representatives were in jail.[7] And it was significant that he was not present in the Mansion House on 21 January when the Dáil formally met for the first time. He felt he had better things to do. He was later accused of being behind an ambush that day at Soloheadbeg, County Tipperary, in which two policemen were killed while escorting a consignment of explosives being delivered to a mine. As organiser of the Volunteers, Collins was blamed for this attack, but it was strictly a local operation.

Feeling that 'the Volunteers were in great danger of becoming merely a political adjunct to the Sinn Féin organisation', some local volunteers led by Seán Treacy and Dan Breen decided to force the pace. 'We had enough of being pushed around and getting our men imprisoned while we remained inactive,' Breen later wrote. 'It was high time that we did a bit of pushing.'[8]

They shot the two policemen with no apparent remorse. 'Our only regret was that the escort had consisted of only two peelers instead of six,' Breen wrote. 'If there had to be dead peelers at all, six would have created a better impression than a mere two.'[9]

'It is said that if Tipperary leads, all Ireland is sure to follow,' the parish priest declared from the pulpit in nearby Tipperary town, 'but God help Ireland if it follows in this trail of blood.'[10] As stated earlier, Collins had no involvement in the ambush; local volunteers were responsible, but one leading British authority was probably right when he wrote that the ambush bore 'the first fruits of a policy of which Michael Collins was the prime mover if not the originator'. He was certainly anxious to resume armed struggle with Britain and it was worth noting that *An t-Óglách*, with which he had been so involved in recent months, actually mentioned that 'a state of war exists with Britain'. In time the Soloheadbeg ambush would be seen as the start of the Anglo-Irish War.[11] Ironically, Collins was not even in the country at the time. He was in England, making plans to spring Eamon de Valera, Seán McGarry and Seán Milroy from Lincoln jail.

The prisoners had managed to send out a drawing of a master key on a postcard. Paddy O'Donoghue, a Killarney man based in Manchester, brought the postcard to Dublin and arrangements were made for him to see Collins. 'I saw Collins that night in Mrs McGarry's house and I showed him the postcard,' O'Donoghue recalled. 'A key was then made from the dimensions given on the postcard by Gerry Boland. Mrs McGarry baked this key in a cake. I took this key with me to England enclosed in the cake and had it sent in to the prison as a gift to the prisoners.'[12]

Collins went to England to personally supervise the escape plans. 'I accompanied him to the vicinity of the prison,' O'Donoghue recalled. 'We walked round the precincts and had a good look at the escape gate selected, and Collins was quite satisfied with everything he saw. Before Collins went back to Dublin I was working out plans for the escape, such as the hiring of taxis and the position they would take up, and where the prisoner would be taken to following the escape.' Collins was satisfied with the plans and returned to Dublin to await the break, which was planned for 3 February.

'A few days before the date fixed for the escape Harry Boland and Michael Collins and Fintan Murphy came over from Dublin,'

O'Donoghue continued his story. 'I was not married then and I had a house to myself. As the Manager of Beecham's Opera Company was a friend of mine we went to an opera on the night before the proposed escape. After the opera we were invited to supper by Sir Thomas Beecham in the Midland Hotel. We were all naturally in very good form. I introduced Collins and Boland to Sir Thomas Beecham under their proper names and he expressed his delight at meeting prominent people interested in the Irish Independence movement.

'On Saturday afternoon the four of us – Collins, Boland, Murphy and myself went to Lincoln. We left Fintan Murphy at Worksop with instructions to have a car at his disposal about the time we would arrive there. Petrol restrictions were very severe at the time and we could not extend beyond Worksop on the first stage. Leaving Murphy behind, the three of us went to Lincoln and I engaged a car there. I had used the driver of this car on several occasions before and had become very friendly with him. I instructed the driver to remain with his car at a certain hotel on the verge of the town. I stayed with the driver and Collins and Boland left me and went to the gates of the gaol which was about a quarter of a mile distant.'[13]

The two men approached the jail from a nearby field and gave a prearranged signal with a flashlight, indicating that everything was ready. Milroy responded from the jail by setting light to a whole box of matches at his cell window. Collins tried to open a side gate with a key he had made, but it jammed. With characteristic impetuousness, he tried to force it, only to have the head of the key snap off in the lock. By this time he could hear de Valera and the others approaching the other side of the gate. 'Dev,' he exclaimed, 'the key's broken in the lock!'[14]

De Valera managed to knock the broken piece out with his own key. The three prisoners then emerged, to the immense relief of those outside. Collins gave de Valera a jubilant thump on the shoulder, and they all made for the taxis. The whole thing had taken less than half an hour by the time they arrived at the hotel with the three prisoners. Collins and Boland left at that point to take a train to London.

O'Donoghue went with the three prisoners to Worksop, where they changed cars and drove to Sheffield. He then escorted de Valera to the Manchester home of a Fr O'Mahony from Tralee. He stayed with O'Mahony for the next two weeks.

After the success of the escape, Collins was hoping for a military confrontation with the British. 'As for us on the outside,' Collins wrote to Stack the following week, 'all ordinary peaceful means are ended and we shall be taking the only alternative actions in a short while now.'[15] The independence movement was entering a new phase. He had played a major role in the reorganisation that would now allow the movement to take up the armed struggle where it had left off in 1916, but his role should not be over-emphasised.

Still in his late twenties, he was a determined, opinionated young man, capable of making fast decisions with all the confidence of youth, but his determination was combined with an arrogance that made him intolerant of differing views. In his desire for action he often failed to realise the significance of symbolic events such as the Proclamation of the Republic by Pearse, or the establishment of Dáil Éireann, or even the importance which de Valera placed on keeping people like MacNeill within the movement. There can be no doubt that 'the Big Fellow' would not have been able to unite Sinn Féin in 1917 as de Valera had done.

Collins recognised de Valera's leadership qualities and looked to him to lead the renewed struggle. After all, in his presidential address at the Sinn Féin Ard Fheis he had promised to 'draw the naked sword' in order to make the British do likewise. But de Valera had no intention of renewing the armed struggle, at least not for the time being. He thought Ireland's best chance of success lay in enlisting American help, based on President Woodrow Wilson's eloquent pronouncements about the rights of small nations, for which Americans had supposedly gone to war in 1917.

As soon as Liam McMahon went to Dublin after de Valera's escape, Collins sent for him and asked him to return to Manchester to try to get de Valera to return to Dublin before going to America. 'He said that differences had developed within the party in Dublin. The only one who could reconcile the difference would be de Valera. He gave me a letter which I was to deliver to him,' McMahon reported. He crossed to Manchester that night and met de Valera the following morning. 'I told him the object of my visit, and handed him the letter,' he continued.[16]

'My own idea is that I should be allowed to go to America, where I could come out in the open,' de Valera replied, 'but if they want me at home, my own ideas do not matter.' He then asked, 'When am I to go?'

'Today,' McMahon replied.[17]

Neil Kerr and Steve Lanigan made arrangements for de Valera to cross from Liverpool to Dublin that night. Collins tried, but failed, to persuade de Valera to stay at home to direct the forthcoming struggle.

'You know what it is to argue with Dev,' Collins told a friend. 'He says he thought it out while in prison, and he feels that the one place where he can be useful to Ireland is in America.'[18]

Collins made arrangements through his shipping contacts for the journey to the United States, and de Valera returned to Britain, where he was to be smuggled onto an America-bound ship. But while he was waiting, the British government suddenly released all the German plot prisoners, with the result that he was free to return openly to Ireland. His impending return was announced with the following statement to the press:

> President de Valera will arrive in Ireland on Wednesday evening next, the 26th inst., and the Executive of Dáil Éireann will offer him a national welcome. It is expected that the home-coming of de Valera will be an occasion of national rejoicing, and full arrangement will be made for marshalling the procession. The Lord Major of Dublin will receive him at the gates of the city, and will escort him to the Mansion House, where he will deliver a message to the Irish people. All organisations and bands wishing to participate in the demonstration should apply to 6 Harcourt Street, on Monday the 24th inst., up to 6 p.m.
>
> H. Boland
> T. Kelly, Honorary Secretaries.[19]

This was the kind of reception normally reserved for royalty, so Dublin Castle banned the reception, and the Sinn Féin executive held an emergency meeting. Arthur Griffith presided at what was for him and

Darrell Figgis the first meeting since their arrest over the so-called German plot. Cathal Brugha had complained privately to Figgis some days earlier that Collins and an IRB clique had essentially taken over the movement from within while the others were in jail. 'He told me that he had seen what had been passing, but that he had been powerless to change events,' Figgis wrote. 'It was at this meeting I saw for the first time the personal hostility between him and Michael Collins.'[20]

Figgis asked to see the record of the executive meeting authorising the honorary secretaries to announce plans to welcome de Valera and was told that the issue had never come up. 'I therefore asked Alderman Tom Kelly on what authority he, as one of the signatories, had attached his name as secretary, and he answered with characteristic bluntness that, in point of fact, he had never seen the announcement and had not known of it, till he read it in the press.'[21]

There followed a 'tangled discussion' before Collins rose. 'Characteristically, he swept aside all pretences, and said that the announcement had been written by him, and that the decision to make it had been made, not by Sinn Féin, though declared in its name, but by "the proper body, the Irish Volunteers",' Figgis wrote. 'He spoke with much vehemence and emphasis, saying that the sooner fighting was forced and a general state of disorder created through the country (his words in this connection are too well printed on my memory ever to be forgotten), the better it would be for the country. Ireland was likely to get more out of a state of general disorder than from a continuance of the situation as it then stood. The proper people to take decisions of that kind were ready to face the British military, and were resolved to force the issue. And they were not to be deterred by weaklings and cowards. For himself he accepted full responsibility for the announcement, and he told the meeting with forceful candour that he held them in no opinion at all, that, in fact, they were only summoned to confirm what the proper people had decided.[22]

'He had always a truculent manner, but in such situations he was certainly candour itself,' Figgis continued. 'As I looked on him while he spoke, for all the hostility between us, I found something refreshing and admirable in his contempt of us all. His brow was gathered in a thunderous frown, and his chin thrust forward, while he emphasised his points on the back of a chair with heavy strokes of his hand.'[23]

Although Figgis may have been impressed by the way that Collins had manipulated the organisation, Arthur Griffith certainly was not. He had no intention of meekly succumbing to this arrogant display. Tapping the table in front of him with a pencil, Griffith emphasised that the decision was one to be taken by the meeting, and by no other body. 'For two hours the debate raged fiercely,' according to Figgis. Going ahead with the announced plans would undoubtedly lead to trouble, while abandoning them could have disastrous implications for the morale of the whole movement. Parallels were drawn with the disastrous consequences of Daniel O'Connell's buckling under similar British pressure at Clontarf some seventy years earlier. The argument was only resolved by deciding to consult de Valera, who asked that the welcoming demonstrations be cancelled. Rather than risk a confrontation in which lives might be lost, he explained that he was sure matters of much greater principle would arise in future.

'We who have waited, know how to wait,' he advised. 'Many a heavy fish is caught even with a fine line if the angler is patient.'[24]

Thus Collins' plans to provoke an early confrontation with the British were frustrated and he was obviously disappointed. 'It is very bad,' he wrote to Stack. 'The chief actor was very firm on the withdrawal, as indeed was Cathal. I used my influence the other way, and was in a practical minority of one. It may be that all arguments were sound, but it seems to me that they have put up a challenge which strikes at the fundamentals of our policy and our attitude.'[25]

Whatever harm Collins had done to his own standing by this arrogant display was more than offset in the following days by his success in organising a sensational prison break from Mountjoy jail. Since the successful springing of de Valera from Lincoln jail, Collins had been devoting considerable attention to organising escapes. He had the help of a number of men who were serving as warders in Mountjoy. They facilitated some of the early escapes, which played a significant part in boosting republican morale. Patrick Joseph Berry, a native of Kilkenny who was in his thirties, was a plumber and a warder on the staff in the jail since 1906. He had also befriended Thomas Ashe in 1917 and testified at his inquest.

'I was more or less their intelligence officer in the prison,' Berry explained. 'I was with Collins day and night carrying dispatches from and to prisoners. These were written dispatches. In spite of the fact that the prison authorities must have been aware of my sympathies following the Ashe Inquiry, no attempt was ever made to search me. Of course I was pretty diplomatic and made no profession of my sympathies.'[26]

Robert Barton had been arrested and Collins tried to arrange his rescue as he was being taken to Mountjoy jail on 12 February 1919, but Barton was not in the van that was stopped. Barton established contact with Collins through Joe Berry and other friendly warders. 'I devised the means of escape,' Barton explained. 'If I had a saw with which to cut one of the bars, I could get out of my cell, they could throw over a rope ladder, and I could climb up the ladder over the wall and get away.'[27]

Collins arranged for Dick Mulcahy, the IRA chief-of-staff, to visit Barton in the jail. He went in posing as a clerk to Barton's solicitor. 'These two came to interview me about my pending court martial and they brought me the tools I was asking for. While the warder was not looking, Dick Mulcahy pushed the tools towards me and I hid them in my riding breeches. It was not in prison garb. With the saw, I cut out the bar.'[28]

On the night of 16 March, Barton made it to the outer wall and threw a bar of soap over the wall at a certain spot, which was a pre-arranged signal for volunteers, led by Rory O'Connor, to throw a rope with a weight attached over the wall. Barton was able to pull over an attached rope ladder and use it to scale the twenty-foot wall. He then jumped into a blanket being held by the volunteers. 'Mick Collins was in a street near by waiting to congratulate me,' Barton added.

'This is only the beginning,' a jubilant Collins declared at Batt O'Connor's home at 1 Brendan Road, Donnybrook, that night. 'We're going to get Béaslaí and Fleming out next.'[29]

Barton's escape was like a trial run for a more ambitious break set for the afternoon of 29 March. The plan was to spring Piaras Béaslaí, J.J. Walsh, Paddy Fleming, Thomas Malone and whoever else could get out with them. Paddy O'Daly was involved from the inside, though he had no intention of trying to escape himself. His wife was dying in a Dublin hospice and he had only been sentenced to six months in jail. If he escaped and went on the run, he would not be able to visit her. Under the circumstances, the prison authorities granted him parole to visit his wife, and he used this to contact republican leaders on the outside, including the chief-of-staff of the volunteers, Richard Mulcahy, and Peadar Clancy who was in charge of those designated to help the escape from the outside.

A Saturday afternoon was selected because the prisoners had more freedom then than on any other afternoon and there would be fewer warders on duty. 'All the criminal sections of the prison were locked up from dinner-time, and we had the grounds to ourselves, with only one or two warders,' O'Daly noted. 'We were supposed to be good boys then and were not causing any trouble.'[30]

With Clancy and his party outside, everything was ready. O'Daly was to give the signal from a window for the stone with the rope attached to the rope ladder to be thrown over the wall, as in the Barton escape.

The men were staging a snowball fight in the prison yard and jumped the three warders and held them on the ground. Fleming pulled the ladder over the wall. 'Everything went according to plan,' according to O'Daly. As the last man stood at the end of the ladder he asked, 'Any more of you coming?'

'I believe that if everyone of us had tried to escape we could have managed it.' The only reason the other five did not go was that they did not want to get the warders in trouble, because they might need their help in the future.

'Damn it, Joe,' a warder named Kelly said to Joe Leonard, 'that's no way to hold a man on the ground. Tear my coat a bit.' Leonard duly pulled the buttons of Kelly's coat to make it look as though they really had struggled.[31]

'I think, Paddy, that you had better sit on me,' warder Murphy said to O'Daly. 'Get another man to hold me as well.'[32]

Having observed the escape Joe O'Reilly peddled off furiously on his bicycle to the Wicklow Hotel, where Collins was waiting impatiently.

'Is Fleming out?' he asked.[33]

'The whole jail is out.'

'What! How many?'

'About twenty when I came away.'[34]

That evening, as Collins sat in his office at Cullenswood House, he put down his pen and burst out laughing every so often. They had accomplished a major coup, which boosted party morale and more than offset whatever damage had been done by the cancellation of the welcoming demonstration for de Valera.

8

'Too Many of the Bargaining Type'

In early 1919 Collins was appointed director of intelligence of the Irish Volunteers. It was here he made his greatest mark.

For centuries the British were renowned for their secret services. In the world war that had just ended, British intelligence had functioned magnificently, breaking German codes and using the information to steer the United States into the war against Germany. During the Second World War, Britain would again break German codes, but in between those two wars British intelligence suffered at the hands of Collins, who made them look like bungling amateurs – for a time, at any rate.

As director of organisation, Collins had put together an escape network that was later copied by Britain's MI9. Éamonn Duggan had been appointed the first director of intelligence for the Volunteers, but this was never much more than an adjunct to his legal practice.

Collins, on the other hand, set up a far-reaching network, incorporating intelligence-gathering, counter-intelligence, and matters relating to prison escapes and smuggling – both arms and people. He was the brains behind the whole network and his industry was phenomenal. He retained personal control over work similar to that done by three different intelligence agencies in Britain: MI5, MI6, and MI9.

An intelligence office was opened over the print shop of J.F. Fowler at 3 Crow Street, which was just off Dame Street and under the figurative shadow of Dublin Castle. Collins generally stayed away from that office. Joe O'Reilly acted as his main courier with the office and everyone in it. Members of staff were supposedly manufacturing agents, but they spent much of their time in the office decoding intercepted police messages.

Liam Tobin, another Cork man, was in charge of the intelligence headquarters. He was an inconspicuous individual, tall and gaunt, with a tragic expression. He walked without moving his arms, which made him seem deceptively listless, in marked contrast with Collins, who bounded from place to place. Tobin's deputy was Tom Cullen, an affable, quick-witted individual from Wicklow who had taken part in the Easter Rising. He was a very likeable individual. He was not only intelligent but also a good athlete, and a handsome young man with a fresh complexion and sparkling eyes. Frank Thornton was next in the chain of command at the headquarters, along with Frank Saurin, who stood out as one of the best-dressed men in the movement. He dressed in impeccable suits and often wore lavender gloves. Some of the British made the mistake of assuming he looked too respectable to be a rebel, with the result that his sense of dress often allowed him to saunter through enemy cordons.

The developing staff of intelligence officers included people like Joe Guilfoyle, a veteran of Frongoch, and Joe Dolan, who wore a British army badge in his lapel with a red, white and blue ribbon. The badge, which was inscribed 'For King & Country', frequently allowed him to get out of sticky situations, as the British assumed he was a loyalist. Charlie Byrne, another of the new men, was called 'the Count' by colleagues, because of his appearance and his sense of humour. They were later joined by Paddy Kennedy from Tipperary, Ned Kelliher, Charlie Dalton and Dan McDonnell from Dublin and Peter McGee.

With their help Collins set about demoralising the crown police forces. There were two separate police forces in Ireland at the time, the Royal Irish Constabulary (RIC) and the Dublin Metropolitan Police (DMP). The latter, which functioned only in the Dublin area, was divided into seven divisions, lettered A through G. Divisions A, B, C and D were uniformed police dealing with different sections of the city, while E and F dealt with the outskirts, and G was an overall division of plainclothes detectives dealing with all types of crime, not just political crimes.

The intelligence staff were Collins' aides. Their initial task was to gather as much information as possible about the police, especially G division. Information about where they lived, and the names of members of their families would prove invaluable to Collins in the coming months.

His agents were a whole range of people, with no one too humble to be of use. Maids in guest houses and hotels, porters, bar-tenders, sailors, railwaymen, postmen, sorters, telephone and telegraph operators, warders, and ordinary policemen all played an important part, and he had the splendid ability of making each feel important, even though he rarely, if ever, thanked them for what they were doing.

'Why should I thank people for doing their part?' he would ask. 'Isn't Ireland their country as well as mine?'[1]

When Collins gave Tom Gay £5 for Detective Sergeant Kavanagh after the latter supplied the names of those about to be arrested in connection with the so-called German plot, there was something contemptuous about the gesture. Gay recognised this and returned the money to Collins a few days later.

'You didn't give him the money!' Collins exclaimed.[2]

'No.'

'You didn't think he'd take it?'

'No.'

'A bloody queer G man!'[3]

It was, of course, early days yet and Collins was still very raw. In his contempt for the police, it did not seem to occur to him that there could be patriotic Irishmen in the police as much as in any other walk of life. But, unlike others in the movement, he soon learned this lesson and turned it to the advantage of the cause.

At the heart of his intelligence-gathering network were his police spies. The first to be recruited were the two G men Joe Kavanagh and Ned Broy, who had warned about impending arrests at the time of the so-called German plot. However, Kavanagh did not have long to live. He died of a heart attack in 1920, by which time he had been of invaluable service to Collins.

Broy, on the other hand, was only in his mid-twenties. A rather stooped individual with a broad face, he thought of himself strictly as an Irishman and he had been looking for somebody within Sinn Féin who could make proper use of important information that he was prepared to pass on. Thinking Collins might be the ideal man, Broy asked to meet him. They met one night in January 1919 at the home of Michael Foley on 5 Cabra Road.

'I had studied for so long the type of man that I would need to act efficiently, that the moment I saw Michael at the door, before he had time to walk across and shake hands, I knew he was the man,' Broy noted. 'I knew he was the man who could beat the British and I decided to work for him from then on.'[4]

As a confidential typist Broy was in a position to be particularly helpful to Collins. When he typed any report likely to be of interest to Collins, he simply inserted an extra carbon and made an additional copy. He then passed this on at weekly meetings at the home of the librarian Thomas Gay.

Broy 'agreed entirely' with Collins that force was necessary to achieve independence. The Volunteers should adopt a twin psychological approach of trying to convince members of the RIC and DMP that even if they were not prepared to assist the volunteers in the coming struggle for Irish independence, they should at least not hinder those efforts. Morale within the police was not high, because even though the majority were Roman Catholic, there was a distinct bias against promoting Catholics. As result a great many of them were actually anti-British. Moreover, many had relatives in the Volunteers.

'As regards the DMP,' Broy argued, 'no attack should be made on the uniformed service.' Only one division of the DMP was involved in political work, and that was the plainclothes G division for which Broy worked. He advocated that 'no attack should be made on the members of the G division who were not on political duty and active on that duty. In this way, the DMP would come to realise that, as long as they did not display zeal against the Volunteers, they were perfectly safe from attack.' He suggested a warning, like tying them to a railing, should be given to those members of G division who remained active, and 'a ruthless war' should then be waged on the hardcore who persisted in resisting the independence struggle.[5]

The Dáil met on 1 April 1919 and de Valera was elected *Príomh Aire* (prime minister). The next day he named a cabinet, representative of the various shades of opinion within Sinn Féin. It included Griffith, Plunkett, MacNeill, Brugha, Cosgrave, Barton, Countess Markievicz and Collins, who was appointed Minister for Finance because he had gathered banking experience before the Easter Rising.

De Valera had plans for Collins to raise money for the movement by issuing bonds. 'It is obvious that the work of our government cannot be carried out without funds,' de Valera told the Dáil. 'The Minister for Finance is accordingly preparing a prospectus which will shortly be published for the issue of a loan of one million pounds sterling – £500,000 to be offered to the public for immediate subscription, £250,000 at home and £325,000 abroad, in bonds and such amounts as to meet the needs of the small subscriber.'[6]

Despite what had happened with the planned welcoming ceremony, Collins still expected great things now that de Valera had taken over the leadership of Sinn Féin from Fr O'Flanagan. For instance, de Valera privately expressed antipathy towards conventional politics in conversation with Collins and Mulcahy.

'You're a young man going into politics,' he told Mulcahy. 'I'll give you two pieces of advice, study economics and read *The Prince*' – Machiavelli's classical study of political duplicity. Mulcahy would later come to appreciate the advice as a key to understanding de Valera, who tended to be a militant among militants and a moderate among moderates, with the result that people with very different outlooks actually thought he shared their views.[7]

Collins had a fairly clear vision of the way he wished to go. He wanted a military confrontation, but not a conventional war. 'If we were to stand up against the powerful military organisation arrayed against us,' Collins later explained, 'something more was necessary than a guerrilla war in which small bands of our warriors, aided by their knowledge of the country, attacked the larger forces of the enemy and reduced their numbers. England could always reinforce her army ... She could replace every soldier that she lost.[8]

'But,' he added, 'there were others indispensable for her purposes which [*sic*] were not so easily replaced. To paralyse the British machine it was necessary to strike at individuals. Without her spies England was helpless. It was only by means of their accumulated and accumulating knowledge that the British machine could operate.' He basically considered the DMP and RIC spies.[9]

Detectives from G division had, after all, segregated the leaders from the rank and file at Richmond barracks after the Easter Rising. And the British had relied on the RIC to select those who were deported from other parts of the island in the aftermath of the rebellion. 'Without their police throughout the country, how could they find the men they "wanted"?' he asked.[10]

The British administration was dependent on such people and would be virtually blind without them. Thus Collins determined that the first step should be to undermine the political detectives in G division of the DMP. Of course, he first had to learn who were the most effective detectives.

His audacity seemed to know no bounds. He arranged for Broy to smuggle him into G division headquarters on the night of 7 April 1919. Earlier that evening Collins met with some IRB colleagues at Vaughan's Hotel and afterwards he asked Seán Nunan to accompany him, and on the way he told him where they were going.

'I duly let them in, showed them the back way and the yard door to Townsend Street, in case anything happened, and gave them the general lie of the land,' Broy recalled. 'No sooner had I done so than a stone came through the window.

'I told them to go into a dark passage and to wait near the back door, in the shadow,' Broy continued. 'On looking out on Great Brunswick Street I saw a British soldier in custody of a policeman. I opened the door and inquired of the constable what was wrong.

'This fellow is drunk and he is after throwing a stone in through the window next door,' the constable replied.

Broy took charge of the soldier and brought him to the police station next door and went back to Collins and Nunan. He brought them upstairs and pilfered a box of candles and matches, because Collins had thought he was joking about bringing a candle. Broy locked the dormitory room on the top floor and used a master key to open the detective's room, and he opened the steel safe with the records. He left Collins and Nunan in the room with the candles and then went downstairs again, when there was a loud knock on the door. 'I opened it and found the same constable back again, inquiring as to the value of the window broken glass. I gave him a rough estimate and he left. I went upstairs, told the boys what the noise was about, and came down to look after telephones, etc.'

Collins and Nunan stayed in the office until about 5 a.m. The files gave Collins an invaluable insight into what the G division knew, and into its most active detectives. He later bragged that his own file mentioned he came from 'a brainy' Cork family 'who are disloyal and of advanced Sinn Féin sympathies.' This report, written by the RIC district inspector in Bandon, was dated 31 December 1916.[11]

When leaving, Collins took with him a bound book of telephone messages received by G division during the Easter Rising. 'Some of the messages were from loyal people, giving information as to where the Irish Volunteers had occupied positions in small numbers or where they had posted snipers on roofs or in windows, but many exactly similar ones were received from persons who posed, then and afterwards, as sympathisers of the Volunteers,' Broy noted. 'Collins had many a cynical laugh, after reading these.'[12]

Although Collins had no sleep, he was in fine form the next day when Sinn Féin held a special Ard Fheis at the Mansion House. De Valera was trying to perform a balancing act in attempting to keep militants like Collins in check by ensuring the Ard Fheis gave the standing committee of Sinn Féin a strong voice in policy matters, and by debarring members of the cabinet, other than himself and Griffith, from membership of the party's standing committee. He undoubtedly had Collins in mind when he said, for example, that if a minister decided the Irish people should no longer pay income tax to the crown, the proposal would first need the standing committee's approval.

Collins had been arguing in favour of such a scheme within the cabinet, but he had come up against the resolute obstinacy of Brugha. De Valera, as was his wont, had assumed an aloof position in the dispute, but his remarks at the Ard Fheis certainly leaned towards Brugha's more cautious approach. Collins was busy lobbying for the election of his friend and IRB colleague Harry Boland to become one of the joint national secretaries of Sinn Féin. When it was all over and Boland had won and thus ousted Darrell Figgis, Collins seemed quite pleased with himself.

'As I left the great hall, the Convention over, I was suddenly stopped by a strange sight,' Figgis wrote. 'Behind one of the statues with which it was surrounded stood Michael Collins and Harry Boland. Their arms were about one another, their heads bowed on one another's shoulders, and they were shaking with laughter. They did not see me. Their thoughts were with their triumph.'[13]

A young man, and always in such a hurry, the Big Fellow made no effort to placate the vanquished and in the process he made more and more personal enemies. Of course, he was operating at a breakneck pace within at least three different spheres – within Sinn Féin he was trying to position IRB colleagues, while in his ministerial capacity he was charged with organising a national loan, and as director of both organisation and intelligence in the Volunteers, he was preparing for a war with Britain.

On the night following the Ard Fheis the detectives of the DMP were given a very public warning of the kind suggested by Broy. Volunteers raided the home of Detective Sergeant Nicholas Halley, and they held up Detective Constable Denis O'Brien in the street and bound and gagged him. O'Brien, a native of Kanturk, had been particularly active, especially against his fellow Corkmen in the city. Neither man was hurt, but it was a warning to them and their colleagues that the Volunteers could and would strike at them in the streets or in their homes. 'They were damned decent men not to shoot me,' O'Brien later told Broy and other colleagues. 'I am not doing any more against them.'

Addressing the Dáil the next day, 10 April, de Valera advocated moral rather than armed resistance. 'We shall conduct ourselves with all needful forbearance,' he declared.[14] While Collins was anxious to kill those policemen who did not heed the warnings to lay off, de Valera called for the ostracism of all policemen, whom he accused of 'brutal treason', because they were acting as 'the main instruments' in keeping the Irish people in subjection. 'They are spies in our midst,' he added, echoing the sentiments of Collins. 'They are the eyes and ears of the enemy.'[15]

Of course, Broy and Detective Sergeant Joe Kavanagh, who was working out of Dublin Castle, were invaluable to Collins. They were friendly with each other, but neither realised the other was helping Collins. The Big Fellow did ask Broy about Kavanagh once or twice. One evening while walking in Stephen's Green they suddenly realised they were both giving information to Collins. 'Michael was glad the two of us knew and understood each other. Thereafter Kavanagh joined Broy's meetings with Collins at the Clontarf home of Thomas Gay. The detectives would go to Clontarf separately by tram, while Collins usually cycled there. If any of them wished to contact Collins at other times, they would leave a message with Gay at the Capel Street library.[16]

De Valera still believed that the best hope of securing international recognition lay with the United States, in view of the war aims pronounced by President Woodrow Wilson. De Valera exhibited a good grasp of the international situation.

'We are here on behalf of the Irish people, and we are quite ready to take our part in a League of Nations which has as its foundation equality and right amongst nations,' he said. 'If we want a Covenant to be really lasting it must be based on the principles which occupied ten of the fourteen points of President Wilson – the right of every nation to self-determination. We take up these principles because they are right, and we take them up particularly because the acceptance of these principles will mean that the long fight for Irish liberty is at an end.'[17]

'What we seek is the reign of law based upon the consent of the governed and sustained by the organised opinion of mankind,' President Wilson had declared on 4 July 1918. The next day Lloyd George affirmed that Britain was fighting for the same thing, and now the Irish were trying to hold them to their words.

It was a measure of Collins' growing influence within the movement that he was chosen to propose the Dáil motion to secure approval for the policy being outlined by de Valera. The motion, which was seconded by W.T. Cosgrave, read:

> The elected Parliament and Government of the Irish Republic pledged the active support of the Irish nation in translating into deeds the principles enunciated by the president of the U.S. at Washington's Tomb on July 4th, 1918, and wholeheartedly accepted by the people of America during the war. We are eager and ready to enter a World League of Nations based on equality of rights, in which the guarantees exchanged neither recognise nor imply a difference between big nations and small, between those that are powerful and those that are weak. We are willing to accept all the duties, responsibilities and burdens which inclusion in such a League implies.[18]

The occasion afforded the Dáil enormous publicity, and Collins – despite his dislike of formal occasions – sensed something momentous about the proceedings. 'The week which has passed has been a busy one for us – perhaps it has been a historical one for very often we are actors in events that have very much more meaning and consequence than we realise,' he wrote next day to his sister Lena, who was by then a nun in England. 'Last week did, I feel, mark the inception of something new. The elected representatives of the people have definitely turned their backs on the old order and the developments are sure to be interesting. Generally the situation is working out to the satisfaction of Ireland – that is in foreign countries. At home we go from success to success in our own guerrilla way.[19]

'It is a most interesting thing to watch from day to day the downfall of the stern government regime,' he added. 'Not indeed that it is ended, not even that it won't flash forth occasionally again, but the impotence of the military governors is gradually taking them into a position which is almost chaotic. Certain it is that we are fast reaching the breaking-point.

'Whether we achieve our object or whether we fail gloriously,' he believed, 'a mark has been made that can never be effaced'. He was rather melodramatic about his own appointment as Minister for Finance, which, he told his sister, would 'simply ensure the hanging that was only probable had we remained merely members of the Dáil.'[20]

In the following weeks Collins became somewhat exasperated with de Valera's style of government, which was to allow endless debate and to give a much greater voice to the politicians within the movement. Once de Valera made up his own mind on any matter he was virtually impossible to shift, though he was usually prepared to allow others to make futile efforts to dissuade him. Of course, sitting through such arguments required an equal amount of patience on the part of other cabinet members, and this kind of patience was not Collins' forte.

As Minister for Finance he had to organise funds and he did so with characteristic thoroughness. He drafted a prospectus for the national loan, but not without some problems. He was irritated by de Valera's habit of considering and weighing every word carefully on the notional scale of history before agreeing to it. Collins was mindful of history, too, but he sought a definite historical link, not mere words that would stand the test of time. He wanted the Dáil to honour similar bonds issued by the Fenians, but de Valera compelled him to delete a reference to those from the prospectus.

De Valera also agonised over the wording of the Irish submission to the Paris Peace Conference. 'The damned Peace Conference will be over before he's satisfied,' Collins grumbled in frustration.[21] An Irish-American delegation tried unsuccessfully to secure a hearing for a delegation from the Dáil, but President Wilson had no intention of going out on a limb for Ireland, notwithstanding his own words about fighting for the self-determination of small nations. He privately admitted, however, that Ireland was 'the outstanding case of a small nationality', but there were much bigger issues at stake and he did not think he could afford to antagonise his British allies by pressing the Irish case.

As there was no chance of getting a meaningful hearing in Paris without the help of the American president, Collins thought that agonising over the text of the submission to the Peace Conference was a waste of time. The three-man Irish-American delegation visited Ireland in early May. The Dáil held a special public session for them at the Mansion House on 9 May 1919, and there were some dramatic developments involving Collins.

'A few of us had a very interesting experience,' he wrote to Stack a couple of days later. During the morning Broy telephoned to warn that the Dáil would be raided that afternoon in an effort to capture Collins and a couple of others. As the telephone service of the day was notoriously insecure, Broy gave the warning to Béaslaí in French.

'We'll have our lunch first,' Collins replied rather nonchalantly after Béaslaí passed on the warning. The Big Fellow was obviously enjoying the prospect of becoming the centre of attention. He sent Joe O'Reilly to fetch his uniform.[22]

'About 5 o'clock the enemy came along with three motor lorries, small armoured car, small armoured car machine guns and probably 200 or 250 troops,' Collins wrote. 'They surrounded the building with great attention to every military detail. They entered the Mansion House and searched it with great care and thoroughness but they got nobody inside. The wanted ones codded them again.'[23]

Collins, Robert Barton and Ted Kelly had slipped out a back window and hid in an adjoining building. When the military left, they returned, only this time Collins was dressed in his volunteer's uniform. It was a show of bravado that went down well with most of the gathering, though some felt the Big Fellow was showing off again.

'By this time everybody should know that it is by naked force that England holds this country,' Collins wrote with obvious satisfaction. 'Our American friends got an exhibition of the truth while they were here.'[24]

Collins was growing increasingly impatient for a fight. He encouraged local units of the Volunteers to raid police barracks for arms. This, in addition to affording an opportunity to acquire much-needed weapons, had the advantage of being a kind of training operation for the Volunteers. It soon led to the withdrawal of the RIC from isolated areas and the abandonment of literally hundreds of police barracks throughout the country.

He was impatient for a fight. Desmond Ryan recalled an incident at Cullenswood House one day when Collins picked up an old copy of *An Cleidheam Soluis* in which Pearse had extolled the virtues of armed conflict. 'We must accustom ourselves to the thought of arms, to the sight of arms, to the use of arms,' Collins read aloud with enthusiasm. 'We may make mistakes in the beginning and shoot the wrong people, but bloodshed is a cleansing and sanctifying thing, and the nation which regards it as the final horror has lost its manhood. There are things more horrible than bloodshed; and slavery is one of them.' With that Collins slapped down the paper and walked out. No matter what he thought of Pearse himself, Collins liked those sentiments.[25]

'When you ask me for ammunition for guns which have never fired a shot in this fight, my answer is a simple one,' he wrote to a brigade commander on 17 May 1919. 'Fire shots at some useful target or get the hell out of it.'[26]

The same day he complained bitterly to Austin Stack about Sinn Féin politicians making things 'intolerable' for militants. 'The policy now seems to be to squeeze out anyone who is tainted with strong fighting ideas, or should I say the utility of fighting.' He was particularly critical of the party's executive committee, which he described as 'a Standing Committee of malcontents' who were 'inclined to be ever less militant and more political and theoretical'. In short, they were talkers and thinkers, rather than men of action, and he was a man of action. 'We have too many of the bargaining type already,' Collins grumbled. 'I am not sure that our movement or part of it at any rate is alive to the developing situation.'[27]

Describing himself as 'only an onlooker' at the executive committee meetings, he complained that the moderates were in control. When Harry Boland went to the United States to make preparations for de Valera's forthcoming tour, the party replaced him as national secretary with Hannah Sheehy-Skeffington, the wife of a pacifist murdered during the Easter Rising. Collins was appalled. Not only had a woman replaced Boland, but the party went on to announce that his replacement was necessary because Boland was out of the country. With this announcement, Collins fumed, 'our people give away in a moment what the detective division had been unable to find out in five weeks'.[28]

He clearly felt that there was a lot of hostility towards him and his militant views. There were 'rumours, whisperings, suggestions of differences between certain people,' he wrote. He described all of this as 'rather pitiful and disheartening.' It belied the national unity of which de Valera boasted, and it tended towards confusion about the best way of achieving national aims. 'At the moment,' Collins exclaimed, 'I'm awfully fed up.'[29]

'Things are not going very smoothly', he was still writing three weeks later. 'All sort of miserable little under currents are working and the effect is anything but good.'[30]

He was, for instance, critical of Boland for talking too much about de Valera's arrival in the United States, because it would allow the ship on which he had travelled to be identified.

'You should not be so communicative over there,' Collins wrote to Boland on 19 July. 'Other people may want to go in the same manner.'[31]

Being New York-born, de Valera attracted a considerable amount of press attention. Instead of his proper title – *Príomh Aire* of Dáil Éireann – he described himself as president of the Irish Republic, a title that Americans could more readily understand. The IRB had claimed that title for the head of its supreme council. Collins was holding that post, but he certainly had no objections. Indeed, he referred quite matter-of-factly to de Valera as 'the president' in a letter to his IRB colleague.

'The president is getting tremendous receptions and the press in its entirety has thrown itself open to Irish propaganda,' Collins wrote. He clearly accepted de Valera as a legitimate successor to Pearse.[32]

9

'We Struck at Individuals'

In the face of organised public ostracism of the police, many resigned. Most had spent their whole working lives in the police force, and many were too old to find other employment. Some sought ways of quietly assisting the Volunteers, while others just kept their heads down and ignored political activities. Of course, there were some who were not terrorised by the Volunteers.

'I'm not letting any young scuts tell me how to do my duty,' Detective Sergeant Patrick Smyth declared. A native of Dromard, County Longford, he was fifty-two years old. He and Detective Constable Daniel Hoey had not only helped to identify leaders of the Easter Rising, but had arrested Thomas Ashe shortly before his death.[1] In addition, Smyth and his colleague Detective Sergeant Thomas Wharton had arrested Piaras Béaslaí for making a seditious speech and found notes on him about how to cut railways and telegraph lines and put railway locomotives out of action.

Collins and Harry Boland tried to get Smyth not to produce those notes in court, but the detective ignored their warning, and Wharton supported his testimony in court. As a result Béaslaí was sentenced to two years in jail, instead of the two months he might have otherwise expected.[2]

Collins was authorised by chief-of-staff Richard Mulcahy and Defence Minister Cathal Brugha to kill Smyth. Around the middle of July 1919, some selected volunteers were invited to a meeting at 35 North Great George's Street. Dick McKee and Mick McDonnell took charge of the team to carry out the assassination. Tom Keogh, Tom Kilcoyne, Jim Slattery and Joe Leonard were selected to assist them.

'We were merely told that we were to be given special duties,' Slattery said. They were ordered to shoot Detective Sergeant Smyth, who was living in Millmount Avenue. 'McDonnell instructed me to go to Drumcondra Bridge and take with me Tom Keogh, Tom Ennis and Mick Kennedy, who knew Smyth by sight,' according to Slattery. 'McDonnell told us that Smyth usually came home by tram, alighted at Botanic Avenue, and walked across the bridge. We were to wait at the bridge and shoot Smyth when the opportunity offered. We waited at Drumcondra bridge for about five nights.'

When he came along they did not strike because Kennedy was not sure it was Smyth. They expected him to turn into Millmount Avenue where he lived, but he was suspicious of them and passed the entrance and took another route. It was too late by the time they realised what had happened. Fearing that they had aroused Smyth's suspicion, they did not come back for about a week, until the night of 30 July.

They waited with .38 revolvers, which they soon found were not powerful enough. They expected that Smyth would fall as soon he was shot. 'But after we hit him he ran,' Slattery noted. 'The four of us fired at him. Keogh and myself ran after him right to his own door and I think he fell at the door, but he got into the house.'[3]

Smyth's teenage son Thomas witnessed the attack, as he was little over 5 yards from his father when he was first shot. Although mortally wounded, Smyth lingered for five weeks before he died.

Meanwhile Collins pressed ahead with plans to launch the national loan. As mentioned previously, he had initially been anxious to include a commitment to honour similar bonds issued by the Fenians more than half a century earlier, but had been forced by de Valera to drop this idea. It was therefore with some satisfaction that he learned that de Valera had an apparent change of heart in America. 'I was very pleased to get from your side a cutting out of the *Evening Sun*,' he wrote to de Valera on 12 July 1919. 'It contained a big announcement saying, "De Valera to pay Bonds of 1866." That, of course, is quite right. It was worth going to America to be converted to that idea.'[4]

'What did you mean by saying it was worth going to America to be "converted" to the idea of paying up the Fenian bonds?' de Valera replied in apparent indignation. 'Surely I never opposed acknowledging that as a national debt. You must mean something else. What is it?'[5]

'I meant about the Fenian bonds, that it was worth going to America to be converted to my idea,' Collins explained. 'Honestly I did not think the fact that I was practically forced to delete a certain paragraph from the prospectus looked much in favour of the idea. For God's sake, Dev, don't start an argument about its being from the prospectus only, etc. Don't please. It's quite all right.'[6]

The republican loan was formally announced at a meeting of the Sinn Féin Executive in the Mansion House on 21 August. Griffith presided and there were delegates from all over the country, including Collins who announced that the $1.25 million being sought in the USA had been upped to $5 million. The prospectus, which was issued in the names of de Valera and Collins, explained that 'the proceeds of this loan will be used for propagating the Irish Case all over the World, for establishing in Foreign Countries Consular services, to promote Irish Trade and Commerce, for fostering Irish Industries, and, generally for National Purposes as directed by Dáil Éireann.'

The British proscribed the loan and ordered that no newspaper should carry any advertisements of the loan. Newspapers that tried to defy this ban were promptly suppressed and copies of the offending editions seized. The suppressions, of course, had the effect of actually advertising the loan. Indeed, it was almost as if the whole edition had been published with nothing but advertisements promoting the loan. In addition, people selling the bonds or even speaking publicly about the scheme were arrested.

Collins was under pressure from two sides, from the British and from within his own side, because some thought he needed to be reined in. On 20 August Cathal Brugha moved to curtail the growing influence of Collins and the IRB by proposing in the Dáil that the next convention of the Volunteers should be asked to swear allegiance to Dáil Éireann. As things stood, the Volunteers were an autonomous organisation. De Valera was president of both the Volunteers and Sinn Féin as well as being *Príomh Aire* of the Dáil, so there was already a considerable amount of overlap, but Brugha and many others were deeply suspicious of Collins and the IRB. During the summer Collins had assumed the presidency of the Supreme Council of the IRB and as such could claim to be a successor to Pearse as president of the Irish Republic. To eliminate the anomalies, Brugha suggested that all Volunteers swear 'true faith and allegiance' to the Irish Republic and to the Dáil as its government.

Collins and some of his IRB colleagues had been arguing that an oath to the republic should be enough, without an oath to the Dáil, but Griffith supported Brugha strongly and this was enough to carry the day. The Dáil passed Brugha's proposal on the suggested form of the oath. 'The Volunteer affair is now fixed,' Collins wrote to de Valera on 25 August 1919.[7]

De Valera took issue with Collins shortly afterwards in relation to the interest to be paid on the bond issue. The prospectus had already been published over a fortnight ago when de Valera wrote to complain that he had only just noticed that it contained a promise to pay interest on the bonds from the date of purchase. 'It should be of course from the date of recognition and evacuation,' he wrote. 'I hope you have not made that mistake in your proposed issue in Ireland. The debt accumulated might be a very serious handicap later. We must look to the future.'[8] He followed this with a further letter three days later. He realised it was too late to do anything about the bonds already on sale in Ireland. 'I am sorry it is so, but I suppose it is too late now to change it,' he wrote. 'It must not be so in any foreign subscriptions. It will not be so in America.'[9]

Collins stood up to de Valera on the issue of the payment of interest on the bonds both in Ireland and the United States. 'I was fully aware at the time of the liability we were incurring, and deliberately drafted the particular paragraph accordingly,' Collins replied. 'We are responsible for an accumulated interest, at a rate of six per cent per annum, from varying dates during the period 1864–1867. This was in my mind when we were going over the original draft prospectus. You remember I talked a good deal of "continuity of responsibility". I am sorry to be always fighting with you on these matters.'[10]

When the Dáil cabinet discussed the situation on 10 October, it agreed with Collins. 'We are, I think, definitely committed to this liability. You will, I am sure, agree that, having in mind all this, it is not possible to alter the conditions of the Loan anywhere.'[11]

Meanwhile things had taken a distinct turn at home. As the British sought to suppress the loan they inevitably antagonised local volunteers, who became anxious to strike back. On 7 September Liam Lynch and fourteen others, armed mostly with clubs and a few rifles, attacked a similar number of British soldiers for their weapons in Fermoy, County Cork. One soldier was killed and three wounded as the Volunteers captured their fifteen rifles. This was the first organised action against British military forces in Ireland since 1916.

By 11 September Collins was writing to Donal Hales in Italy of 'the usual daily round – raids and counter raids, and repression'.[12] The British were gradually being sucked into the confrontation that Collins had been seeking for months. 'The repressions have been of benefit to us,' Collins wrote to de Valera. 'On our side the spirit is if anything improving to meet the ever increasing demands which the enemy make.'[13]

On the same day Detective Sergeant Smyth died, some five weeks after he had been shot. The British reaction essentially cut the ground from under the moderates within Sinn Féin. Dublin Castle proscribed Dáil Éireann, Sinn Féin, Cumann na mBan and the Gaelic League. In the next nine months the Dáil met only once. In this vacuum the militants gained firm control, and Collins would soon have that state of general disorder he had called for back in March.

The ill-conceived British reaction played directly into the hands of Collins, who henceforth had little difficulty outmanoeuvring Sinn Féin moderates and implementing his own more militant policy. The checks and balances that de Valera had placed on the militants were wiped out by the banning of the political wing of the movement. This prompted one leading British civil servant to conclude that the Castle regime was 'almost woodenly stupid and quite devoid of imagination'. He found it demoralised, mired in sectarian bigotry and bureaucratic to the point of incredible ineptitude. 'Imagine,' Fisher wrote, 'the result on public opinion in Great Britain of a similar act by the executive towards a political party (or the women's suffrage movement)!'[14]

At 10.30 a.m. following Smyth's death the DMP raided Sinn Féin headquarters at 6 Harcourt Street, backed up by two army lorries with British soldiers. Collins was in his finance office upstairs 'We had no warning of this raid at all,' Eibhlín Lawless, one of the young women secretaries, recalled. 'Collins was upstairs in our room.' J.J. 'Ginger' O'Connell had just left having talked with Collins and did not close the door of the room.

'I was getting up to shut it when I saw a policeman standing on guard outside,' Lawless said. 'I shut the door and told Mick it looked like a raid.'[15]

'There was no means of escape,' she noted, 'as the military had occupied the narrow entrance in the back as well as the front. The police had locked the front door and they were not letting anyone in or out. Detective Inspector George Love was in charge of the raid.

'I think only Mick was armed,' she continued. 'I stuck Mick's revolver down my stocking and anything else incriminating we girls took charge of. The police seemed to start the raid systematically from the bottom up thus giving us time to take these precautions. When they arrived, we had disposed of everything and they found nothing of any importance. They searched the men but not us.'[16]

'We are caught like rats in a trap and there is no escape,' Collins said. Detective Inspector Neil McFeely entered the office. 'He went round searching the different desks, and seemed desperately anxious to finish his task and get out. Mick sat very casually on his desk with one leg swinging and told him in no measured terms what sort of work he was engaged on. He was scathing in his remarks about it.'

McFeely had only recently been promoted to inspector in charge of political duty. He had always been a desk man before his promotion, doing reports and making maps of accident scenes, burglaries and the like. 'He was told to arrest people like Paudeen O'Keeffe or Paddy Sheehan, but nobody suggested arresting Michael Collins because they would not have believed he would be at such a well-known Sinn Féin address as party headquarters,' Broy noted. The other detectives accompanying him recognised the people on the ground floor, but McFeely wandered upstairs alone. He did not know Collins and he apparently made the mistake of assuming that Collins could not be of much importance if he was upstairs working with a bunch of women.

Collins had prepared himself by learning all he could about G division. Broy had told him that McFeely was a staunch home ruler and the way to handle him would be to say that his activities against Sinn Féin were 'sowing up disgrace for himself, his family and descendants for years to come'. Collins therefore responded with a torrent of abuse when McFeely asked him about some documents.

'What have they got to do with you?' the Big Fellow snapped. 'A nice job you've got, spying on your countrymen.' He then bombarded him. 'What sort of a legacy will you leave to your family, looking for blood money? Could you not find some honest work to do?'[17]

'The inspector was writhing under the attack,' Lawless noted. After McFeely left the office and went downstairs, Collins slipped upstairs to the caretaker's rooms. He then climbed out the skylight and hid on the roof of the nearby Ivanhoe Hotel. Other police then came into the office but they just looked around and did not question anybody.

'It was Mick's coolness that saved him from being recognised,' Lawless assumed.[18] 'It was only by almost a miracle I was not landed,' Collins wrote the next day. 'It so happened the particular detective who came into the room where I was did not know me, which gave me an opportunity of eluding him.'[19]

Pádraig O'Keeffe, the general secretary of Sinn Féin, was arrested along with Ernest Blythe, who was found hiding in a small storeroom. One of those involved in the raid was Detective Constable Daniel Hoey, a native of King's County (now Offaly). Although he was only in his early thirties, he had been a particular thorn in the side of the Volunteers going back to before 1916. He was also with Smyth when he arrested Thomas Ashe.

'You're for it tonight, Hoey,' O'Keeffe warned.[20]

Hoey would have recognised Collins, but he had missed his chance, and he would not get another chance. Jim Slattery said that he received a call that night from Mick McDonnell. 'They very nearly got the man we want to guard,' McDonnell said. He went on to explain that 'Collins had a very narrow escape' that afternoon.[21]

'That was the first inkling I got that Collins was the heart of things,' Slattery noted.

Hoey had been 'the leading spirit' of the raiders, because he was the detective on the ground with the most knowledge about the active Volunteers. He was a nine-year veteran of the DMP. McDonnell said they were going to have to kill him that night. Tom Ennis, McDonnell and Slattery went down to the vicinity of the G division headquarters on Brunswick Street to kill Hoey as he went off duty around 10 p.m. They shot him at the door of the garage at the back of the police station.

'We had better go to Mick Collins and report to him,' McDonnell said after the shooting.[22]

Although the nucleus of what would become known as 'the Squad' had been formally established to kill Smyth, there was no actual mention of any 'Squad' at the time. Dick McKee invited a number of people to report to 46 Parnell Square – the meeting place of a branch of the Gaelic League – on 19 September 1919. Paddy O'Daly Mick McDonnell, Joe Leonard, Ben Barrett, Seàn Doyle, Tom Keogh and Jim Slattery attended the meeting, which was addressed by Collins and chief-of-staff Mulcahy. 'They told us it was proposed to form a Squad,' O'Daly said. 'The Squad would take orders directly from Michael Collins, and, in the absence of Collins, the orders would be given to us through either Dick McKee or Dick Mulcahy. We were told that we were not to discuss our movements or actions with Volunteer officers or with anybody else. Collins told us that we were being formed to deal with spies and informers and that he had authority from the government to have this matter carried out.'[23]

The Squad was established on a part-time basis but by March 1920 it had become a permanent full-time service unit to undertake the assassination of selected members of the enemy, along with 'spies' helping the enemy. It was basically the counter-intelligence arm of Collins' network. It was soon extended to twelve men – Mick McDonnell, Tom Keogh, Jimmy Slattery, Paddy Daly, Joe Leonard, Ben Barrett, Vincent Byrne, Seán Doyle, Paddy Griffith, Eddie Byrne, Mick Reilly and Jimmy Conroy. They were sometimes irreverently known as The Twelve Apostles, and the name stuck even after other were included – Ben

Byrne, Frank Bolster, Mick Keogh, Mick Kennedy, Bill Stapleton, and Sam Robinson.

Detectives and their would-be touts were warned to desist from political work, or they would be shot. 'Spies are not so ready to step into the shoes of their departed confederates as are soldiers to fill up the front line in honourable battle,' Collins noted. 'And even when the new spy stepped into the shoes of the old one, he could not step into the old one's knowledge.[24]

'We struck at individuals and by so doing we cut their lines of communication and we shook their morale,' he explained afterwards.[25]

The Squad was never intended as a bodyguard for Collins, as has been suggested. Instead it was a full-time assassination team, made up of clerks, tradesmen, and general workers, who were paid £4-10 a week. Initially the Squad's meeting place was in Oriel House, but it soon moved to a builder's yard near Dublin Castle. There was a sign over the main gate, 'Geo. Moreland Cabinet Maker'. Vinny Byrne was a master carpenter and did carpentry work in the yard while not engaged in Squad business, but most prospective customers who ventured into the yard were discouraged by outrageously long delivery dates.

Before ordering the Squad to kill any detective, the consequences were carefully considered. 'Collins would always work out how the public would react to the shooting of a G man first,' Broy noted. 'And then he'd hang back for a while before he'd have another one shot.'[26]

Usually one of his intelligence people would accompany the Squad to identify the quarry. 'We'd go out in pairs, walk up to the target and do it, and then split,' Byrne recalled. 'You wouldn't be nervous while you'd be waiting to plug him, but you'd imagine that everyone was looking into your face. On a typical job we'd use about eight, including the back up. Nobody got in our way. One of us would knock him over with the first shot, and the other would knock him off with a shot to the head.'[27]

Byrne recalled confessing one such killing to a priest.

'Did you think you were doing right?' the priest asked.

Byrne said that he confidently replied that he did. They priest might have asked why he was confessing if he was so confident, but, instead, in the face of British confrontation, the priest essentially endorsed the killing.

'Carry on the good work,' the priest replied, giving Byrne absolution.[28]

'The enemy's chief offensive here at the moment is directed against the loan,' Collins wrote to de Valera on 14 October. The more the crown authorities tried to interfere with Collins' efforts to promote the national loan, however, the more determined he became to ensure its success, despite mounting promotional problems. 'We are having extreme difficulties in advertising as far as newspapers are concerned,' he noted. It was illegal for the press to carry advertisements for the loan, and the *Cork Examiner* and some twenty-one local newspapers were suppressed between 17 September and 7 October for carrying such ads.

Of course, he was impatient with those newspapers that were not prepared to risk suppression by defying the law. 'The *Independent* is particularly objectionable and hostile – in its own cowardly and sneaking way,' he wrote to Donal Hales. 'It has not the courage to express its hostility openly, but does so with carefully conceived innuendo. We will meet that position too in due time.'[29]

Collins found a novel way of promoting the campaign. John McDonagh, a brother of one of the executed leaders of 1915, made a short film clip of Collins and Diarmuid O'Hegarty sitting at a table outside Pearse's old school, signing bonds for Pearse's mother, Clarke's widow and Connolly's daughter. Armed Volunteers then raided cinemas throughout the country and ordered projectionists to run the brief clip. They would then hightail it with the film before the police or military could be called. Hitherto the name of Michael Collins had been largely unknown outside separatist circles, but the film brought his name to public attention as never before and, as the crown forces concentrated on suppressing the loan, his reputation grew to the point where he became the most wanted man in the country.

'That film of yourself and Hegarty selling Bonds brought tears to me eyes,' Harry Boland wrote from the US. 'Gee Boy! You are some movie actor. Nobody could resist buying a Bond and we having such a handsome Minister for Finance.'[30]

As Collins was building a reputation for himself, there were people inside the movement looking for leadership and those outside, like Ned Broy, who were looking for somebody they could trust. Kavanagh and Broy introduced a new detective, James McNamara, who was administrative assistant to the assistant police commissioner in Dublin Castle. The son of a policeman, McNamara was a light-hearted, charming individual who won the trust of his superiors. He joined Kavanagh and Broy in their weekly meetings with Collins in Tom Gay's home.

In September Collins learned that a Sergeant Jerry Maher of the RIC in Naas might be sympathetic. When an emissary approached Maher about working for Collins, his eyes immediately lit up.

'You're the man I've been waiting for,' Maher replied.[31]

He was working as a clerk for the district inspector of the RIC, and he was able to feed Collins with information about various circulars from headquarters, as well as current codes being used. At times in the coming months, Collins would have dispatches decoded and circulated to brigade intelligence officers before some of the RIC inspectors had decoded their own messages.

Thomas O'Rourke, the crimes special sergeant of the RIC in Tralee, actually approached Tadhg Kennedy, the intelligence office with the local brigade, and offered his services. Collins asked him to supply the code, which he did every time it was changed. Collins also had at least two other sources for the police codes. Maurice McCarthy, an RIC sergeant stationed in Belfast was one, and the other was a cousin of his, Nancy O'Brien, who worked as a cipher clerk decoding messages. She had spent some years working in the post office in London and had been brought to Dublin. She later married Michael's brother Johnny after his first wife died. The file that the DMP kept on Collins has evidence that the police were aware that he was friendly with her.

Others within the movement also looked to Collins for more action. Dan Breen and three of the colleagues, who had killed the two RIC men escorting the explosive consignment at Soloheadbeg in January,

Michael [aged eleven] *with his mother, grandmother and sister*

Left:
Collins in 1917

Below:
Collins [marked by x] *in Stafford Jail*

Group of British soldiers, including RIC, Black and Tans, auxiliaries and British army

Collins photographed as Minister for Home Affairs. The RIC later used this photograph in their gazette when they were searching for Collins

Members of the Squad: [left to right, front] *Mick McDonnell, Tom Kehoe, Vinny Byrne,* [back] *Paddy O'Daly and Jim Slattery*

[Left to right] *Joe Leonard, Jim Slattery, Joe Dolan, Gearóid O'Sullivan, Bill Stapleton and Charlie Dalton*

POLICE GAZETTE

OR

HUE-AND-CRY.

Published (by Authority) for Ireland on every Tuesday and Friday.

REGULATIONS.

☞ All Notices intended for insertion in the "Hue-and-Cry" are to be transmitted, under cover, addressed to the Inspector-General, Royal Irish Constabulary, Dublin Castle, *authenticated by a Separate Communication*. No Description can be inserted unless an Information shall have been sworn; and it is not necessary to forward the Information to the Inspector-General.

Notices respecting all Felonies and such Misdemeanours as are of an aggravated nature will be inserted.

All Descriptions of persons whose apprehension is sought on a charge of Misdemeanour should be accompanied by a statement that a Warrant has been issued, and by the name of the person in whose hands it is. But the Constabulary should remember that they cannot arrest a person charged with an offence of this nature unless they have the Warrant in their possession when making the arrest.

** Should irregularities arise in the delivery of the "Hue-and-Cry" it will be necessary to forward one of the covers, or give the number it bears, as without this information the mistake cannot be rectified.

Prison and Police Authorities are particularly requested to be good enough to inform the Inspector-General, Royal Irish Constabulary, Dublin Castle, of the abolition of Gaols, Statutes, &c. and of any circumstances rendering the supply of the "Hue-and-Cry" no longer necessary.

Postage should be prepaid at the ordinary rates for printed matter on any copies of this Gazette, which may be sent by post within the United Kingdom, except such as are dispatched in proper course from a Metropolitan Government Office, or from the Publishing Office of the Gazette. Copies sent abroad should be prepaid at the rate of a half-penny for every two ounces.

DUBLIN, FRIDAY, DECEMBER 24, 1920.

NOTICE

The Composition of the Hue-and-Cry will be found arranged for easy reference as follows:—

(a.) Regulations on top of first page.
(b.) Apprehensions Sought.
   (1.) Royal Irish Constabulary
   (2.) Dublin Metropolitan Police
   (3.) English Police
   (4.) Scotch Police
(c.) Animals Stolen.
(d.) Property Stolen.
(e.) Apprehensions

APPREHENSIONS SOUGHT.

DESCRIPTIONS and PHOTOGRAPHS of persons who are wanted.

If any of them be found they should be detained and a telegram sent to Head Quarters.

ERNEST BLYTHE, M.P. (Dublin City), age 31, 5 ft. 8 in., grey eyes, broad face, Roman nose, medium make, long dark hair, brown, clean shaven. Marks—Wart on right cheek, 1 in. from lobe of ear.

DENIS GALVIN (Cork F.R.), age 21 yrs., height 6 ft. 1 in., hair dark brown.

PIERCE F. BEASLEY, M.P. (Dublin City), age 40 yrs., 5 ft. 8 in., complexion sallow, brown eyes, long face, long nose, medium make. Marks—usually dressed in dark grey clothes and brown hat.

RICHARD MULCAHY, M.P. (Dublin City), age 35 yrs., height 6 ft. 8 in., fair hair, has slight stoop when walking.

MICHAEL COLLINS, M.P. (Dublin City and Cork W.R.), age 28, height 5 ft. 11, complexion fresh.

The RIC searching for Collins

Tom Cullen, Michael Collins and Liam Tobin

Collins being followed by Joe O'Reilly

Right:
Collins with his bicycle

Below:
Collins [with Diarmuid O'Hegarty] *signing Loan Bonds outside St Enda's*

Collins at his desk as Minister for Finance

In memory of two good
friends – Dick + Peadar-
two of Irelands best
soldiers'

Mícheál Ó Coileáin

25/11/20

Message on Collins' wreath for Dick McKee and Peadar Clancy

came to Dublin in search of more meaningful action. 'We felt bigger game was needed,' he wrote.[32] As a teenager Collins had spoken about the assassination of the Lord Lieutenant in the Phoenix Park in 1882, and he now endorsed a plot to assassinate the current Lord Lieutenant, Lord French. He believed in striking at individuals who were providing useful service to the British. The person with the highest profile in this regard was Lord French, a symbol of Britain's domination as well as Lloyd George's most influential adviser on Irish matters at the time. Brugha and Mulcahy agreed, so Collins ordered members of the Squad to join the four Tipperary men in a plan to assassinate the viceroy.

'For three long months we watched, planned and waited,' according to Breen. 'Mick Collins was with us on the first occasion that we lay in ambush.' He had learned that French was returning from England through Dun Laoghaire that night and the ambush was set up at the junction of Suffolk and Trinity Street. They waited until dawn but the viceroy never showed. Nothing happened on a number of other occasions either because French – mindful of the need for extreme caution – repeatedly altered his route at the last moment.[33]

'The ready comradeship' between Collins and his military colleagues was particularly striking around this time. Liam Deasy visited Dublin on 14 October, with instructions to go to Vaughan's Hotel, where he met Collins and Gearóid O'Sullivan, Seán Ó Muirthile, Peadar Clancy, Diarmuid O'Hegarty, Dick McKee, Liam Tobin and Frank Thornton. 'My recollection,' Deasy wrote, 'is of a very informal meeting where GHQ staff were constantly coming and going, and it was a surprise to me to see how nonchalantly they seemed to accept the constant risk that was theirs.'[34]

The next day Deasy was introduced to Brugha and Mulcahy by Collins at Lalor's on Upper Ormond Quay: 'It was quite clear to me that these men were anticipating an early development of hostilities on the part of the enemy,' Deasy wrote. Plans were made to transfer the allegiance of the volunteers to Dáil Eireann at a convention called for December and Deasy was informed that they would be changing the name of the volunteers to the Irish Republican Army (IRA).[35]

Of course, Collins was busy with other matters, like building up his intelligence network and releasing Stack from jail. He was already taking a particularly active interest in supervising arrangements for the escape of Stack. For more than a year he had been planning to spring him, first from Dundalk jail and then Belfast jail, but on each occasion Stack was moved before arrangements could be finalised. Now he was in Strangeways jail in Manchester. Collins actually visited Stack in the prison to discuss plans for the escape, which was finally set for 26 October. Some twenty men were posted outside the jail under Rory O'Connor.

Basically the same technique was used as in the mass escape from Mountjoy. A rope with a weight attached to it was thrown over the wall and the prisoners were able to pull over a rope ladder and scale the wall. Piaras Béaslaí, who had escaped from Mountjoy in the earlier break, was also involved in the Strangeways escape. He followed Stack over the wall and four others came after them. Stack and Béaslaí were taken to the Prestwich home of George Lodge, who was a chemist with the Imperial Chemical Company. Collins visited Stack and Béaslaí at Lodge's on 2 November, and he brought along Neil Kerr and Liam MacMahon to finalise arrangements for Stack and Béaslaí to return to Dublin. This was a measure of how highly he thought of Stack. He actually used his influence to have Stack appointed deputy chief-of-staff to Richard Mulcahy.

On the eve of their return to Dublin the following week, Collins had Detective Sergeant Thomas Wharton, a native of Ballyhar near Killarney, shot by Paddy O'Daly of the Squad. Wharton had assisted the ill-fated Detective Sergeant Smyth in arresting Béaslaí. O'Daly and Joe Leonard had been looking for Wharton for hours and had actually given up on finding him that day. Leonard had already dumped his pistol when suddenly they saw Wharton near the corner of Harcourt Street and St Stephen's Green. O'Daly walked up behind him and shot him in the back. The bullet passed through Wharton's right lung and struck a young female student from Sligo, Gertrude O'Hanlon, who was walking in front of him. She was very lucky, because the bullet tore through her velvet cap and drew a considerable amount of blood from what was fortunately only a scalp wound.

10

'Spies Beware'

Collins opened new offices at 76 Harcourt Street. This time certain precautions were taken to ensure there was an escape route and a hiding place for important papers. Batt O'Connor built a small secret closet into a wall to store documents.

'I also provided a means of escape for Collins,' O'Connor wrote. 'We had an alarm bell on the top landing, so that, when the caretaker saw the enemy coming, he could ring the alarm bell outside the room where Collins worked. I had also provided a light ladder on the top landing, hanging on two hooks, so that he could immediately get through a skylight. On the outside of the skylight we had bolts, so that it could be bolted from the outside after the ladder has been pulled up after him.'

O'Connor told Collins that the owner of the Standard Hotel, two doors away, was sympathetic. 'It is not the friendship of the proprietor I want, but the friendship of the boots,' Collins said.

'So I approached the boots and we took him into our confidence. He promised to leave the skylight on their roof always unbolted.'[1]

On 8 November 1919 Collins was in his new Harcourt Street office when it was raided. The staff managed to get the important papers into the secret closet while he headed for the skylight with an attaché case, but his escape route and procedures was not nearly as carefully planned as they should have been. For one thing, Collins did not lift the ladder behind him and he obviously forgot to bolt the skylight from the outside. To make matters worse he found that while the skylight of the Standard Hotel was unlocked as arranged, it was directly above a stairwell, which meant that he had to make a dangerous jump across to the landing.

'Just as I got through the hotel skylight I saw a khaki helmet appear out of the skylight of No. 76,' he told colleagues that evening. 'I flung my bag across, commended myself to Providence, and jumped.'[2] Although he hurt himself a little in the process, he was in great spirits afterwards as he recounted what happened to Batt O'Connor and Joe O'Reilly, as well as Piaras Béaslaí, who had just arrived back in Dublin that day from his escape from Strangeways. The Big Fellow was in his element – he too had just had a daring escape.

Three members of the Dáil were arrested in the latest raid, along with three members of the Volunteer headquarters staff, but the police failed to find the secret closet. One of the uniformed policemen ordered to search the building was Constable David Neligan, who had no intention of trying to find anything. 'I went upstairs and counted the roses on the wallpaper until the raid was over,' he later explained.[3]

'They got no document of importance, so that the only disorganisation is through the seizure of the staff,' Collins wrote. 'The enemy is certainly very keen at the moment in preventing the Dáil loan being a success, so that it becomes a more pressing duty than ever that every supporter of the Republic should increase his efforts.'[4]

Although Wharton survived his shooting, his injuries forced him to resign from the police force. He was luckier than his fellow Kerryman, Detective Sergeant Johnny Barton, who wrongly arrested news vendor James Hurley. Hurley was charged with, and subsequently convicted of, shooting Wharton, even though he had had no involvement whatsoever. William F. Bachelor, a former British army officer stated that he witnessed Hurley shoot Wharton. He picked Hurley out on the street for Barton. 'I can swear he is the man,' Bachelor said to Barton, who promptly arrested Hurley.[5]

The arrest of the news vendor suggested that Barton was not afraid to investigate such attacks, while Collins wanted the DMP to realise that anyone investigating such a matter was a legitimate target. Jim Slattery had no idea why Collins wanted Barton out of the way. 'I have nothing much to say about him except that I received orders (again through Mick McDonnell) that Barton was to be eliminated,' Slattery said. As usual, none of the Squad asked why.[6]

Barton was shot in the back from such close range that there were powder burns on his coat. As he crumpled to the ground, mortally wounded he cried, 'Oh, God what did I do to deserve this?' He was near G division headquarters and it was the height of the evening rush hour at 6.10 p.m. on 30 November. 'What did I do?' he repeated as he lay dying. He had been in G division for only two months. Why Collins ordered the killing is not clear, but it was assumed that Barton's unforgivable sin had been trying to find Wharton's assailants.

While it was believed that Collins moved about in disguise, highly armed and well protected, he usually went alone, unarmed, on a bicycle and without any disguise. Some of the detectives knew him, but he had so terrorised G division that they were afraid to apprehend him, lest the faceless people supposedly protecting him would come to his rescue, or take revenge on the detective or his family at some later date. Of course, attacking members of anyone's family would have been totally out of character for Collins, but his enemies were not to know this. They knew only of his ruthless reputation, and he exploited it to the full.

One can imagine the scene as Collins recognised a detective on a tram. He would sit down next to him, ask about specific members of the detective's family, or colleagues in the DMP, and – before alighting – assure the detective it would be safe for him to get off the tram at some later stop.

Many of the detectives and policemen knew him by sight, but their failure to arrest him could not be explained by fear alone. Like the police who were working for him, others were undoubtedly secret sympathisers. He had come across Inspector Lowry of the uniformed branch of the DMP as early as 1917, when he delivered the oration at Thomas Ashe's funeral, and ever since Lowry always seemed to salute and show Collins great respect, but there was never much more between them than the inspector's polite 'Mr Collins'. One night as Collins was cycling before curfew, a couple of uniformed policemen were standing by the road, and one of them shouted, 'More power, me Corkman!'[7]

On another occasion, in the street, Batt O'Connor became uneasy at the way two DMPs looked at Collins. They seemed to recognise him, but Collins was unperturbed. 'Even if they recognised me,' Collins said, 'they would be afraid to report they saw me.' And, if they did report, it would take the DMP an hour to muster the necessary force to seize him. 'And, of course,' he added, 'all the time I would wait here until they were ready to come along!'[8]

He never stayed in any one place for very long; he had difficulty sitting still. He always had something to do, somebody to see, or somewhere to go. He was always on the go, though he never thought of himself as being 'on the run'. Wanted men frequently developed a habit of venturing forth only with care. Before leaving a building they sneak a furtive glance to make sure there is no police around, whereas Collins had contempt for such practices. He just bounded out of doors in a carefree, self-confident manner, without betraying the slightest indication he was trying to evade anybody.

'I do not allow myself to feel I am on the run,' he explained. 'That is my safeguard. It prevents me from acting in a manner likely to arouse suspicion.'[9]

When the police started looking for him in May, he moved from the Munster Hotel, but the proprietress, Myra McCarthy, continued to do his laundry, so he visited the hotel frequently. By acting as he did he gave the distinct impression of not being afraid of the detectives; they were left to ponder whether he was crazy or just very well protected. In either case he was not someone to mess with.

Faced with the demise of the DMP's most active detectives, Lord French set up a three-man committee – consisting of T.J. Smith, the acting inspector general of the RIC; assistant under-secretary Sir John J. Taylor at Dublin Castle, and a resident magistrate named Alan Bell – to consider what to do about the deteriorating intelligence situation from the British point of view. Bell, a former RIC man, was particularly close to French and had a great deal of investigative experience going back to the troubles of the 1880s.

The committee reported on 7 December that 'an organised conspiracy of murder, outrage and intimidation has existed for sometime past' with the aim of undermining the police forces. Even though the first police had been killed in Tipperary, the committee concluded that 'Dublin City is the storm centre and mainspring of it all.'[10] To remedy the situation it was proposed that the Sinn Féin movement should be infiltrated and selected leaders should be assassinated.

'We are inclined to think that the shooting of a few would-be assassins would have an excellent effect,' the committee reported. 'Up to the present they have escaped with impunity. We think that this should be tried as soon as possible.'[11]

This was really a very important day in Collins' life. He went to the Munster Hotel to collect his laundry, but found a police raid in progress. The DMP were looking for him while he mingled with spectators on the street outside. He knew that Detective Inspector Bruton was aware he lived there, and he apparently blamed him for the raid. The Squad was ordered to kill Bruton, though this was easier ordered than done, because he ventured out of Dublin Castle only under armed escort, and he took the precaution of not developing a routine. In any event the finger of suspicion was soon transferred from Bruton to a spy who had infiltrated Collins' network.

Timothy A. Quinlisk from Wexford had been one of the prisoners-of-war recruited by Casement for his Irish brigade in Germany. He was a corporal in the Royal Irish Regiment when the Germans captured him in 1915. His father was a former member of the RIC who had been stationed in Cork for some twenty years and in Wexford during his later years before retiring to Waterford. With credentials in the Casement brigade, Quinlisk was easily accepted in Sinn Féin quarters, especially after Robert Brennan introduced him to Seán Ó Muirthile, the secretary of the Supreme Council of the IRB. Quinlisk, or Quinn as he called himself, cut a dashing figure and was quite a man for the ladies. 'He was always immaculately dressed and one would have said that with his good looks, his self-assurance and general bonhomie, he would have got anywhere,' according to Brennan. 'He liked to give the impression that he was in on all of Mick Collins' secrets.'

As a result of his enlistment in the Irish brigade, he had been denied back pay for the period of his imprisonment in Germany. Collins helped him out financially, and Quinlisk stayed for a time at the Munster Hotel, but he wanted more. On 11 November he wrote to the under-secretary at Dublin Castle, mentioning his background and offering to provide information.

'I was the man who assisted Casement in Germany and since coming home I have been connected with Sinn Féin,' he wrote. 'I have decided to tell all I know of that organisation and my information would be of use to the authorities. The scoundrel Michael Collins has treated me scurvily and I now am going to wash my hands of the whole business.'[12]

He was brought to G division headquarters to make a statement, which Broy typed up and, of course, passed on to Collins. But Quinlisk had taken the precaution of telling Collins that he had gone to the DMP merely to get a passport so he could emigrate to the United States. He said the police put pressure on him to inform on Collins, offering money, promising to make arrangements for him to get his wartime back-pay. He told Collins that he was merely pretending to go along with police.

Collins had moved from the Munster Hotel some months previously but returned there weekly for his laundry. He apparently moved about, never staying in any one place for very long. 'Living in such turmoil,' he wrote to Hannie, 'it's not all that easy to be clear on all matters at all times.' Yet he maintained a very regular daily routine.[13]

After his office at 76 Harcourt Street was raided in November, he opened a new finance office at 22 Henry Street. Like his other offices, it was on a busy thoroughfare with a lot of passing traffic, so that the comings and goings of strangers would not attract attention, as they would if the offices had been in some quiet, out-of-the-way location. The Henry Street office survived for about eighteen months. He also had another finance office at 29 Mary Street and he set up a new intelligence office at 5 Mespil Road. He kept papers in Eileen McGrane's home at 21 Dawson Street, and had gold hidden in a house owned by Batt O'Connor at 3 St Andrew's Terrace, and also in O'Connor's home at 1 Brendan's Road, Donnybrook.

In the morning he would go to his intelligence office in Mespil Road. This was only known to his secretary Susan Mason, Tobin, O'Reilly and a couple of other people. He did not meet people there. Afterwards he would cycle over to his finance office in Mary Street, and he would have lunch at either Batt O'Connor's home in Donnybrook, or in Pádraig O'Keeffe's wife's restaurant in Camden Street. He would meet people in either of those two places or in one of the many 'joints' that he used around the city.

There was a whole cluster of these on the north side of the city around the Rutland (now Parnell) Square area. 'Joint No. 1' was Vaughan's Hotel at 29 Rutland Square. It was a kind of clearing house for him. People visiting from outside Dublin wishing to meet him for the first time would go to Vaughan's, where the porter, Christy Hart, was usually able to pass on a message to him. 'Joint No. 2' was Liam Devlin's pub at 69 Parnell Street on the south side of the square. Here Collins met a more select group of people, like members of the Dublin brigade. He met warders from Mountjoy jail in Jim Kirwin's Bar on the same street. Other 'joints' around the square included No. 4, the old headquarters of the Irish Volunteers; No. 20, Bamba Hall; No. 41, Irish National Forresters Hall; and No. 46, the Keating Branch of the Gaelic League. Nearby were other joints, like Barry's Hotel on Great Denmark Street and Fleming's Hotel in Gardiner Row. He met railway men carrying dispatches to and from Belfast at Phil Sheerin's Coolevin Dairies in Amiens Street, and police contacts in the Bannon brother's pub in Upper Abbey Street, and sailors with news from Britain in Foley Street at Pat Shanahan's bar, which was also the haunt of Dan Breen and the Soloheadbeg gang.

They and the Squad finally caught up with Lord French on 19 December. He had gone to his country residence in Roscommon, and Collins sent a man there to report back when the Lord Lieutenant left for Dublin. An ambush was then prepared at Ashtown Cross, not far from the Viceregal Lodge in Phoenix Park, Dublin. The attempt was bungled, however, and the only fatality was one of the ambushers who apparently was caught in crossfire.

After his escape French was highly critical of G division. 'Our Secret service is simply non-existent,' he complained. 'What masquerades for such a service is nothing but a delusion and a snare. The DMP are absolutely demoralised and the RIC will be in the same case very soon if we do not quickly set our house in order.'[14]

Detective Inspector W.C. Forbes Redmond was brought from Belfast as assistant commissioner to reorganise G division, and he brought a number of his own people to work undercover. He made the capture of Collins a priority. He called all DMP detectives, from sergeants up, and told them 'that they were not doing their duty, that he would give them one month to get Michael Collins and those responsible for the shooting the various detectives, or else he would order them to resign.' They need not have worried, because Redmond did not last the month himself.

Not knowing Dublin, he had to have someone as a guide to the city, so he naturally used his administrative assistant, Jim McNamara. Redmond set about trying to capture Collins, and he came quite close with the help of a secret service agent who wormed his way into Collins' confidence.

Sergeant T.J. McElligott, who had been dismissed from the RIC because of his Sinn Féin sympathies, secretly went to work for Collins as a kind of police union organiser. Ostensibly, he was trying to improve the pay and conditions of the RIC, but in fact he was engaged in propaganda, trying to undermine the morale of the force by sowing seeds of discord. When the police went on strike in London, Collins sent McElligott there to make some useful contacts. At strike headquarters he met a man using the name of John Jameson, who was posing as a Marxist sympathiser but was actually a secret service agent. Shortly afterwards Jameson turned up in Dublin with an introduction from Art O'Brian, the Sinn Féin representative in Britain.

Jameson, whose real name was John Charles Byrne, was a Londoner living in Romford, Essex, and posing as a revolutionary anxious to undermine the British system. He offered to supply weapons, and arrangements were made for him to meet Collins, Mulcahy and Rory O'Connor at the Home Farm Produce Shop in Camden Street. They met again the following day at the Ranelagh home of Mrs Wyse Power, a member of the Sinn Féin executive.

'What he was delaying about that prevented him getting us caught with him, at least on the second of these occasions, I don't know,' Mulcahy remarked.[15] Byrne did make arrangements to have Collins arrested after a third meeting at the home of Batt O'Connor on 16 January 1920.

D.I. Redmond had one of his own undercover men watching the house, but that man did not know Collins and by a stroke of good luck Liam Tobin, who also happened to be at the house, left with Byrne and the lookout – assuming that Tobin was Collins – intercepted Redmond on Morehampton Road as he approached with a lorry-load of troops to raid O'Connor's house. The raid was promptly called off, but Redmond had brought Jim McNamara with him, and also used him as a guide that night when he decided to keep O'Connor's house under observation.

By the next day Collins had been briefed. He was due to have dinner again at O'Connor's house, but he gave it a miss. When Redmond and the police arrived, there was no one in the house, other than O'Connor's wife and children. He left, promising not to bother her again, a prophetic promise as it turned out.

Redmond had already made a fatal mistake when a detective had come to him with a grievance over some of his changes in G division, and he dismissed the complaint with some disparaging comments about G division as a whole. 'You are a bright lot!' Redmond reportedly said. 'Not one of you has been able to get on to Collins' track for a month, and here is a man only two days in Dublin and has already seen him.'[16]

The disgruntled detective mentioned this to Broy, who promptly informed Collins. Together with the information from McNamara, they immediately became suspicious of Byrne. He had not only arrived from London recently but had also had a meeting with Collins at Batt O'Connor's house.

Tobin had disliked Byrne from the outset, but had problems convincing Collins, who liked the unusual visitor. The thirty-four-year-old Byrne was clearly an adventurer. Small, with a very muscular build, he had a whole series of tattoos on his arms and hands. There were Japanese women, snakes, flowers and a bird. He had a snake ring tattooed on the third finger of his right hand and two rings tattooed on his left hand. He also had a strange fascination with birds, the feathered variety, which he kept in cages in his hotel room.

Collins and Tobin decided to set a trap for Byrne, by leading him to believe that important documents were being stored in the home of a former Lord Mayor of Dublin, J.J. Farrell of 9 Iona Road. The castle authorities had no grounds for suspecting him, because he had no sympathy whatever for Sinn Féin. The greatest moment of his life had been when he received King Edward VII on a visit to Dublin. Collins' men kept an eye on Farrell's house, and had a great laugh when the police raided it and forced the former mayor to stand outside in his night attire. 'You are raiding your friends,' Farrell protested. 'Do you know I received the King? I had twenty minutes conversation with him.'[17]

The raid looked particularly bad for Jameson, who promptly left the country. It was Art O'Brien who introduced Jameson to Sinn Féin. 'What I have to say with regard to him will probably be somewhat of a thunderbolt to you,' Collins wrote to O'Brien. 'I have absolutely certain information that the man who came from London met me and spoke to me and reported that I was growing a moustache to Basil Thompson.'[18]

On the night of 20 January 1920 Collins was tipped off that Redmond planned a raid that night on Cullenswood House, where Collins had a basement office and Mulcahy had a top-floor flat with his wife. Cullen and Thornton roused Mulcahy from his bed, and he spent the remainder of the night with a friend a short distance away. Redmond was becoming a real thorn, and Collins gave the Squad orders to eliminate him.

'If we don't get that man, he'll get us and soon,' Collins warned the Squad.[19]

Redmond really made a soft target, because he underestimated his opponents. Nattily dressed in civilian clothes, topped off by a bowler hat, he looked more like a stockbroker than a policeman. He stayed at the Standard Hotel in Harcourt Street and walked to work at Dublin Castle and back without an escort, though he did take the precaution of wearing a bullet-proof vest.

With Forbes Redmond as the second assistant commissioner of the DMP and head of G division, a serious effort was made by some of the police to find Collins. Quinlisk was told that things had become so hot in Dublin that Collins had moved to Cork, so then concerted efforts were made to find him in Cork. On 1 January 1920 William Mulhern, the crimes special sergeant in Bandon produced a letter that Collins had written to someone in his area in relation to the Dáil loan. His return address was the Mansion House, and Mulhern suggested that Collins was 'seemingly at present staying in Dublin'.[20] The county inspector of the RIC reported from Cork the next day that 'Michael Collins, M.P. is carrying on operations from the Mansion House. I am putting all my DI's on the alert re the matter + taking steps to deal with the men likely to be appointed to further the loan in different districts. It is clear that Collins is in communication with the Sinn Féin organisation in all counties in Ireland in regard to the loan.'[21]

But Detective Superintendent Owen Brien telephoned Cork to say that Collins was in the Clonakilty area on 5 January. That was true, but he was back in Dublin by the time word reached Cork.

'Collins cannot be found in this district,' District Inspector Henry Connor reported three days later. He noted that careful enquiries had been made and a number of houses searched without result. 'A close watch will be kept and if Collins appears I will have him arrested,' the district inspector concluded.[22] Bandon and Skibbereen reported the following week that 'no trace of Collins has been found in their districts', Sergeant William Mulhern stated on 15 January. 'There is reason to believe this man is in Dublin still according to local information in Skibbereen,' the county inspector added at the end of the report, which was shown to Redmond.[23]

Even Redmond had extensive inquiries made in the West Cork area, as the DMP had obtained a letter written by Collins on 30 December expressing 'the greatest regret' that he was unable to meet with supporters in south Cork. 'You will understand that the enemy anxiety to stop my activities is so great,' he wrote, 'that I cannot make the journey, even if I could spare time from the duties which fall on me through having to organise the loan effort for all Ireland.'[24]

One report from the country suggested that Collins was staying at the Clarence Hotel in Dublin, but Detective Officer Denis O'Brien could find no trace of him there, or at Mountjoy Street. But by then Redmond learned that an undercover agent had made contact with Collins.

In the Michael Collins movie, Redmond was killed by a car bomb, but the IRA never used car bombs at the time, though Redmond ended up just as dead. As mentioned previously, he stayed at the Standard Hotel in Harcourt Street while a residence was being renovated for him in Dublin Castle. Collins had Tom Cullen book into the hotel to keep an eye on Redmond and gather information about his habits, such as when he left the hotel and returned, and what he did in the evening and at night. He continued to walk to and from work at the Castle without an escort every day.

Members of the Squad got their chance on 21 January 1920. 'I saw Redmond coming down from the Castle but he turned back and went in again,' Joe Dolan recalled. 'Tom Keogh, Vinny Byrne and myself were waiting and Redmond came out again. Tom Keogh turned to Vinny Byrne and myself and told us to cover them off. Redmond went straight up Dame Street, Grafton Street and Harcourt Street, and we followed him.'[25]

'Michael Collins picked Joe Leonard, Seán Doyle and myself to be between the Standard Hotel and the foot of Harcourt Street,' Paddy O'Daly recalled. 'Joe Leonard and myself were walking up and down one side of the street, and Seán Doyle was on the other side. It was nearly 6 p.m. when O'Daly spotted other members of the Squad, walking briskly. 'I saw Tom Keogh and another man crossing the road to the railings side of the Green.'[26]

'Look out, Joe, here is Keogh and the gang,' O'Daly said to Leonard.

'I had hardly spoken these words when I turned and saw Redmond crossing Harcourt Street about six yards away,' O'Daly continued. 'When Redmond was about two yards from me I fired and he fell mortally wounded, shot through the head.' Keogh was about twenty yards away when he started running and arrived moments after O'Daly had hit Redmond behind the left ear, and Keogh proceeded to shoot him in the back. Byrne and Slattery watched, acting as a covering party.

The shot behind the ear was fatal because it severed Redmond's spinal cord at the second vertebrae. The other bullet went through his liver, a lung and his stomach. 'The area was full of British military and Air Force men, but no attempt was made to follow us and we got away,' Dolan noted.[27]

Following Redmond's death, his own undercover detectives pulled out and returned to Belfast, and thereafter G division 'ceased to affect the situation', according to British military intelligence.[28] Dublin Castle offered £10,000 for information leading to the arrest and conviction of the person responsible for his death. This was probably where the story about the big reward for Collins' arrest originated. He was the one who had given the order to kill Redmond. Rewards of £5,000 had already been offered in connection with the deaths of the three other DMP detectives, Smyth, Hoey and Barton, and these rewards were now doubled. As Collins had ordered all four killings, there was a handsome accumulative reward for the evidence to convict him, though the authorities never officially offered a reward for his actual capture.

11

'Well Shoot Him So'

The British began to fight back. On 24 February a curfew was introduced from midnight until 5 a.m. 'Last night,' Collins wrote the next day, 'the city of Dublin was like a city of the dead. It is the English way of restoring peace to this country.'[1]

In the following weeks he would complain of growing repression. 'By night the streets of Dublin are like streets of a beleaguered city – no one abroad save the military forces of the enemy fully equipped for all the purposes and usages of war.'[2]

British undercover people were infiltrating Ireland, and were desperate to entrap Collins. Quinlisk, who had lost touch with him, began making anxious efforts to contact him. By then, however, Collins had firm evidence of his treachery – having got his hands on Quinlisk's actual letter offering his services to Dublin Castle. Rather than asking the Squad to take him out immediately, Collins tried to use Quinlisk as bait to get at Detective Superintendent Owen Brien of the DMP. The Squad had been trying to kill him, but he rarely moved outside the walls of Dublin Castle.

Seán Ó Muirthile was assigned to keep Quinlisk busy while one of the Squad telephoned the castle to say that Quinlisk had vital information and would meet Brien outside the offices of the *Evening Mail*, just outside the castle, at a certain time. Brien turned up, but something spooked him and he darted back into the cover of Dublin Castle before the Squad could get a shot at him.

Collins learned afterwards that the superintendent had twigged he was being set up. He blamed Quinlisk, who explained that he had been detained all night by Ó Muirthile. 'You're in the soup,' Collins told Ó Muirthile with a laugh.[3]

Quinlisk should have had the good sense to quit at that point, but he persisted in his efforts to see Collins. So a trap was set. He was told that Collins was out of town and would meet him that night at Wren's Hotel in Cork City.

Liam Archer, one of Collins' telegraph agents at the GPO duly intercepted a coded message to the district inspector of the RIC at Union Quay, Cork. 'Tonight at midnight surround Wren's Hotel, Wintrop Street, Cork', the message read when decoded. 'Collins and others will be there. Expect shooting as he is a dangerous man and heavily armed.'[4]

'That ****** has signed his death warrant,' Collins said when Archer showed him the message. He was amused, however, at what was likely to happen at Wren's Hotel. 'They'll play *síghle caoch* with the place,' he added.[5]

The RIC raided the hotel and, of course, found nothing. Quinlisk stayed in Cork searching for Collins. On the night of 18 February he was met by some members of the IRA, who – promising to take him to Collins – took him outside the city to Ballyphehane and shot him dead in a field and pinned a note to his body – 'Spies Beware'.

'The body presented a gruesome spectacle,' according to the *Cork Examiner*. 'There are about five bullet marks on the forehead and one bullet went through the right eye and found an exit on the left side of the neck. He was also shot in the neighbourhood of the ear, and another bullet entered his chest.' In all he was shot eleven times.[6] 'The medical evidence was that the wounds could not have been self-inflicted', the *Cork Examiner* added.[7]

District Inspector P.W. MacDonagh of the RIC had made the mistake of looking for Collins in Cork at the beginning of the year. He was shot and seriously wounded at Infirmary Road while walking from Blackrock to Union Quay with Head Constable John Patrick Ferris on 10 March. Ferris gave chase and emptied his revolver in the direction of the fleeing assailant. No evidence was ever produced to suggest Collins had called for the attempt on his life. But even if the IRA in Cork had done so without directions from Dublin, the ultimate message to the police was still the same – looking for Collins was dangerous.

Around this time Byrne, alias Jameson, returned with a suitcase of revolvers. Tobin took the guns and pretended to leave them in a business premises on Bachelor's Walk, which he said was an arms dump for the IRA. When the premises were raided that night, Collins was finally convinced of Byrne's duplicity. Members of the Squad called for Byrne at the Granville Hotel on Sackville Street on the afternoon of 2 March on the pretext of taking him to Collins' hideout, but they brought him to the grounds of a lunatic asylum in Glasnevin instead.

Realising what was about to happen, he tried to bluff about his friendship with Collins and Tobin, but the Squad members knew better. They asked him if he wished to pray.

'No,' he replied.

'We are only doing our duty,' one said to him.

'And I have done mine,' he replied, drawing himself to attention as they shot him twice, once in the head and again through the heart. Some weeks later the British cabinet were told that Byrne had been 'the best secret service man we had'.[8]

Robert Farnan, a member of the Dáil, introduced another British agent to Collins at the home of Batt O'Connor. Private Fergus Bryan Molloy was offering to procure arms. He depicted himself as the son of a Mayo man who had been forced to emigrate. He was planning to infiltrate the IRA as a double agent for the British. He was working for Colonel Hill Dillon, the chief intelligence officer of the British army at Park Gate Street.

Lily Mernin, a cousin of Piaras Béaslaí, was supplying information to Collins on the British army similar to that which Broy was supplying on the DMP. She was a typist for Major Stratford Burton, the garrison adjutant for the Dublin district at Ship Street barracks. Burton assigned her to type reports in connection with the Volunteers and court martial proceedings. Her duty included typing reports on the strength of various military posts throughout Dublin. Béaslaí introduced Collins to her.

'I promised to give him all the assistance that I possibly could,' she later recalled. 'Each week I prepared a carbon or a typed copy which ever

I was able to get. Sometimes I would bring these to the office placed at my disposal', in a house on Clonliffe Road. She typed copies of reports and other correspondence that she thought would be of interest to Collins. 'I left them on the machine and they were collected by some person whom I did not know,' she said. 'If anything special required urgent delivery to the intelligence staff then I would deliver it at Vaughan's between certain hours and Máire Ní Raghalleigh's book shop, Dorset Street.' She also left messages at a shop on Parnell Street.[9]

Lily warned that Molloy was really working for the British. At one point he asked one of his Irish contacts to write the names and addresses of prominent members of Sinn Féin, such as Count Plunkett and Countess Markievicz, on Dáil Éireann notepaper that had been seized during the raids on Sinn Féin headquarters.

'We have to shoot that fellow,' Tobin told Collins.

'Well shoot him so,' Collins replied.[10]

Frank Saurin, who was Lily Mernin's handler, was due to meet Molloy on 23 March 1920, and Vinny Byrne was told to get a good look at him so that he could identify him for other Squad members afterwards. Saurin and Molloy went into the Cairo Café on Grafton Street, and when Byrne sauntered in, Saurin invited him to sit with them. 'Our friend is very anxious to met Liam Tobin and I am sure you could arrange it,' Saurin said.[11]

Vinny Byrne arranged to meet Molloy at 5.30 p.m. next day at the corner of South King Street and Grafton Street. 'We would each wear a flower on our coats,' Byrne recalled.[12] McDonnell and Slattery were to do the killing while Keogh and Byrne covered them. Molloy waited for Byrne for three-quarters of an hour. When Byrne did not show, Molloy moved off down Grafton Street and into Wicklow Street. At the corner of South William Street Slattery brushed aside Annie Hughes, a young domestic servant, as he moved in for the kill. She shouted for him not to kill the man. As Molloy turned to look, he was shot in the right knee, and he fell to the ground. McDonnell and Slattery then shot Molloy two more times, once in the abdomen and once in the right temple.

'The crowd started shouting and made attempts to stop us getting away,' Slattery recalled. Keogh and Byrne drew their guns, forcing those people to back off and let all of them escape.[13]

This was the first time civilians had behaved in this way. When they discussed what had happened among themselves afterwards, the Squad concluded that people mistook them for British military dressed in civilian clothes.

Alan Bell – a resident magistrate and one of the secret committee, as we saw earlier, that had called for 'the shooting of a few would-be assassins' – was in charge of some covert agents. He was reporting to Sir Basil Thompson at Scotland Yard. 'In the course of moving about,' Bell wrote to Viscount French, 'my men have picked up a good deal of useful information which leads to raids.'

Bell was empowered to examine bank accounts to locate money deposited in the names of a number of party sympathisers, and he opened a much-publicised inquiry into Sinn Féin funds. He was from Banagher, King's County (now Offaly), and had served in the RIC during the Land League troubles of the 1880s. He rose to the rank of district inspector, before leaving the constabulary to become a resident magistrate in Claremorris and later in Lurgan. Transferred to Dublin in 1919, he lived in Monkstown and travelled into the city each day on a tram. A police guard escorted him to and from the tram, but he travelled into the city alone. He was coming into the city as usual on the morning of 26 March when four men approached him as the tram reached Ballsbridge.

Horrified passengers watched while Guilfoyle stopped the tram and McDonnell, Tobin and Dolan dragged the elderly man into the street. McDonnell and Tobin shot him dead on the pavement. They then escaped, but later concluded that shooting him in this relatively quiet area of the city had been a mistake, because it was more difficult to escape than in a crowded area.

'We always felt very secure when a wanted man was shot in a thickly populated district, because when the shooting was over we could easily mix with the crowd and escape the watchful eyes of enemy agents,' Slattery noted. 'Such was not the case in the shooting of Bell.

There was scarcely anybody on the road that morning, and if enemy forces had come along we would have had no chance of escaping. That was a lesson that we took deeply to heart and remembered for future occasions.'[14]

The killing of the elderly man provoked a storm of revulsion. It was widely believed that he was killed because he was trying to find the national loan money, though there were also rumours that he had been investigating the attempt on the life of his friend, Viscount French. One rather colourful story published in the United States suggested that Bell had 'arranged for a Scotland Yard detective to go to Mountjoy Prison, pose as a priest and "hear" confessions of political prisoners there.' The IRA supposedly shot Bell and the detective the next day. No detective was killed the next day, or in the whole of March, but the story was published anyway.[15]

Bell's killing was taken as a very public warning not to look for the loan money. Despite early misgivings, Collins achieved the goal of raising a quarter of a million pounds. In fact the loan was over-subscribed by more than forty per cent. More than £357,000 was collected. Of that the British only captured a mere £18,000. 'From any point of view the seizure was insignificant,' Collins wrote, 'but you may rely upon it we shall see to the return of this money just as someday Ireland will exact her full reparation for all the stealings and seizures by the British in the past.'[16]

The British retaliated by using some of the IRA's tactics. After the killing of Constable Joseph Murtagh, a twenty-three-year veteran of the RIC from County Meath, on Pope's Quay, Cork at around 10.40 p.m. on the night of 19 March 1920, the police retaliated. Murtagh, who was off duty, was shot dead while returning from the Palace Theatre in civilian clothes. A few hours later MacCurtain would pay for this with his life, even though he had had no involvement.

The RIC cut off the street on which his shop was located and men with blackened faces raided his home over the shop and killed him. The coroner's jury returned 'a verdict of wilful murder against David Lloyd George, Prime Minister of England; Lord French, Lord Lieutenant of Ireland; Ian McPherson, late Chief Secretary of Ireland, Acting Inspector

General Smith of RIC; Divisional Inspector Clayton of RIC; District Inspector Swanzy and some unknown members of the RIC.' Swanzy was one of a large number of Orangemen from Ulster stationed in Cork. He and Head Constable Ferris were promptly transferred to the north for their own protection.[17]

Collins was deeply upset by the death of his friend MacCurtain; they had been quite close ever since their internment together in Frongoch. 'I have not very much heart in what I am doing today, thinking of poor Tomás,' Collins wrote to Terence MacSwiney, took over from MacCurtain. 'It is surely the most appalling thing that has been done yet.'[18] He was particularly annoyed that the RIC was trying to make it appear that the IRA was responsible. 'The English, in their usual way, are trying to make the world believe that poor Tomás was shot by his own friends,' Collins wrote. 'That is the English way.'[19]

Two similar killings took place on the following nights in the Thurles area, where the RIC also had a strong contingent of Orangemen. Collins complained that the British and 'their agents here, whether military, police or civil, are doing all they can to goad the people into premature action'.[20] Mulcahy and Collins had already had to persuade MacCurtain not to stage a 1916-style rebellion in Cork to commemorate the fourth anniversary of the Easter Rising.

The Squad shot and killed Detective Constable Henry Kells at the corner of Upper Camden Street and Pleasant Street, where he lived, on the morning of 14 April. He had been in the DMP for over twenty years but he had only transferred to G division a couple of months earlier. It was reported that 'he was concerned solely with criminal work, and had no connection with duties of a political or semi-political description'.[21] Peadar Clancy, the vice-brigadier of the Dublin brigade, had sent word to Collins from Mountjoy jail, however, that Harry Kells was conducting identity parades within the prison looking for anyone involved in the killing of Alan Bell. The Squad waited to ambush Kells as he went to work as usual between 9.30 and 10 a.m. He had to walk to work that morning, as were no trams running due to a one-day general strike.

'On our way we picked up Hugo McNeill,' Paddy O'Daly recalled. McNeill, a brother of Eoin MacNeill, was not a member of the Squad but asked to come along. 'We told him he could help us,' O'Daly added. 'We divided up and patrolled in twos.'[22]

MacNeill went with Joe Leonard. O'Daly heard some shooting and saw McNeill sauntering down Pleasant Street as if nothing had happened.

'What was the shooting about? O'Daly asked.

'Kells is up there if you want him,' MacNeill replied.

'Where?'

'On the footpath.'

Apparently nobody witnessed the killing other than the assailants.

Detective Constable Laurence Dalton had also only been a member of G division for some months. He was a stout man with a charming disposition, according to David Neligan, with whom he was quite friendly. Dalton watched the trains coming into the Broadstone (now Connolly) railroad station. There was later a suggestion that he had arrested J.J. Walsh, who had escaped from Mountjoy having been sentenced to five years in jail in March 1920, but he was not actually re-arrested until some months after Dalton's death. However, Dalton was suspected of fingering IRB people arriving at the station.

'The intelligence section got to know of his activities, with the result that we were instructed to have him put away,' according to Jim Slattery. 'Liam Tobin was the man who pointed Dalton out to us.' Mick McDonnell, Tom Keogh and Jim Slattery were detailed to shoot him, while Vinny Byrne and Joe Dolan covered them.[23]

Dalton was walking towards Broadstone station with Detective Constable Robert Spencer. They were planning to meet the 1.10 train from the west on the afternoon of 20 April 1920. They were fired on from behind while passing St Mary's church.

Spencer raced off towards Dorset Street, while Dalton headed towards the railroad station. Two of the men followed him. One brought him to the ground with a shot to the leg, as they believed he was wearing a steel vest.

'Let me alone,' the wounded detective pleaded. One of the gunmen fired three shots at him on the ground from a short distance, according to a witness.[24] Dalton was fatally wounded and died at the Mater Hospital about two hours later.

Some of the Squad were unhappy that they were merely providing back-up cover and not doing the actual shooting. They feared headquarters would think they were doing nothing of importance.

'I promised that they would carry out the next operation,' O'Daly noted.[25] This was to be the elimination of Sergeant Richard J. Revell. He had been employed exclusively on clerical work in the detective department of Dublin Castle for the past six years.

'As in the majority of the executions which we carried out, we were not aware of the reason for his elimination,' O'Daly added. 'We simply got orders to carry out the execution of Revell. The reason did not concern us.'[26]

The Squad took up position to kill him as he cycled to work on 8 May. Three men stepped out into the road and began shooting. He veered across the road and came down heavily on his head. He tried to get up but collapsed, bleeding profusely from a neck wound. They left him on the road for dead. But he survived.

Prior to 1920 the British cabinet had been too preoccupied with other problems to devote much attention to Ireland, but the need to do something about the deteriorating situation gradually became clear to Lloyd George and his colleagues. They set about changing their policy with a thorough spring-cleaning of the Dublin Castle administration.

Sir Hamar Greenwood was appointed chief secretary, Sir John Anderson under secretary, and Alfred 'Andy' Cope assistant under secretary. General Sir Nevil Macready became commander-in-chief of British forces in Ireland, Major-General Henry Tudor took over at the head of the police and General Sir Ormonde Winter became chief of combined intelligence services.

From the outset Greenwood was determined to implement a hard-line policy. Even before visiting Ireland he 'talked the most awful tosh about shooting Sinn Féiners on sight, and without evidence, and frightfulness generally,' according to the cabinet secretary.[27]

Terence MacSwiney, who succeeded MacCurtain as lord mayor, was a stoic individual who was quite prepared to suffer. 'This contest is one of endurance,' he declared in his inaugural address. 'It is not they who can inflict most, but they who can suffer most who will conquer.'[28]

The other side's capacity for suffering was already showing signs of stress. Members of the RIC were not prepared to put up with the ostracism and attacks to which they were being subjected. Resignations from the force were running at more than 200 a month in early 1920. It was not long before the British found it necessary to bring in new recruits from outside. The first of these arrived in Ireland on 25 March 1920. They had been recruited so hastily that there was no time to get them proper uniforms.

All wore the dark green caps and belts of the RIC, and some had dark green tunics with military khaki pants, while others had khaki tunics and dark green pants. Most were veterans of the First World War who had been unable either to find civilian employment or to adjust to civilian life. The ten shillings a day, all found, were a relatively good wage for the time, especially for men who were desperate for a job. In view of the colour of their uniforms and the ruthless reputation they quickly acquired, they were called the Black and Tans after a pack of hounds. The more active undoubtedly welcomed the name, because they – like Dan Breen – tended to see their enemies in terms of hunting 'game'.

Faced with the choice of British or Irish terrorists, the Irish people preferred their own; they hid them and supported them. As a result the Black and Tans quickly began to look on all civilians as their enemies and acted accordingly, thereby further alienating the Irish people from the crown government.

The week after the arrival of the first contingent of Black and Tans, the IRA intensified its campaign. At Collins' suggestion tax offices throughout the country were fire-bombed on the night of 3 April in an attempt to disrupt the British tax-collecting apparatus. At the same time more than 350 unoccupied RIC barracks were burned to the ground.

When the British government discussed what to do about the Irish situation, General Macready advocated making the security forces mobile enough to surprise IRA bands, but Sir Henry Wilson, the chief of the imperial general staff, dismissed this idea as useless. He wanted instead 'to collect the names of Sinn Féiners by districts: proclaim them on church doors all over the country; and whenever a policeman is murdered, pick five by lot and shoot them!'[29] One could hardly imagine anything more likely to provoke the indignation of Irish people than defiling their churches in such a barbarous manner.

'Somehow or other terror must be met by greater terror,' Wilson argued according to the cabinet secretary. And this is precisely what happened.[30] When members of the new Dublin Castle administration met on 31 May to discuss the Irish situation with Lloyd George and War Minister Winston Churchill, the new chief secretary complained of 'thugs' going about shooting people in Dublin, Cork and Limerick.[31]

'We are certain that these are handsomely paid,' Greenwood said, 'the money comes from the USA.' According to him, Collins paid 'the murderers in public houses'.[32]

'It is monstrous that we have 200 murders and no one hung,' Churchill cried. 'After a person is caught he should pay the penalty within a week. Look at the tribunals which the Russian government have devised. You should get three or four judges whose scope should be universal and they should move quickly over the country and do summary justice.'[33] It was ironic that he, of all people, should privately advocate imitating the Bolshevik system, against which he railed in his public speeches.

'You agreed six or seven months ago that there should be hanging,' he said to Lloyd George.

'I feel certain you must hang,' the prime minister replied, but he doubted that an Irish jury would convict any rebel of a capital offence. In the interim, he therefore advocated economic pressure.

'Increase their pecuniary burdens,' he said. 'There is nothing farmers so much dislike as the rates.'

'Why not make life intolerable in a particular area?' Churchill asked.

'We are at present in very much of a fog,' Macready explained. The old system of intelligence had broken down, as the DMP's 'morale had been destroyed by the murders'. There was no longer an effective detective division in Ireland, though he added that a new system was being built.[34]

Neligan was greatly disillusioned by the killing of Detective Constable Laurence Dalton, who he believed had been improperly targeted. 'All that can be said now is that personal antagonism brought about this man's death, which I deeply regret,' Neligan wrote in *The Spy in the Castle*. 'It was one of the tragedies of the time.'[35]

Neligan wished to get out of the DMP but feared that he might be targeted if he returned to his native west Limerick because local republicans were liable to suspect him of being a British spy. His brother Maurice, a member of the IRB and a transport union organiser in Tralee, tried to help Dave by seeking the assistance of Tadhg Kennedy, the local IRA intelligence officer.

Kennedy, the accountant for Kerry County Council, was a small man with a cherubic face and bright eyes. He had already recruited Thomas O'Rourke, the crime special sergeant in Tralee, to provide the RIC cipher on a regular basis. The Neligan brothers met Kennedy one day and explained that Dave was looking for Collins to secure safe conduct so that he could return home. Kennedy, who spent much of his time working in Dublin between March and October 1920, was unable to locate Collins, so he turned to Stack with unfortunate consequences.

'I saw Stack and said that this fellow should not resign,' Kennedy related. Stack arranged for an aide, Paddy Sheehan, to meet the Neligan brothers. After Sheehan questioned Dave, however, Stack dismissed the idea of using Neligan as a spy.[36]

'Get him to resign,' Stack told Kennedy. 'He's no good.'[37]

Neligan duly resigned from the DMP on 11 May 1920, and he was provided with a note from the IRA for his own protection. Collins was furious when he learned what had happened.

'I got a flaming letter from Mick asking why the hell did I take Stack's/Sheehan's advice,' Kennedy noted. 'The result was that I went to Maurice and I told him that I had been sacked for letting Dave leave.'[38]

Kennedy also set up a meeting for Dave Neligan with Stack at the Clarence Hotel in Dublin. 'He told me that Collins wanted to meet me and that arrangements would be made,' Neligan wrote.[39]

Neligan suggested that he would have an excuse to get back into the force if the IRA pretended to intimidate him by sending him threatening letters to get out of Limerick. This was done and he even burned some hay that his father had at the back of the family home as a supposed warning. Neligan re-applied to the DMP and produced the threatening letters that had been sent to him. That was good enough and he was accepted back.

'I thought he was the best intelligence officer I ever met in my life,' Tadhg Kennedy explained. 'I discussed plans with Michael Collins for the re-establishment of Neligan into favour with the castle authorities.' Collins had stuff planted in Findlaters, a loyalist business house. When the auxiliaries raided the place and found the planted material, they nearly wrecked the building, much to the amusement of Collins and company. 'A number of such stunts put up Dave's stock with the Castle people,' Kennedy explained, 'and when the Castle were looking for one of their G men to train and lead the military raids, they asked for volunteers and Dave came to me, and he volunteered, and I understand with dire consequences to the military.'[40]

Before being invited to re-join, Neligan was interviewed by the Inspector-General Colonel Walter Edworth-Johnson, who asked him about conditions in the country. 'I told him the truth, which was unpalatable to him,' Neligan explained. Of course he knew the state of affairs himself, better than I did.' He offered Neligan any division he desired. 'I replied that G division would suit me,' Neligan noted. 'He agreed.' Hence Neligan went back as a detective working on political crime – the classic double agent. His initial task was protecting Thomas O'Shaughnessy, the recorder of Dublin. Dan MacDonnell was Neligan's handler, carrying messages from him back to intelligence headquarters.

Each of the G division detectives kept a journal in which they entered the names of suspects that they had seen that day. Neligan and McNamara used to check the journals of the detectives based in Dublin

Castle and note information that would be of interest to the IRA. 'We used to convey this information to Collins which served as a warning to those political suspects to watch themselves, that they were being seen by the police or under observation with a view to being picked up later,' Neligan explained.[41]

When Joe Kavanagh died in September 1920 from a blood clot after an operation for appendicitis in Jervis Street hospital, Neligan began attending meetings with Collins, Broy and McNamara at Tom Gay's home in Clontarf. One night the four of them returned to the city in a car driven by Joe Hyland.

They were stopped by a patrol near the Tolka Bridge. 'A British military sergeant ordered us all out of the car,' according to Broy. 'I produced a detective's card and said we were all detectives.'

'You'll have to see the officer,' sergeant replied.

The officers said that a bomb had been thrown at their military truck. Broy realised he could hoodwink the young military officer. If the auxiliaries arrived, however, he was afraid they might bring them all to Dublin Castle for identification. He asked the officer if the Drumcondra area was safe. The officer said he believed it was.

'We had better go that way so,' Broy said to the others. 'This bombing might be intended for us.' They then changed over to the Richmond Road, and sped up that road 'and got away while the going was good'.[42]

12

Settling Old Scores

While the British were re-organising, Collins' network was able to settle an old score on 15 June 1920. Joe Sweeney was in the bar of the Wicklow Hotel when Collins stomped in.

'We got the bugger, Joe.'[1]

'What are you taking about?' Sweeney asked.

'Do you remember that first night outside the Rotunda? Lea Wilson?'

'I'll never forget it.'

'Well,' said Collins, 'we got him today in Gorey.'[2]

He had tracked Percival Lea Wilson to Gorey, County Wexford, where he was an RIC district inspector. Three members of the Squad specially selected for the job had shot him dead that morning.

'Captain Lea Wilson was not shot because he had ill-treated Seán McDermott and other prisoners in 1916, because there were other British officers just as bad as he had been and no attempt was made to shoot them,' Paddy O'Daly later contended. 'I believe he was shot because of the position he held at the time, and for no other reason. I am satisfied from my long experience with the Squad that no man was shot merely for revenge and that any execution sanctioned by Michael Collins was perfectly justified.'[3] But Frank Thornton, one of the Big Fellow's main intelligence aides, told a very different story. He said that Wilson was shot because of his 'brutal treatment of IRA leaders during 1916, the treatment of Cumann na mBan prisoners whom he herded with the men like sheep on the Rotunda Gardens, and finally because he renewed activity in the Gorey district in 1920.'[4]

'Sinn Féin has had all the sport up to the present, and we are going to have sport now,' Colonel Ferguson Smyth, the newly appointed RIC divisional commissioner for Munster, told the assembled police at the RIC station in Listowel on 19 June. A highly decorated veteran, he was scarred by the First World War in which he had been shot six times and had lost an arm as result of his injuries. He seemed a rather embittered man as he advocated that the RIC should shoot first and ask questions later, but his remarks were obviously authorised, because General Tudor was present.[5]

'We must take the offensive and beat Sinn Féin at its own tactics,' Smyth said. 'If persons approaching carry their hands in their pockets or are suspicious-looking, shoot them down. You may make mistakes occasionally, and innocent people may be shot, but that cannot be helped. No policeman will get into trouble for shooting any man.'[6]

'By your accent I take it you are an Englishman, and in your ignorance you forget you are addressing Irishmen,' Constable Jeremiah Mee replied, appalled by the thought of such a policy. He took off his cap and belt and threw them on a table.[7]

'These too, are English,' he said. 'Take them.'[8]

Smyth, a native of Banbridge, County Down, denied he was English. He ordered that Mee be arrested, but the constable's colleagues shared his indignation and ignored the order. Afterwards Mee drew up an account of what had happened and thirteen of those present testified to its accuracy by signing the statement.

Mee and a colleague met Collins and others in Dublin on 15 July. Those present included the editor of *The Bulletin*, Erskine Childers and Countess Markievicz, along with the editor and managing director of the *The Freeman's Journal*, which had recently published details of Smyth's speech and was being sued for libel as a result.

'I had always imagined that the IRA leaders who were "on the run" were in hiding in cellars or in some out of the way place far removed from the scene of hostilities,' Mee recalled. 'I was somewhat surprised, then, as I sat with some of these same leaders, and calmly discussed the current situation, while military lorries were speeding through the street under the very windows of the room where our conference was taking place. As a matter of fact there seemed to be nothing to prevent anybody walking into that room and finding Michael Collins and Countess Markievicz.[9]

'For at least three hours we sat there under a cross-examination,' Mee wrote. The representatives of *The Freeman's Journal* were trying to build a defence against the libel action, and the republicans were seeking to exploit the Listowel incident for all that it was worth.[10] But Smyth never got the chance to press his libel suit. He was shot and killed by the IRA on 18 July in the County Club in Cork City.

'Were not your orders to shoot at sight?' his assassin asked. 'Well, you are in sight now, so prepare.'

The one-armed Smyth did not have a chance. He was shot five times and died at the scene. When the authorities sought to hold an inquest afterwards, they were unable to find enough people to serve on a jury. But the killing was used as an excuse for a week of rioting in the north in Bangor, Lisburn and Newtownards, where seventeen people were killed in the ensuing unrest.

Sergeant William Mulhern, the RIC crimes special sergeant who had been looking for Collins in the Bandon area back in January was shot as he was entering the local Catholic church for 8 a.m. mass on 25 June 1920. Daniel Cohalan, the Catholic bishop of Cork, roundly denounced the killing.

'His murder was singularly heinous, for he was murdered in circumstances which added to murder an awful irreverence and disrespect to God,' the bishop declared. 'God's House was selected as the place of safety for committing the murder.'[11] He pronounced the murderers excommunicated from the Catholic church.

The following Friday the Squad killed Frank Brooke, a railroad company executive. He was another of those who advised Lord Lieutenant French, and was a frequent overnight guest at the Viceregal Lodge.

Tom Keogh, Jim Slattery and Vinny Byrne were sent to kill Brooke at the railway company's offices at Westland Row on July 30, 1920. 'I do not know much about him except that we received instructions to shoot him,' Jim Slattery explained. 'Brooke was sitting at his table when we entered his office. We immediately opened fired on him and he fell.'[12]

Brooke was actually armed with a loaded revolver in his right pocket, but he never got a chance to use it before he was repeatedly hit.

Although O'Daly, the head of the Squad, argued that Collins was not motivated by vengeance, the events surrounding the killing of District Inspector Oswald R. Swanzy would seem to suggest otherwise. He was suspected of involvement in the murder of Tomás MacCurtain. Collins' intelligence network traced District Inspector Swanzy to Lisburn, County Antrim. The Squad had no operational involvement in the killing of Smyth, but Collins did have direct input in the subsequent killing on 22 August. 'Inspector Swanzy and his associates put Lord Mayor MacCurtain away,' Collins later explained, 'so I got Swanzy and all his associates wiped out, one by one, in all parts of the Ireland to which they had been secretly dispersed'.[13]

Roger E. McCorley of Befast was given the task of preparing the groundwork to kill Swanzy, and he concluded that the best time to shoot him was coming from church on Sunday 15 August 1920. Five men from MacCurtain's own brigade were selected to kill Swanzy.

'I met Mick Collins and, after a frank discussion, he remarked that the job was much too big for me,' recalled Seán Culhane, one of those men selected. 'I probably looked immature as at the time I was not yet twenty years of age. He said it was a job for experienced men and mentioned about picking selected men from Dublin. I made a strong protest to him and informed him that my orders were very emphatic and that it was solely a Cork brigade job. After thinking it over he said he would leave the decision to the Minister for Defence.'[14]

Culhane met Cathal Brugha with Mulcahy and Collins. 'The Minister questioned me very closely as to my proposed plan of action, which I fully detailed to him,' Culhane related. After many questions, Brugha relented. 'Go ahead and do the job,' he said.

The assassination team hijacked a taxi for the operation but it broke down and they had to abandon the attempt. All of the Corkmen left Belfast that evening, and just two – Culhane and Dick Murphy – returned for the next attempt the following Sunday. As Swanzy left the church, McCorley pointed him out to Culhane and Murphy. Culhane was to fire the first shot from MacCurtain's own gun. Swanzy was walking between his father and an army major. The father and major were knocked to either side from the rear by two of the back-up team as Culhane and Murphy moved in for the kill.

'I fired the first shot, getting him in the head, and Dick fired almost simultaneously into his body,' Culhane recalled. The first shot, fired from almost point black range, hit Swanzy behind the right ear and the bullet exited on the other side of his head between his ear and his eye. 'Immediately after, we all opened fire on him,' McCorley said. 'When we were satisfied that the execution had been carried out we started off for the taxi.'[15]

The killing of Swanzy in Lisburn further inflamed the situation. Roman Catholics were burned out of their homes in mixed areas and some 8,000 Catholic workers were expelled from the shipyards and other industries. The Dáil retaliated by sanctioning a boycott of Northern Irish goods.

A number of subsequent efforts were made to get District Inspector Ferris, but he seemed to have luck on his side. He came out of the first two attempts unscathed, but the third time he was shot at point blank range in Cavendish Street in the Falls Road having left St Paul's presbytery on 7 May 1921. He was hit in the neck and the hip. 'We left him perfectly satisfied that the execution had been carried out,' McCorley lamented. 'To our astonishment, although he was seriously wounded, he recovered.'[16]

Flying squads were established by the IRA in several areas to cope with the increasing mobility of crown forces. Local leaders like Tom Barry and Liam Lynch in Cork, Tom Maguire in Mayo, and Seán MacEoin in the Longford area generally acted independently of IRA headquarters, but Collins was always quick to endorse their actions, and this created the impression that their efforts were being orchestrated centrally. As a result Collins was often credited with, or accused of, involvement in skirmishes that he only learned about later.

Dick Mulcahy resented the wild and undisciplined approach of Breen and the Soloheadbeg gang, especially their unauthorised killing of the two policemen on the day the Dáil was established. They were not generally welcome even within the IRA in Dublin. 'The only place in which they could find association and some kind of scope for their activities was on the fringe of Collins' intelligence activity work,' according to Mulcahy.[17]

Collins adopted a friendly attitude towards them. 'It would have been a comfort to them at all times compared with the natural attitude of Gearóid O'Sullivan and Diarmuid O'Hegarty,' Mulcahy wrote. Of course, Collins' 'rough breezy manner' afforded him 'greater flexibility in being able, while putting up with them when he liked, to get away with pushing them unceremoniously out of his way when he didn't want them.'[18]

Lloyd George's initial hope of using economic pressure to turn the Irish people against the rebels by putting the cost of fighting on the local rates was undermined when Sinn Féin won control of all but five of the island's thirty-three county councils in May 1920. As a result the party controlled the striking of rates throughout all but the north-east corner of Ireland. The following month Collins outmanoeuvred the British on the income tax front by getting the Dáil to establish a tax department.

All Irish people were called upon to pay income tax to this new department rather than to the British government, and the Dáil promised to indemnify anyone against loss. The call was partly effective, as people avoided crown taxes by exploiting the chaos caused by the burning of tax offices in April. Some did pay the Sinn Féin regime, but most simply used the opportunity to evade income tax altogether.

With economic pressure holding little prospect for success, Lloyd George gave enormous freedom to militants like Churchill and Greenwood. On 23 July Churchill told his cabinet colleagues 'it was necessary to raise the temperature of the conflict'. One of his pet schemes was to recruit 'a special force' of carefully selected men to act in Ireland. The cabinet authorised this during the summer, and advertisements were placed for a *corps d'elite* in which the recruits were supposed to be veteran officers from any of the services.[19]

Known as auxiliaries, they contained a mixture of fine men and scoundrels. On the whole they were more intelligent than the Black and

Tans and received twice the pay. Like the Black and Tans they wore a blend of police and military uniforms, with their own distinctive head-gear, a Glengarry cap. They were heavily armed, as each man carried two revolvers, some on low-slung holsters, wild-west style, and they also had a rifle each, as well as a Sam Brown belt. They usually travelled in Crossley tenders, seated in two rows, sitting back-to-back, and they had at their disposal fast armoured cars with revolving turrets and Vickers machine guns. It made them a formidable force as far as the IRA was concerned. Although sometimes accused of having started the counter-terror, the policy was already in operation for some time before the auxiliaries took up duty in September 1920.

During August the Black and Tans took revenge for attacks on their forces by 'shooting up' towns and burning the business premises or homes of people known to be sympathetic to Sinn Féin. In towns like Bantry, Fermoy, Thurles, Limerick, Enniscorthy, Tuam and other towns and villages, they rampaged about the streets, shooting indiscriminately into buildings, and generally terrorising those communities. In the process nine civilians were killed.

Even Field Marshal Wilson was disgusted at the undisciplined conduct of the Black and Tans. 'I told Lloyd George that the authorities were gravely miscalculating the situation but he reverted to his amazing theory that someone was murdering two Sinn Féiners to every loyalist the Sinn Féiners were murdering,' Wilson wrote on 1 September. 'He seemed to be satisfied that a counter-murder association was the best answer to Sinn Féin murders.'[20]

Collins, for his part, saw the British terror as a kind of mixed blessing, in that it clearly drove any doubting nationalists into the arms of Sinn Féin. 'The enemy continues to be savage and ruthless, and innocent people are murdered and outraged daily,' he wrote on 13 August. 'Apart from the loss which these attacks entail, good is done as it makes clear and clearer to people what both sides stand for.'[21]

Even the DMP betrayed signs of uneasiness with British policy in the coming weeks. Since it was implicit in Collins' attitude towards the force that police would not be attacked if they stayed out of political or military matters, representatives of the DMP approached Sinn Féin for a guarantee that they would not be shot at if they stopped carrying weapons. Collins was consulted and he agreed, provided they also ceased to support the military in raids. The DMP was effectively withdrawn from the ongoing struggle during the month of October.

While the terror and counter-terror were escalating, the British sent out peace 'feelers', and quietly orchestrated press speculation about a possible settlement along the lines of Dominion Home Rule. Fearing that Lloyd George was merely exploiting the speculation to obscure the terrorist policies of British forces, Collins tried to scotch the unfounded rumours by giving a newspaper interview to a celebrated American journalist. Carl Ackermann, who had earlier interviewed Lenin during the Russian revolution, had sought a meeting with Collins because the British considered him 'the most important member of the Irish Republican cabinet'.[22]

'There will be no compromise,' Collins told Ackermann, 'and we will have no negotiations with any British government until Ireland is recognised as an independent republic.'

'But Mr Collins,' the reporter asked, 'would you not consider accepting Dominion Home Rule as an instalment?'

'I see you think we have only to whittle our demand down to Dominion Home Rule and we shall get it. This talk about Dominion Home Rule is not promoted by England with a view to granting it to us, but merely with a view of getting rid of the republican movement. England will give us neither as a gift. The same effort that would get us Dominion Home Rule will get us a Republic.'

Ackermann concluded his scoop with a prediction that 'there will be a real war in Ireland in the not-distant future'. A British officer told him 'the next few weeks will be decisive – one way or the other'.[23]

At the time the Sinn Féin regime was clearly winning the propaganda struggle on the world stage, and the movement received enormous publicity when the new Lord Mayor of Cork, Terence MacSwiney went on hunger strike to protest against his imprisonment. He had been arrested in August having been found in possession of police codes supplied by Collins. Although others were also on hunger strike, MacSwiney received the most extensive publicity because he was an elected member of the British parliament. His seventy-nine-day fast received worldwide publicity, and Lloyd George came under pressure from all sides to do something about MacSwiney and the deteriorating situation in Ireland.

Publicly Lloyd George denied that British forces were killing people illegally, but in private he 'strongly defended the murder reprisals', according to Sir Maurice Hankey, the cabinet secretary. 'The truth is that these reprisals are more or less winked at by the government.'[24]

Winston Churchill became concerned that the security forces were 'getting out of control, drinking, and thieving, and destroying indiscriminately'. He argued that the reprisal policy should be formally regularised. Instead of turning a blind eye while the Black and Tans burned or killed indiscriminately, he wanted it done officially and publicly acknowledged, with the full support of the British government. He wanted official hangings rather than shooting prisoners in cold blood and then contending they were killed while trying to escape.[25]

With events in Ireland in the international spotlight, speculation about a possible settlement commanded growing press attention. The British had been investigating peaceful resolutions ever since July, when a Conservative member of parliament made discreet approaches to Art O'Brien, the Sinn Féin representative in London, about the kind of terms Sinn Féin would be looking for.

Collins was rather dismissive of this approach. He predicted that nothing was likely to develop unless the United States were asked to intervene or 'offered her services as a mediator'. Nevertheless Lloyd George continued to encourage peaceful advances behind the scenes for the remainder of the year through a number of people like John Steele of the *Chicago Tribune*, a Mayo businessman named Patrick Moylett, and George Russell (Æ), the well-known writer. Speculation about peace was boosted when former Prime Minister Asquith wrote to *The Times* in early October advocating that Britain offer Ireland 'the status of an autonomous dominion in the fullest and widest sense.'[26]

Moylett came to Dublin for informal talks with Griffith in mid-October and, upon his return to London, was invited by Lloyd George to sit in on a foreign office meeting at which it was suggested that the Dáil should select three or four people to visit London for preliminary discussions about a formal conference to resolve the Irish situation. Collins was highly sceptical of these proceedings.

Throughout 1920 British secret service agents infiltrated Ireland, intending to take on Collins and the IRA in their own game in line with the scenario outlined in the three-man committee on which Alan Bell had served. Basil Thompson of Scotland Yard recruited most of the members in London, but they were known as the Cairo gang because some of the more notorious members hung out at the Cairo Cafe on Grafton Street.

Members of the gang lived in private houses and guesthouses scattered around the city, and they were given passes so they could move about after curfew. James McNamara furnished the other side with the names of people with curfew passes, and by a process of elimination Collins' network was able to narrow the list down to likely agents.

Many of them stood out because of English accents. 'They were 'mostly "hoy hoy lah-di-dahs",' according to Brigadier General Frank Crozier, the commander of the auxiliaries.[27] Collins, with the help of his own agents in the postal sorting office, had the mail of suspected members of the secret service intercepted and delivered to him.

Amidst the intercepted correspondence was a letter from Captain F. Harper Shrove to Captain William L. King on 2 March 1920. Even though the country was 'in a fearful mess', he wrote that they should be able to put up 'a good show' because they had 'been given a free hand'.[28]

'*Re* our little stunt,' Shrove continued, 'there are possibilities'. In hindsight it seemed that the killing of MacCurtain might have been part of their 'little stunt'.[29] The secret service planned to exterminate prominent members of Sinn Féin and make it appear that they had been killed in an IRA feud. They sent a threatening letter to MacCurtain on Dáil Éireann notepaper that had been seized the previous September in the raid on Sinn Féin headquarters.

'Thomas MacCurtain, prepare for death,' it read. 'You are doomed.'[30]

In the following months most members of the Dáil received threatening letters. One was addressed to Collins at the Mansion House:

AN EYE FOR AN EYE.
A TOOTH FOR A TOOTH.
THEREFORE A LIFE FOR A LIFE.[31]

'I'm quite safe,' Collins joked. 'If they get me, I'll claim I haven't received my death notice yet.'[32]

While Collins made light of the threat against his own life, he took the overall threat posed by the secret service very seriously. In fact, he infiltrated it with at least one agent of his own. Willie Beaumont, a former British army officer, joined the secret service to spy for Collins. The agents from Britain had to rely on touts for information, and Beaumont pretended that members of Collins' intelligence staff – Cullen, Thornton, and Saurin – were his touts. He introduced them to agents, and they in turn got to know other secret service agents. On one occasion Cullen and Thornton were with Beaumont and Neligan in a Grafton Street cafe when one of the Cairo gang joined them.

'Surely you fellows know these men – Liam Tobin, Tom Cullen and Frank Thornton,' he said. 'These are Collins' three officers, and if you can get them we could locate Collins himself.'[33]

Getting Collins had clearly become a priority for the secret service, and they were getting close. They now knew the names of his staff, though they were seriously handicapped in not knowing what some of them looked like.

One of the British secret service agents, going under the name of F. Digby Hardy acted as a provocateur. He met Griffith and offered to set up his intelligence chief on Dun Laoghaire pier so that the IRA could kill him, but Collins was forewarned. Griffith invited reporters, including foreign correspondents, to a secret meeting on 16 September. Before the meeting he briefed them about Hardy.

'This man admits he is in the English secret service, and offered to arrange for the presence of the secret service chief at a lonely point on Dun Laoghaire Pier,' Griffith told the reporters. 'He asked me to let him meet leaders of the movement, especially on the military side, and he is coming here this evening imagining that he is to meet some inner council of the Sinn Féin movement ... I will let him tell you his own story,' Griffith continued, 'but I will ask the foreign gentlemen present not to speak much lest the man's suspicion be aroused.'[34]

Hardy arrived and told the gathering that he was a secret service agent and that upon his arrival in Ireland he had been met by Captain Thompson at Dun Laoghaire pier and given instructions to find Michael Collins. He offered to arrange another meeting with Thompson on the pier so the IRA could kill him. He also said that he could arrange to lead the auxiliaries into an ambush and could locate the arsenals of the Ulster Volunteer Force. If the IRA could give him information about Collins' whereabouts, he said he would withhold the information for a couple of days and could then impress his secret service superiors by giving them the information.

'And, of course,' he added familiarly, 'no harm would come to Mick.'[35]

'Well, gentlemen, you have heard this man's proposal and can judge for yourselves,' Griffith intervened. He then proceeded to expose Hardy as a convicted criminal, with actual details of his criminal record. 'You are a scoundrel, Hardy,' he said, 'but the people who employ you are greater scoundrels. A boat will leave Dublin tonight at 9 o'clock. My advice to you is – catch that boat and never return to Ireland.'[36]

Griffith furnished the press with detailed inside information supplied by Collins about Hardy's criminal record. He had been freed from jail to work for the secret service, and it made for good propaganda to show that the British were using criminal elements to do their dirty work in Ireland. Indeed, the Sinn Féin propaganda department would do such an effective job that many Irish people believed the British had opened their jails for any criminals prepared to serve the crown in Ireland. This was absurd, but incidents like the Hardy affair certainly lent it credibility.

The following week the secret service struck again. John Lynch, a Sinn Féin county councillor from Kilmallock, County Limerick, who had come to Dublin with national loan money for Collins, was shot dead in his room at the Exchange Hotel on the night of 23 September 1920. Secret service agents claimed he had pulled a gun on them, but Collins dismissed this.

'There is not the slightest doubt that there was no intention whatever to arrest Mr Lynch,' he wrote. 'Neither is there the slightest doubt that he was not in possession of a revolver.' Neligan reported to Collins that Captain Bagally, a one-legged court martial officer had telephoned Dublin Castle about Lynch's presence in the hotel, and the men responsible for the actual shooting were two undercover officers using the names MacMahon and Peel, each a *nom de guerre*.[37]

Griffith publicly accused the secret service of planning to kill moderates in Sinn Féin and give the impression that they were victims of an internal feud to undermine the movement's international support. 'A certain number of Sinn Féin leaders have been marked down for assassination,' he said. 'I am first on the list. They intended to kill two birds with the one stone by getting me and circulating the story I have been assassinated by extremists because I am a man of moderate action.'[38]

British intelligence was being co-ordinated in Dublin Castle by Brigadier Ormonde de l'Epée Winter. With his monocle and greased black hair, plastered flat, he was like the prototype for a character in a spy thriller. 'A most amazing original' was how assistant secretary Mark Sturgis described him. 'He looks like a wicked little white snake, and is clever as paint [and] probably entirely non-moral'.[39]

In October Winter arranged for the Central Raid Bureau to coordinate the activities of his agents and the auxiliaries. And they soon began to make their presence felt.

13

'I'll Report You to Michael Collins'

Terence MacSwiney's plight was so protracted that within Dublin Castle the hunger strikes 'faded into insignificance as a topic beside reprisals'. Before the end of September Collins was being goaded into arranging what would have been by far the Squad's most spectacular operation up until then. On the Sunday after the killing of John Lynch, Collins arranged for the Squad and the Tipperary gang of Treacy, Breen, Hogan and Robinson to kill between eight and a dozen senior policemen, including Superintendents Owen Brien and Dennis Barrett, and Inspectors John Bruton, George Love and Denis Barrett, as they went to 8 a.m. mass at a church near Dublin Castle.

At the last moment the attack was called off because Jim McNamara was among the policemen. They were not in a position to tell so many men not to shoot McNamara, as he was a valuable agent, so it was not safe to proceed. The whole thing was re-set for the following Sunday, but the police went to another church – Saint Teresa's in Clarendon Street – that Sunday. The following week the Squad waited in Clarendon Street. 'Misters! They're not here today!' a newsboy shouted at them.[1]

Once again, if the newspaper boy could twig what they were trying to do, they were clearly becoming too obvious. As MacSwiney and ten other hunger strikers approached death, Collins called off plans to shoot the men on the way to mass. But he did manage to exploit the rivalries within the DMP to such an extent that Superintendent Brien was discredited and forced to retire from the force.

The British suspected arms were being smuggled from America into Dublin on the Moore-McCormack line. Inspector McCabe, who was on port duty at the North Wall, was directed to search boats carefully, but the Americans were inclined to make legal trouble for the inspector regarding international law. McCabe wrote a long report, explaining the position and difficulties, legal and otherwise. He asked for instructions. Superintendent Brien submitted a report to Inspector-General Edgeworth-Johnson: 'This subject ought never to have been raised,' Edgeworth-Johnson wrote in the margin. 'All American sailors are now suspect. Their belongings should be searched and a report made in each case.' Broy gave Collins a copy of the correspondence. [2]

'We will make use out of that,' Collins said.

The Americans traditionally resented British interference with American ships, and Collins sought to exploit this. 'I remember seeing Colonel Johnston's minutes in the latest news column of the *Dublin Evening Mail*,' Broy recalled. 'Superintendent Brien hated Inspector McCabe, who was a unionist, and said that he must have been indiscreet and must have shown the file to some disloyal customs officer. Disciplinary action was taken against Inspector McCabe, and he was about to be compelled to retire on pension.

'I settled that fellow's hash at last,' Brien remarked to some colleagues, including Broy. McNamara told McCabe what Brien had said, and McCabe got on to some of his unionist friends in the castle to re-open his dismissal. McCabe was duly reinstated and Brien was forced to retire.

In another incident Major Gerald Smyth, a brother of the one-armed colonel shot in Cork on 18 July, was brought back from the Middle East to avenge his brother's death. It had been incorrectly rumoured that Breen had killed him. So when Winter's people learned that Breen and Seán Treacy were spending the night at the Drumcondra home of Professor John Carolan on 11 October, Smyth was selected to lead the raiding party. They burst into the house, but Smyth and a colleague were killed when Breen and Treacy blindly shot through their bedroom door before making a run for it. Although wounded, Breen still managed to get away. He chose a house at random and asked for help there as he collapsed on the doorstep.

'I don't approve of gunmen,' the man of the house replied. 'I shall call the military.'[3]

'If you do I'll report you to Michael Collins,' came a woman's voice from inside the house.[4] The threat obviously worked because word was sent to the IRA, and Breen was collected and taken to the Mater Hospital, where doctors and nurses colluded to hide his identity and the nature of his wounds. Another patient there was Professor Carolan, whom the raiding party had put up against a wall and shot in the head; he eventually died of his wounds, but not before making a full deathbed statement about what had happened. Treacy escaped from Drumcondra unscathed only to be shot dead a few days later.

Despite his busy schedule and the risk involved, Collins took a keen interest in Breen's recovery. He visited him in hospital and arranged his transfer to the home of Dr Alice Barry in the south side of the city as soon as he was ready to be moved. Breen had been there for about a week when he heard a commotion outside the house. He looked out to find the whole block cordoned off by the auxiliaries. They were searching the houses as a crowd of spectators gathered.

'I concluded there was no chance for me,' Breen wrote. 'As I surveyed the mass of spectators, I recognised the figure of Mick Collins.'[5] He had seen the troops moving in the direction of the house and had followed them in case Breen needed to be rescued. As it happened, the auxiliaries did not bother to search Dr Barry's home, and Breen was spared. At one point the DMP thought they had found Breen's body, so Sergeant Roche of the RIC was brought up from Tipperary to identify him. David Neligan was given the gruesome task of accompanying Roche to the hospital morgue. 'That's not Dan Breen,' Roche said on being shown the body, 'I'd know his ugly mug anywhere.'[6]

That evening Neligan mentioned the incident to Liam Tobin and added that he was due to meet Roche on Ormonde Quay the following afternoon. To his horror, the next day Neligan saw Dolan and Thornton with Keogh and Slattery. He realised they were waiting for Roche. 'For Christ's sake, what has he done?' Neligan asked.

'I don't know,' one of the men replied. 'I've my orders to shoot him and that's what I'm going to do.'[7]

It was not just because he was in Dublin to identify Breen and Treacy that Roche was shot, according to Vinny Byrne. 'There is no doubt there must have been some other reason for the shooting, as it in itself would not warrant such action,' he argued. 'But that was no concern of the Squad's; they got their orders and asked no question.'[8]

Roche was walking with a colleague. 'The two policemen were coming towards us and we let them pass us,' Dolan explained. 'Then I took out my revolver and put six bullets into Roche when he was just in front of me in the passage-way. Tom Keogh and Jim Slattery put a few more bullets into Roche.'[9] Roche's colleague reported that he saw Neligan talking to one of the killers, and Neligan had some difficulty explaining. He was summoned before Inspector-General Thomas J. Smith.

'This constable says he saw you talking to the men who shot Sergeant Roche,' Smith said.[10]

'He is making a mistake, Sir.'

'What did you do?' he asked. 'Did you see the men who attacked Roche?'

'I told him that I had run away as I thought the shots were firing at me,' Neligan later recalled. 'I also told him that I was waiting for a tram to go to the Park. I had no sooner said this than I saw there was a flaw in it as I was on the wrong side of the road for an outgoing tram.' But his mistake went unnoticed.[11]

The inspector general could not understand how the IRA had learned that Roche was in Dublin. 'Didn't you tell me that some woman at the railway station enquired where you were going?' Neligan said to the other constable. 'Yes,' he replied, 'a woman in the magazine stall at Limerick Junction asked me where we were bound for.'[12] At that point Neligan was told he could leave. He was understandably annoyed that Roche being shot in his presence had jeopardised his cover as a spy. It really demonstrated a dangerous blind spot in the Big Fellow's intelligence operations. As a man of action he was so anxious to get things done that he sometimes acted before the dust had settled enough to cover his agent's tracks.

Paddy O'Daly said Roche and the other constable had supposedly been recognised in the lorry that raided the Republican Outfitters, the shop owned by Peadar Clancy, and it was suspected that they were in Dublin to look for Breen. It seemed more likely to Neligan, however, that Roche had simply been shot as a reprisal for the killing of Seán Treacy. 'Identifying a dead man was certainly not an offence at all, but of course it was not for me to question the ins and outs of the matter,' Neligan explained. It should also be noted that Roche was obviously prepared to identify Breen. Whatever the real story, it clearly weighed on Neligan's conscience. 'That was the one day I regretted my role,' he said. 'If for one second I thought the poor wretch would have been shot, not a word of his visit would have been mentioned.'[13]

Believing that Larry Dalton and Daniel Roche had both been unfairly eliminated, Neligan set out to spare Detective Sergeant Denis Coffey, who had picked men for execution in 1916. He knew many of the older volunteers and could pick them out by hanging around the streets, or, even more dangerous, he could be tipped about IRA activities. So he was on the Squad's hit list.

'Although, in my opinion, he richly deserved such a fate, I determined to save his life for the sake of his poor wretch of a wife and young family,' Neligan explained. 'I, therefore, sought him out and told him I'd heard two fellows in a public house saying they'd shoot him next day.' Coffey was terrified. 'He had no stomach for the business after that,' Neligan said. 'He never came out of the Castle (where he lived with his wife and family) again until the Truce.'[14]

As of October 1920 the conflict had turned extremely nasty. Collins was deeply upset when he learned that the Black and Tans had captured and tortured Tom Hales, a brother of his closest friend in Frongoch. Another man tortured at the same time, Pat Harte from Clonakilty went mad and had to be committed to a mental asylum. Tom Hales managed to smuggle out an account of their ill-treatment, which included pulling out nails with pincers.

'I was with Collins when he received the message,' Piaras Béaslaí recalled. 'He was beside himself with rage and pity, and, as he told me afterwards, could not sleep that night for thinking of it.'[15] The whole episode was something 'that no civilised nation can let pass unchallenged',

Collins wrote to Tom's brother Donal in Italy. 'The statement has made a profound impression and will have far-reaching effects,' Collins explained. 'Poor Harte, I am sorry to say, is really bad and I fear he will be a permanent wreck as a result of his treatment.[16]

'In the way of torture nothing worse has occurred since – although any prisoner who is captured now is very fortunate if he does not get similar treatment,' Collins added. 'Naturally there are few men whose physique would allow them to stand as much as Tom did.' The torture was indicative of what Collins might expect if he fell into enemy hands. He was now the most wanted man in the country and the Cairo gang was getting close. 'We were being made to feel that they were very close on the heels of some of us,' Mulcahy explained.[17] It was ironic that Collins should have been so upset, because Tom Hales was the man who helped to organise the ambush to kill him at Béal na Bláth less than two years later.

Collins realised the police officers involved with the Cairo gang's activities had the tacit approval of the British government. This was not just in his imagination, as records on the British side indicate that there was a strong debate going on in the corridors of power. Fearing that escalating reprisals were undermining discipline in the British army, Field Marshall Sir Henry Wilson tried to insist that instead of allowing individual soldiers to select their victims, the British government should assume formal responsibility for the reprisals by ordering that a roster of local hostages be drawn up and those people be formally executed.

'I had 1½ hours this evening with Lloyd George and Bonar Law,' Wilson noted in his diary on 29 September. 'I told them what I thought of reprisals by the "Black and Tans", and how this must lead to chaos and ruin. Lloyd George danced about and was angry, but I never budged. I pointed out that these reprisals were carried out without anybody being responsible; men were murdered, houses burnt, villages wrecked (such as Balbriggan, Ennistymon, Trim, etc.). I said that this was due to want of discipline, and this must be stopped. It was the business of the government to govern. If these men ought to be murdered, then the government ought to murder them. Lloyd

George danced at all this, said no government could possibly take this responsibility.[18]

'I have protested for months against this method of out-terrorising the terrorists by irresponsible persons,' Wilson continued. 'We drift from bad to worse and always under the guidance of Lloyd George. Anyhow, neither Lloyd George nor Bonar can ever say that I have not warned them and very plainly spoken my mind.'

Winston Churchill, who was not renowned for either his political sagacity or sound military judgment at this stage of his career, tended to side with Wilson regarding the need for the government to take responsibility for reprisals. He had been calling for formal executions for months, and he was about to get his way. 'You have been right all along,' Churchill wrote to Wilson, 'the government must shoulder the responsibility for reprisals.'[19]

When Wilson met the prime minister to discuss the Irish situation on 14 October, Lloyd George said that he would 'shoulder the responsibility for reprisals, but wanted to wait until after the American presidential election was over. He did not wish to speak out then, because it would give the Democratic presidential candidate, Governor James M. Cox, an issue he could exploit among Anglophobic elements in the United States. Lloyd George agreed with the reprisals but was not prepared to accept formal responsibility for what British forces were doing in Ireland. Hankey, the cabinet secretary, noted that the prime minister privately argued that 'murder reprisals' had been resorted to from time immemorial in Ireland. 'He gave numerous instances where they had been effective in checking crimes,' Hankey added. There was no use in saying 'I should shoot without mercy,' Churchill argued. 'The question immediately arises "whom would you shoot". And shortly after that "where are they?"'[20] He actually came to the conclusion that Wilson's reprehensible scheme to engage in reprisal by roster was justified.

'You have been right all along,' Churchill told Wilson. 'At last there is some hope that the cabinet will stop whispering from the back parlour and will come into the open.'[21]

The debate about British reprisals was not confined to the corridors of power; it was also taking place in the public domain. 'I do not think that any truthful or sane person can avoid the conclusion that the authorities in Ireland are deliberately encouraging, and, what is more actually screening, reprisals and "counter-murder" by armed force of the Crown,' General Sir Hubert Gough wrote to the *Manchester Guardian* in early October.[22]

'In Ireland at the moment murder and destruction are condoned and winked at, if not actively encouraged,' Gough continued. 'The murders of policemen and others by the "Irish Republicans" have been inexcusable. As you say the leaders of Sinn Féin and the Irish priesthood are very greatly to be condemned for not having taken a far more active part against such methods, but that is no excuse for any government, and especially a government of the great British Empire, adopting such methods.'[23]

Having been attacked, the Black and Tans or military would burn houses in the neighbourhood or the nearest town or village, sometimes shooting up the villages and towns, firing indiscriminately through windows or just up in the air, terrorising the local inhabitants. In a growing number of instances people were taken out and shot even when they might have had nothing to do with the particular attack that the crown forces were avenging.

During September and early October 1920, Collins behaved with a certain amount of restraint in order not to divert the international spotlight form Terence MacSwiney's hunger strike. Collins secretly encouraged MacSwiney to quit the strike because he did not want him to die. It went on longer than anybody anticipated. Many had expected him to die in August, but MacSwiney survived until the fourth week of October. His suffering attracted media attention around the world.

After months of clamouring for executions Churchill finally had his way the week after MacSwiney's death. Kevin Barry, a teenage university student was sentenced to be hanged in Mountjoy jail. He had been captured after an IRA raid in which two teenage British soldiers were killed. In view of his age, there was strong public pressure for his sentence to be commuted. Collins tried to arrange for Barry's escape but all efforts failed. The timing of the execution again demonstrated the 'wooden stupidity' of the Dublin Castle, as exemplified by Warren Fisher, the leading British civil servant. Barry's execution, the first since 1916, was set for a Catholic holiday – All Saints Day. As a result he was virtually canonised by the Irish people who celebrated him in a ballad:

Another martyr for old Ireland,
Another murder for the Crown,
Whose brutal laws may kill the Irish
But can't keep their spirit down.[24]

It was almost as if the British had decided that the next stage of the struggle would begin with the execution of Barry. MacSwiney was buried in Cork on the eve of Barry's execution.

Tadhg Kennedy had returned to Kerry to resume working as head of intelligence in the northern half of the country having spent several months working with Collins in Dublin. Kennedy brought with him orders to mark Barry's execution by killing off as many members of the crown forces as possible. One Black and Tan who had been held captive for some weeks was brought out to Banna and shot and buried in the sand hills on 29 October.

This order to strike at crown forces was subsequently countermanded, but the rescinding order did not reach Kerry until it was too late. On Sunday 31 October, in the hours following the MacSwiney funeral, the IRA in Kerry lashed out at the RIC and some people attached to the British army.

Four RIC men had been killed in Kerry by the republicans since the Easter Rising, but within twenty-four hours of Barry's execution no less than sixteen policemen were shot, seven fatally, and another two were kidnapped within the brigade area stretching from Killorglin in the southern half of Kerry to Ballylongford on the Shannon estuary.

Four policemen were shot in Ballyduff, one fatally, with the other was critically wounded in the head. Two others were shot in Abbeydorney, both fatally; two were shot and wounded in Causeway and in Dingle, while two others were killed near Kilorglin. A British naval radio operator and an RIC man were wounded in Tralee, and two other policemen were kidnapped and secretly killed that night. Another two policemen were kidnapped in Ballylongford the following evening and savagely abused. After the countermanding order came through, the two kidnapped in Ballylongford were released, but one of them never overcame his ordeal. He killed himself by cutting his throat some weeks later.

Meanwhile the Black and Tans reacted with fury. Shortly before 5 p.m. on Monday morning a force of Black and Tans arrived in Ballyduff and proceeded to torch the local creamery and some of the principal business houses. John Houlihan, a teenager, was taken out of his home near the village and killed by the Tans. They apparently singled him out because his brother had recently been on hunger strike in Mountjoy jail. His parents later testified that John was dragged from the house and taken across the road, where he was stabbed in the side with a bayonet and then shot three times. One of the Tans then finished him off with a blow of a rifle butt to the head as the young man's helpless mother looked on.

The Black and Tans also went on the rampage in Killorglin, burning down the Sinn Féin Hall and an adjoining garage, as well as the Temperance Association Hall. They raided the homes of known Sinn Féiners and one man was taken from his home and shot four times.

In Tralee the Black and Tans instituted a reign of terror that was to last for more than a week, during which events in the town prompted a series of parliamentary questions at Westminster and became the subject of some controversy and editorials in the British daily press. In the early hours of Monday morning they burned down the county hall. They drove up and down the streets in lorries, discharging their rifles. Shots were fired as people emerged from mid-day mass at St John's parish church. There was a panic as people stampeded back into the church.

Hearing of the trouble in Tralee a group of foreign journalist who had been in Cork for the MacSwiney funeral decided to visit to see what was happening first hand. They included reporters from the Associated Press of the United States, *Le Journal de Paris*, *The London Times*, *Daily News*, *Manchester Guardian*, and *London Evening News*. The group reached Tralee about 9 p.m. on Monday night and some of them talked to a group of some twenty Tans on the street.

The journalists asked if was safe to walk the main streets.

'What have you come for – to spy on us, I suppose?' one of the men replied, going on to ask what newspapers they represented.[25]

Hugh Martin of the *Daily News* decided on discretion rather than valour. For some time he had been denouncing what he called 'the most grotesque comedy'. He accused the crown forces of engaging in 'the infamy of stamping on freedom in Ireland'. He had been warned by friends in official circles to be very careful, as his reports had infuriated the Black and Tans in particular.

'I decided to lie boldly, and mentioned the name of a coalition journal which both by silence and occasional comment has lent the strongest support to the government's Irish policy,' he explained. 'I also gave my name when it was demanded, as that of an English journalist associated with the coalition.

'Is there a Hugh Martin among you?' one of the police asked, 'because if there is, we mean to do for him. It's him we want, and we're going to get him.'

One of the journalists explained that they had come to Tralee to find out about the burning of the county hall.

'Up to Saturday night we were at peace,' the sergeant in charge of the men explained, 'but they have declared war upon us.' He went on to list the names of his comrades who had been killed recently, and he then ordered the two journalists to get indoors at once.

'Just as we reached the door of the hotel, however, they changed their minds and shouted to us to come back,' Martin continued. 'I feared that they had decided to examine our papers, which must have established my real identity. As escape was impossible, we returned. I spoke in a friendly way to the men, and again succeeded in bluffing them completely, so that after a few minutes' chat we were on fairly good terms, and seemed to have gained their confidence. Finally, we were ordered to walk to the corner of the street and read a typewritten notice affixed to the wall.' It warned that 'reprisal of a nature not yet heard of in Ireland will take place in Tralee and surroundings'.

On returning to the hotel Martin had some trouble sleeping. 'As I lay in bed,' he later wrote, 'I heard the sound, then so common o' nights in Ireland, of plate-glass windows being smashed in the principal shopping street.' Next morning he learned that the word was out that he was in town, and he made a hasty retreat to Cork. The *Daily News* duly printed Martin's report, along with the editorial criticising Greenwood's repeated denials that crown forces were engaged in reprisals in Ireland.[26]

The threat to Martin, which made front page news in *The New York Times*, was denounced as a threat to the freedom of the press in an editorial in *The Times of London*: 'An issue of importance to all independent newspapers and to the public is raised by the account published yesterday in the *Daily News* of the threatening attitude of the Constabulary at Tralee towards a special correspondent and confirmed in all essentials by the special correspondent of the *Evening News* who accompanied him and heard the threats.[27]

'I can corroborate the verbatim accuracy of Hugh Martin's report,' the *Evening News* reporter noted. 'The threats at Tralee were real. I believe Martin's life was in danger at the opening of the interview, but the threats and danger came from three or four of the party and would not have been uttered by their leaders.'

When Greenwood was confronted in Parliament with the latest evidence, he refused to back down. What he had said, he reminded the house, was that 'Ireland is the freest country in the world for journalists'; he repeated this to cheers from the government benches. 'On reflection, I confirm that opinion.'

A French journalist who was with the group visiting Tralee outlined a frightening situation. 'I do not remember, even during the war, having seen a people so profoundly terrified as those of this little town, Tralee,' M. de Marsillac, the London correspondent of *Le Journal* reported. 'The violence of the reprisals undertaken by representatives of authority, so to speak, everywhere, has made everybody beside himself, even before facts justified such a state of mind.'

Shopkeepers were warned by the police to close down for the funerals of their companions, who deserved as much respect as the lord mayor of Cork. All schools were closed and remained closed for over a week. The security forces stalked the deserted streets firing shots into the air, or shooting blindly into windows as they drove up and down the street.

While the siege of Tralee was continuing, Lloyd George referred to Ireland in his address at the Guildhall banquet in London on 9 November. 'There we witness the spectacle of organised assassination of the most cowardly character – firing on men who are unsuspecting, firing from men who are dressed in the garb of peaceable citizens, and are treated as such by the officers of the laws, firing from behind – cowardly murder,' he said. 'Unless I am mistaken by the steps we have taken, we have murder by the throat.'[28]

Next day Churchill had a very hush-hush meeting with Lloyd George, Bonar Law, Greenwood and Francis Short, the former chief secretary for Ireland, to consider his proposal 'advocating the substitution of regular, authorised and legalised reprisals for unauthorised reprisal by police and soldiers'.[29]

When Collins advocated provoking a general state of disorder back in March 1919, could he have envisaged that things would descend to this level? The events in Tralee during those nine days made the front pages of the *Montreal Gazette* for four days and *The New York Times* on three different days. Ireland was in the international spotlight and things were about to get even worse.

In the first two weeks of November crown forces detained some of Collins' closest associates. They had Frank Thornton for ten days, but he managed to convince them that he had nothing to do with Sinn Féin. On the night of 10 November they just missed Richard Mulcahy; he escaped through the skylight of Professor Michael Hayes' house on the South Circular Road around five a.m. Three days later they raided Vaughan's Hotel and questioned Liam Tobin and Tom Cullen, but they managed to bluff their way out of it. In a matter of three days the IRA's chief-of-staff and the three top men of Collins' intelligence network had been arrested and let go. This kind of luck was unlikely to last.

14

'They Got What They Deserved'

Collins prepared detailed files on suspected members of the Cairo gang. One of his sources – referred to merely as 'Lt. G', helped identify the members of the gang. Collins planned on killing those he called 'the particular ones', and his Lt. G suggested the coming Sunday morning was the best to strike.[1]

'Arrangements should now be made about the matter,' Collins wrote to McKee on 17 November. 'Lt. G is aware of things. He suggests the 21st. A most suitable date and day I think.' Although Collins was not always as careful as he should have been about protecting the identity of his spies, he kept their names to himself.[2]

On Saturday night, 20 November, Collins met with Brugha, Mulcahy, McKee, Clancy and Seán Russell, the quartermaster general of the IRA. The meeting was at the headquarters of the printer's union at 35 Lower Gardiner Street, where the Dublin brigade normally held meetings. They finalised arrangements to attack members of British intelligence operations. Russell selected the men to head the various assassinations teams. He put a member of the Squad in charge of each, with the exception of the group assigned to kill three men in the Gresham Hotel. Brugha felt there was insufficient evidence against some of those named by Collins, but there was no room for doubt in relation to others, such as Peter Ames and George Bennett, the two men who had questioned Tobin and Cullen, nor with Captain Bagally and the two men who had shot John Lynch at the Exchange Hotel – MacMahon and Peel. Brugha authorised their killings along with over thirty others.

'It's to be done exactly at nine,' Collins insisted. 'Neither before not after. These whores, the British, have got to learn that Irishmen can turn up on time.' The killings were to be a joint operation of the Squad and the Dublin brigade, under the command of Dick McKee.[3]

After the meeting Collins, McKee and some of the others went over to Vaughan's Hotel for a drink. There was a group of them in an upstairs room when Christy Harte, the porter, became suspicious of one of the hotel guests, a Mr Edwards, who had booked in three days earlier. He made a late night telephone call and then left the hotel, a rather ominous sign as it was after curfew. Harte immediately went upstairs to where Collins and the others were gathered.

'I think, sirs, ye ought to be going.'[4]

Collins trusted Harte's instincts and didn't hesitate. 'Come on boys, quick,' he said, and all promptly headed for the door.

Collins took refuge a few doors down in the top floor flat of Dr Paddy Browne of Maynooth college at 39 Parnell Square. From there he watched the raid on Vaughan's Hotel a few minutes later. By then all the guests in the hotel were legitimately registered, with the exception of Conor Clune, a football supporter in Dublin for a game the next day. He had come to the hotel with Peadar Clancy, and had apparently been forgotten. Clune was not registered. Although he was not a member of the IRA, he was obviously nervous when questioned because he made some rather inane comment about being prepared to die for Ireland. He was therefore taken away for further questioning.

During the night McKee and Clancy were arrested where they were staying for the night, but everything had already been set in motion for the morning. Eleven different assassination teams took part. Some used church bells, and others waited for clocks to strike before they began the operations at exactly 9 p.m. Each team was composed of a member of the Squad as well as an intelligence officer assigned to search the bodies and rooms for documents.

Fifteen of the Cairo Gang were shot, ten fatally, at eight different locations, some in the presence of their families. Captain W.F. Newbury's heavily pregnant wife was in the room with him at the time; the following week their child was stillborn. The killing of Captain MacCormack of the Royal Army Veterinary Corps was apparently a mistake. He was shot dead in the Gresham Hotel, but Collins had no evidence against him. 'We have no evidence he was a secret service agent,' he later wrote. 'Some of the names were put on by the Dublin brigade.' In this instance, however, it would seem that the men got the room numbers confused in the hotel.[5]

Two auxiliaries were also killed. They happened to pass the scene of one of the killings at 22 Lower Mount Street as the gunmen were trying to escape while a maid was screaming hysterically from an upstairs window. One of Lynch's killers was shot there, but his colleague managed to escape by barricading himself in his room while some twenty shots were fired into the door. Frank Teeling of the Dublin brigade was wounded and captured by auxiliaries.

General Crozier, the commander of the auxiliaries, was nearby and he visited the house on Mount Street. He then went to Dublin Castle to report what had happened. While there, word was received by telephone of the other killings.

'What!' the officer, who answered the telephone, exclaimed, turning deathly pale. He staggered as he turned around after hanging up and had to clutch a table for support.

'About fifty officers are shot in all parts of the city,' he said. 'Collins has done in most of the secret service people.'[6]

'In Dublin Castle panic reigned. For the next week the gates were choked with incoming traffic – all military, their wives and agents,' according to Neligan. One distraught agent, whose pals had been killed, shot and killed himself and was buried with the others in England, where they were given a state funeral, with services at Westminster Abbey.

Collins certainly had no regrets about his part in what would become known as Bloody Sunday. 'My own intention was the destruction of the undesirables who continued to make miserable the lives of ordinary decent citizens,' he wrote. 'I have proof enough to assure myself of the atrocities which this gang of spies and informers have committed. Perjury and torture are words too easily known to them.' If he had another motive, he added, 'it was no more than a feeling such as I would have for a dangerous reptile.'[7]

'That should be the future's judgment on this particular event,' he wrote. 'For myself my conscience is clear. There is no crime in detecting and destroying in wartime, the spy and the informer. They have destroyed without trial. I have paid them back in their own coin.'

'The attack was so well organised, so unexpected, and so ruthlessly executed that the effect was paralysing,' according to Neligan. 'It can be said that the enemy never recovered from the blow. While some of the worst killers escaped, they were thoroughly frightened.'[8]

Two of those who escaped were Captain King and Lieutenant Hardy, who were particularly despised by the IRA, because of their brutal treatment of prisoners. They were not in their residences when the hit-teams called. Todd Andrews of the Dublin brigade burst into King's room to find only his half-naked mistress. Shocked by the sudden intrusion, she sat bolt upright in bed and looked terrified. 'I felt a sense of shame and embarrassment for the woman's sake,' Todd noted, but the two Squad members with him were too frustrated at missing King to have any sympathy for the unfortunate woman. 'I was so angry I gave the poor girl a right scourging with the sword scabbard,' Joe Dolan recalled. 'Then I set the room on fire.' Andrews was horrified at the conduct of Dolan and the other Squad member. They 'behaved like Black and Tans', he noted.[9]

Hardy and King, on the other hand, gave vent to their rage some hours later by torturing and killing McKee, Clancy and Clune in Dublin Castle.

Elsewhere in the city the auxiliaries went on a rampage at Croke Park. They raided a football game and began firing indiscriminately into the crowd. Fifteen people were killed outright, or fatally wounded, including ten-year-old Jeremiah O'Leary, who was shot in the head. Fourteen-year-old John Scott was also killed, along with Jane Boyle, who had gone to the game with her fiancée. They were due to marry five days later. Others killed included Michael Hogan, one of the players on the field.

The auxiliaries said they were fired upon, but Crozier publicly refuted the claim. 'It was the most disgraceful show I have ever seen,' one of his officers told him. 'Black and Tans fired into the crowd without any provocation whatever.'

In London Lloyd George and members of his cabinet were very jittery, according to Sir Maurice Hankey. Hamar Greenwood provided weapons for all his domestic staff, though – unlike the prime minister – he was able to joke about his own predicament. 'All my household are armed,' the chief secretary told the cabinet, 'my valet, my butler, and my cook. So if you have any complaints about the soup you may know what to expect.'[10]

There were good reasons to be fearful. Brugha, who had planned to go into the House of Commons and kill as many members of the government as possible if conscription had been enforced in 1918, resurrected this plan as a possible response to the death of Terence MacSwiney and had not really given up on the idea, which he would raise again in the coming weeks.

In the interim arrangements were made for a large-scale operation in Britain, where the IRA planned incendiary attacks on warehouses in the Liverpool and Manchester areas. Wishing to send an important message to the IRA in Britain, Collins arranged for Jeremiah Mee – who had been working for Countess Markievicz since his resignation from the RIC over the late Colonel Smyth's remarks in Listowel – to take the message personally. He was selected because he had a military look about him, but Mee had been trying to conceal this.

'What happened to your little moustache?' Collins asked.[11]

Mee explained he had shaved it off because the countess thought it looked too military.

'Be damn to her,' snapped Collins. 'She should know by now that a military appearance is the best disguise for our men at the present time.'

He proceeded to outline the best way for Mee to behave so as to avoid detection. The advice provided a real insight into how Collins had been able to move about Dublin so freely in recent months. He told Mee to dress up in spats with good creases on his pants and carry a walking stick and a supply of cigars.

'Get into friendly chat with some of the military officers,' he added.

'You can do this by passing round your cigars and even if they do not smoke cigars it will at least be an introduction and will save you being questioned or searched. That is how I get across myself and you should have no difficulty if you keep your head screwed on.'[12]

Collins might well have gone himself except that he was anxious to pay his last respects to McKee and Clancy. Their deaths had been a terrible blow to him. They were 'two men who fully understood the inside of his work and his mind, and who were ever ready and able to link up their resources of the Dublin brigade to any work that Collins had in hand, and to do so promptly, effectively and sympathetically,' Mulcahy noted.[13]

Collins was so upset by their deaths that he seemed to become quite reckless. He went to the cathedral to dress the bodies in IRA uniforms and took a prominent part in the funeral.

The next morning Collins, Cullen, Thornton and Gearóid O'Sullivan helped to carry the bodies out to the waiting hearses. A photograph of Collins and Cullen at the head of one of the coffins actually appeared in the *Evening Herald*. He attended the requiem mass and went on to the graveside, where he was actually filmed as he stepped out of the crowd to lay a wreath on the grave. Attached was a note signed by him: 'In memory of two good friends – Dick and Peadar – and two of Ireland's best soldiers.'

'Look,' a woman said as he stepped forward, 'there's Michael Collins.'

'You bloody bitch,' he snarled, glaring at her.[14]

Given his state of mind, it was a measure of his respect for Griffith that he was still ready to go along with Lloyd George's continuing tentative peace offers, even though he had no faith in them himself.

Moylett had visited Dublin again in November and returned to London with a letter from Griffith to the prime minister on the eve of Bloody Sunday. One might have thought the events of the next day would have killed the peace initiative at this point, but this was not the case at all. When Moylett met Lloyd George the next day, the prime minister did not seem unduly perturbed. 'They got what they deserved,' Lloyd George supposedly said. That, at any rate, was Moylett's story, but

Art O'Brien, the Sinn Féin representative in London, warned Collins that the Mayo man was just a 'Big Blower' and a damn fool.

'Your view is shared by me,' Collins replied, 'but Mr Griffith thinks differently, therefore, I am keeping in touch with this man for the present.'

While Moylett was meeting with Lloyd George, Steele was talking with Griffith about a possible ceasefire on both sides. 'I'll do all I can [to] stop murders but you must call off reprisals at the same time,' was Griffith's message for the prime minister.

Lloyd George met the Irish writer George Russell (Æ) on 26 November and told him that he would negotiate with anybody but Collins, and somebody called 'Gallagher'. Presumably the prime minister was referring to Mulcahy, and either he or Russell got the name mixed up. Lloyd George's message to Russell was basically that he would call off military operations if there were three weeks of peace. Then negotiations could begin, though he indicated there were limits to what the British would consider.

'We will not tolerate a Republic,' he emphasised, 'but anything short of that.'[15]

Whatever hope Lloyd George entertained for his proposals was seriously upset that day by the arrest of Griffith, who had been picked up in a nationwide swoop on Sinn Féin supporters.

When the Dáil met to elect his replacement, the cabinet secretary produced a letter from Griffith's solicitor nominating Cathal Brugha to take office, or Austin Stack in the event of Brugha being unable or unwilling to fill the post, and Michael Collins, should Stack not wish to serve. J.J. (Sceilg) O'Kelly presided at the meeting. 'Cathal would not act; his army work engaged all his thoughts and all his energy,' O'Kelly wrote. Brugha explained that he had already served as president before de Valera's election. Stack said that he could not act, as he was too busy setting up republican courts and organising a republican police force.

'Come, Micheál,' O'Kelly said to Collins, 'sit in this chair, and we'll all do our best to help you.'

'As no one else will,' he said, 'I suppose I must.'[16]

Collins was acting president for four hectic weeks, amid a wave of rumours of peace. The strain was tremendous. 'Those of us who were in constant touch with him always possessed the fear that he would collapse under it,' Seán Ó Muirthile wrote. Those fears became all the more real when Collins – still deeply upset over the brutal killings of McKee and Clancy – assumed the extra strain of the presidency.

He was not even in the new post two full days when the British-based IRA fire-bombed more than a dozen warehouses in the Liverpool docks area, causing millions of pounds worth of damage. That same day in Kilmichael, County Cork, Tom Barry led an IRA ambush on a convoy of auxiliaries and killed seventeen of them, much to the delight of Collins.

'Good man Barry!' he exclaimed on hearing the news.[17]

Lloyd George clearly intimated earlier in the month that British forces were coming to grips with things in Ireland, but he was now confronted with irrefutable evidence that the rebels were far from finished. The last full week of November was, in fact, the bloodiest in Ireland since 1916.

Lloyd George told his cabinet that the Kilmichael ambush was indicative of a change in the nature of the conflict in Ireland. Previous killings were selective assassinations, but Kilmichael was a military operations. 'We ought to regularise the proceedings which had been taking place there,' Churchill argued. In other words, the British should authorise and take responsibility for reprisals. Lloyd George was thinking of introducing martial law in Cork and Kerry, but according to Churchill, Field Marshal Wilson thought this would be useless unless it covered all of Ireland. The prime minister had reservations about this, because there had been no murders in twelve counties. Austen Chamberlain was opposed to martial law unless he could be assured that relatively junior officers would not be able to exercise control.[18]

'The real danger is drink,' Lloyd George said. He was clearly worried about the behaviour of British forces under the influence of drink.[19]

'It is a very moist climate,' Churchill interjected with a smile. He was more concerned about the danger that the IRA would extend its campaign to Britain. He asked if the home secretary had thought of encouraging people 'to keep their eyes open for suspicious strangers' by offering large rewards for the capture of Sinn Féiners before they were installed in Britain. 'I would pay up to £5,000 for a hanging case and proportionally for the others,' Churchill said.[20]

That same day Lloyd George opened up a new peace channel, this time through the Irish-born Roman Catholic Archbishop of Perth, Patrick J. Clune. He asked the archbishop to meet the Irish leaders in Dublin and sound them out about negotiations and a possible ceasefire.

Clune met with Griffith in Mountjoy jail. Griffith advised Collins against a meeting with the archbishop because of the danger that British agents would be tailing him, but Collins met him without difficulty on 4 December at a school run by Louise Gavan Duffy on St Stephen's Green.

Even if the secret service were keeping an eye on the archbishop, they would have considered his visit to her school quite natural as she was a daughter of Sir Charles Gavan Duffy, a former Young Ireland leader who had risen to the top in Australian politics having migrated there in the mid-nineteenth century.

'I wonder how it is that the archbishop sees Collins apparently without difficulty in Dublin and our intelligence fails to find him after weeks of search,' Mark Sturgis wrote in obvious exasperation.[21]

Collins gave Clune a written outline of ceasefire terms agreeable to the Dáil cabinet. 'If it is understood that the acts of violence (attacks, counter-attacks, reprisals, arrests, pursuits) are called off on both sides,' he wrote, 'we are agreeable to issue the necessary instructions on our side, it being understood that the entire Dáil shall be free to meet and that its peaceful activities be not interfered with.'[22]

Before the archbishop could return to Britain, a spanner was thrown in the works when some Sinn Féin members of Galway County Council called publicly for peace talks, and Fr Michael O'Flanagan, the Sinn Féin vice-president, wrote to Lloyd George asking for peace terms. Although both acts were unauthorised, Collins realised their significance immediately. He asked the secretary of the party to inform the press 'that Father O'Flanagan acted without any authority from the Sinn Féin Standing Committee, and without consulting that body.

'We must not allow ourselves to be rushed by these foolish productions, or foolish people, who are tumbling over themselves to talk about a "truce", when there is no truce,' Collins wrote.[23]

The *Irish Independent* suggested a hitch had developed in secret talks because of the difficulty in organising a truce in which Collins' safety could be assured. He forcefully denied the report and lashed out against the recent unauthorised overtures in a short letter to the newspaper's editor. 'My personal safety does not matter and does not count as a factor in the question of Ireland's right,' he explained. 'I thank no one for refraining from murdering me. At the moment there is a very grave danger that the country may be stampeded on false promises and foolish, ill-timed actions. We must stand up against that danger. My advice to the people is, "Hold fast".'

People in the movement were rushing 'to talk of truce' when there was no indication the British were ready to call off their aggression, he complained in another letter to the press. As far as he was concerned, the Irish side was merely acting in self-defence. 'If the aggression ceases there will be no longer any need for defence,' he argued. 'But is the aggression ceasing?[24]

'Everywhere the enemy has gone on with his attack,' Collins added, answering his own question. 'Let us drop talking and get on with our work.[25]

'Everyone in Ireland has reason to be profoundly distrustful of British politicians of all schools, and we have learned to be more distrustful of their promises than of their threats,' he continued. 'Prepare to meet their threats, but let their promises be realised. Then, we can bestow thanks according to value.'

His scepticism was well founded. When Clune returned to London, he found Lloyd George's attitude had stiffened. Passions were so roused over the recent killings, the prime minister said, it was necessary to hold off on actual talks for a while longer. If the Irish would keep things quiet for about a month, he predicted the atmosphere would be more conducive to negotiations. He also added it would help matters if Collins and Mulcahy left the country for a while. The archbishop concluded the British attitude had changed because they believed O'Flanagan's letter and the telegram from the six members of the Galway County Council were indications Sinn Féin was 'showing the white feather'.[26]

Clune heard the prime minister call a meeting with his hard-liners, and it was worth noting that when Lloyd George spoke in the House of Commons afterwards, he said that the 'extremists must first be broken up' before there could be a negotiated settlement, and he announced the introduction of martial law throughout the southern counties of Ireland.[27]

The next evening the Black and Tans and auxiliaries ran amok in Cork, burning much of the business centre of the city in a frightening rampage of arson and looting. The outcry was such that the government ordered a formal military inquiry.

When Clune returned to Mountjoy for further discussions with Griffith on 12 December, Collins was clearly disillusioned. 'It seems to me that no additional good result can come from further continuing these discussions,' he wrote to Griffith. 'We have clearly demonstrated our willingness to have peace on honourable terms. Lloyd George insists upon capitulation. Between these there is no mean, and it is only a waste of time continuing.'

Collins was afraid that his willingness to continue with such talks might be interpreted in Britain as an indication that the Irish side was on the verge of collapse and was therefore desperate for peace. 'Let Lloyd George make no mistake,' Collins continued, 'the IRA is not broken.'[28]

Although Lloyd George's coalition government had been given a handsome majority in the last general election, his own political position was really precarious because his Liberal Party had been decimated at the polls, and the Conservative Party, with which he was in coalition, had won an overwhelming majority of it own within Westminster. Thus the prime minister was really a political prisoner of the Conservatives who traditionally tended to take a hard line on Irish matters.

Clune was convinced that Lloyd George was 'genuinely anxious' for a settlement and was being hampered by diehards in his government, but their position had been weakened by the recent outrageous behaviour of crown forces. 'The Cork burnings have strengthened his hands against the diehards,' the archbishop argued. In addition, there was also the senseless killing of a Catholic priest, Cannon Magner. He had been shot in Cork by the Black and Tans after he had stopped to help a local magistrate who was having car trouble.

'His sole offence was to have helped a Resident Magistrate to get his motor car going, and here comes a drunken beast of a soldier who makes him kneel down and shoots him,' Lloyd George told his cabinet.[29]

Griffith tended to agree with Clune about the prime minister's desire for a settlement. 'Lloyd George, apparently wants peace,' he wrote to Collins, 'but is afraid of his militarists.'

All this was 'being too credulous of Lloyd George's intentions', in the opinion of Collins. 'My own feeling about Lloyd George is that we should not allow him to disassociate himself from his public actions, as head of his cabinet, and from the actions resulting from decisions of his cabinet,' Collins wrote to Art O'Brien on 15 December. 'Particularly on this side, there is far too great a tendency to believe that Lloyd George is wishful for peace, and that it is only his own wild men prevent him from accomplishing his desires.'

Nevertheless the archbishop now brought proposals from Dublin Castle that the British were willing to stop arrests, raids or reprisals for a month in return for a ceasefire on the Irish side, but they were not prepared to agree formally that the Dáil should be allowed to meet. It was not that they wanted to prevent such meetings but rather they did not want to be seen to formally approve of them.

'A truce on the terms specified cannot possibly do us any harm,' Collins wrote to Griffith. He had consulted Brugha and Stack and both were agreeable. Stack was ready to accept if Collins was, while Brugha merely insisted that 'it must be definitely understood that our peaceful activities are not to be interfered with'.[30]

Just as everything seemed ready for a truce, the British again scuttled the process. Clune returned to Griffith on 17 December with news that Dublin Castle was now insisting that the IRA should first surrender its arms. This, of course, was tantamount to demanding capitulation, and Griffith told him without hesitation that it would not even be considered.

That evening the Squad killed RIC District Inspector Philip J. O'Sullivan, a native of Bantry, County Cork. He had serve in the Royal Navy during the Great War, was just twenty-three years old. He had only been in the RIC for five months and was based in the office of the RIC's deputy inspector general at Dublin Castle.

'I was instructed, with others, to proceed to Henry Street to assist in the shooting of D.I. O'Sullivan,' Joe Byrne of the Squad recalled. 'About four of us comprised the party.'

O'Sullivan met his fiancée in Henry Street as usual around 6.15 p.m. She had been waiting for him. Shortly after he came along, two men crossed the street, took out revolvers and shot him at close range. She grappled with one of the men while the other stood over O'Sullivan who lay on the ground and fired another shot at him. A passing military lorry's took the wounded officer to Jervis Street Hospital, where he died shortly afterwards.

The two assailants casually walked away and promptly disappeared into the rush-hour crowd. 'We returned to Morelands,' Byrne added.[31]

The next day, Collins met Clune for a second time. 'Our interview was not a lengthy one,' Collins wrote. 'We had both, practically speaking, come to the conclusion that no talk was necessary, seeing that the new proposal from the British government was a proposal that we should surrender.'[32]

A number of factors contributed to Lloyd George's change of heart, but in the last instance the main reason was unwillingness to confront his cabinet hard-liners, who were predicting that they were on the verge of victory. 'Stress was laid on the importance of doing nothing to check the surrender of arms at a time when the forces of the Crown had at last definitely established the upper hand,' the cabinet secretary noted in his diary.[33]

The talk about getting the upper hand was strengthened by the antics of Fr O'Flanagan and six members of Galway County Council clamouring for peace, followed by the bitter denunciation of ambushes by the Roman Catholic Bishop of Cork, Daniel Cohalan, who announced the excommunication of anyone engaging in ambushes.

'Anyone who shall within the Diocese of Cork, organise or take part in an ambush or in a kidnapping, or otherwise shall be guilty of murder or attempt at murder,' Bishop Daniel Cohalan said, 'and shall incur by the very fact the censure of excommunication.'[34]

'That is pretty serious,' Lloyd George noted. He saw the sermon as an indication that the hierarchy was turning away from Sinn Féin.[35]

On top of all this the British had their own intelligence reports that de Valera was on his way back from the United States, and they believed he would be easier to deal with than a militant like Collins. As things stood Clune told the British that Collins was 'the only one with whom business could be done', but they gave the archbishop the impression they thought de Valera and O'Flanagan and would be more ready to compromise.

The British cabinet was told on 20 December that de Valera would be landing at Liverpool that day and Lloyd George suggested that no effort should be made to arrest him.

'I cannot guarantee de Valera's safety now,' Greenwood declared.

'That is his look out,' the prime minister replied.

'How can you let de Valera loose when we have arrested Arthur Griffith?' Greenwood asked.

'That was a piece of impertinence on the part of the military and if it had not been for the fact that we want support of the military we would have repudiated it,' Lloyd George explained.[36]

The Clune talks were only one of the issues that Collins had to concern himself with during his month as acting president. In addition to being acting president of the Dáil, he was still Minister for Finance, president of the IRB and director of intelligence in the IRA.

He was really an administrative genius, able to compartmentalise all matters and keep them separate, while at the same time slicing through bureaucratic red tape. He believed in getting right to the heart of a matter and baulked at the paper shuffling on which civil servants often spend so much of their time.

'Look here,' he wrote to the cabinet secretary, Diarmuid O'Hegarty, 'I am not going to have any more of the parcels of miscellanies dumped on me. If anything concerns this department, or the general aspect, it should be sent to me and no more about it – I have something else to do than to wade through a miscellaneous collection of cuttings, surmounted by a letter from the Propaganda Department to you, a letter from you to the propaganda Department, and another letter to myself. If a little common sense is applied, the situation will be very much simplified,' he declared. [37]

He had the neat, orderly mind of a trained civil servant. He liked his reports typed, or at least written in ink.

'For God's sake,' he wrote to one intelligence officer in the habit of sending pencilled reports, 'buy a pen and a bottle of ink.'[38]

Collins returned an illegible report to another officer. 'What in Heaven's name is the use of mystifying me with a thing like this?' he asked.[39]

His own letters were a model of businesslike clarity – short and to the point, with numbered paragraphs for different items, and separate letters dealing with intelligence and financial matters.

His good friend Harry Boland used to irritate him by including Sinn Féin, IRB and personal matters in the same letters, which caused problems if Collins wished to pass on the letters to someone else. But try as he might, there was no way some people would adopt the kind of reporting habits Collins desired.

'I undertook to fight for you, not to write for you,' Seán MacEoin snapped back in irritation one day.

15

'He's No Big Fella to Me'

'Got plenty of staff, Austin?' Collins asked Austin Stack, the Minister for Home Affairs.

'Yes,' replied the Kerryman.

'Well I have just received the following,' Collins snarled, dumping a bundle of complaints on his desk. 'Your department, Austin, is nothing but a bloody joke.'

The rather sensitive Stack resented the remark. A few days later, when someone referred to Collins as the Big Fellow, Stack betrayed his bitterness. 'Big Fella!' he said. 'He's no Big Fella to me.'[1]

The nickname, born out of derision, had become a term of affection, but there was no longer any affection between Collins and Stack. Their once warm friendship was developing into bitter animosity.

Pádraic O'Keeffe, who served with Stack as joint national secretary of Sinn Féin, noted it was 'easy to work with' Stack. 'Of course,' O'Keeffe added pointedly, 'he did no work'. Within the IRB it seemed to be the same story. 'Stack was County Centre for Kerry, for instance, in all these years but neither Crowe nor Diarmuid Lynch who succeeded him as divisional Representatives for Munster, could get him to do anything, and his removal from office for laziness was many times mooted – but there was nobody else on offer,' P.S. O'Hegarty recalled.[2]

Collins would have been quite content to leave Stack alone if he had been working properly, but Stack never got on top of his job. He never even attended a meeting of the headquarters staff after Collins had been instrumental in appointing him deputy chief-of-staff. He antagonised Collins by transmitting routine material though the IRA's express communications network. This was a kind of fast-track service in which railway men carried sensitive IRA messages all over the country.

Collins had set up the network and was very protective of it. He would not have minded it being used for important matters, but he resented Stack endangering the process just to transmit routine matters.

Collins 'never crossed the boughs of anybody who was doing work and particularly anybody in authority,' according to Mulcahy. This was probably an exaggeration, but it was particularly significant coming from the IRA chief-of-staff, who noted that Collins 'set himself out to serve unreservedly in every possible way'.[3] He certainly had an excellent working relationship not only with Mulcahy but also with Griffith, during the period of the latter's acting presidency.

Collins was a demanding taskmaster, always pushing and shoving to get things done. He pushed everyone, especially himself. People throughout the movement looked to him for action. 'There was no burden too big to put on Mick's shoulders, and there was no job too small for him to do,' according to Dan Breen.[4]

'Whenever anybody wanted anything done they were told to see Mick,' Tom Barry noted. 'He was very good-hearted and generous, but he was also a man you could easily dislike. He was very domineering.'[5]

Witnesses were often embarrassed by the way Collins bullied his aide Joe O'Reilly. The latter was everything to him, confidant, messenger, nurse, sometime bodyguard and the person who bore the brunt of the Big Fellow's rages when he left off steam as things went wrong, which was quite often for a perfectionist like Collins. They had been friends since their emigrant days in London and O'Reilly was a perfect sidekick, totally devoted to Collins, though at times the bullying did get to him. O'Reilly would announce he was leaving and Collins would act indifferently, making no effort to change his friend's mind.

'Here!' Collins would say. 'Take this letter on your way.'[6]

'Do you know what you're doing to that boy?' one disgusted woman asked Collins.

'I know his value better than you do,' he replied. 'He goes to Mass for me every morning. Jesus Christ, do you think I don't know what he's worth to me?'[7]

O'Reilly always returned, for course, because in spite of everything he knew that Collins valued his services. Maybe the reason Collins would not ask him to stay was because he recognised that nobody should be pressed to take the risks that O'Reilly took for him. Collins trusted him with his life because O'Reilly always knew where the find Collins; he was the only person who knew where Collins was sleeping on any given night.

Finding a bed for the night was usually a problem for someone like Collins. The Munster Hotel was subject to regular raids, so it was too dangerous for him to stay there throughout 1920, and Vaughan's Hotel became much too dangerous after Bloody Sunday. Anyone putting him up for the night had to be particularly brave because they were endangering their own lives and those of their families.

On the evening of de Valera's return to Ireland, Collins arranged a party with some friends in the Gresham Hotel. That day the *Police Gazette: Hue and Cry* came out with a good photograph of him on its front page. The gathering at the Gresham was exclusively male. It included Rory O'Connor, Gearóid O'Sullivan, Liam Tobin, Tom Cullen and Collins. He also invited David Neligan, his spy in Dublin Castle, but Neligan declined.

'Dave's getting windy,' Collins exclaimed.[8]

During the evening the hotel was raided by the auxiliaries, and all were questioned and searched.

'What is your name?' the auxiliary officer asked Collins.[9]

'John Grace.'

'What is your job?'

'I am an accountant.'

'Where do you work?'

'My office is in Dame Street.'[10]

Collins had an ordnance survey map in his possession with the words '6 refills' written in a corner. The officer suggested it said rifles, but the neat handwriting left little room for confusion.

'They were very suspicious of me,' Collins told friends the next day. 'I was questioned over and over again. One officer actually drew an old photograph of me out of his pocket, and compared it with my face, drawing my hair down as it was in the picture. It was touch and go. They were not quite satisfied, and hesitated long before they left us.'[11]

Throughout it all Collins remained cheerful, and the raiding party eventually departed, leaving him to get very drunk indeed. Afterwards they went to Vaughan's hotel. Cullen left to get a car, and Béaslaí arrived to find O'Sullivan sprawled on a chair, while O'Connor and Collins were embraced on the floor.

Once Collins launched the loan campaign in Ireland, de Valera asked him to come to the United States to help arrange things there, but Collins declined. Although realising that America afforded enormous opportunities for propaganda and financial help, Collins was convinced that all this would only happened if the right atmosphere were generated by events in Ireland. 'Our hope is here and must be here,' he wrote. 'The job will be to prevent eyes turning to Paris or New York as a substitute for London.'[12] In short, they should not make the mistake of concentrating on efforts to secure international recognition, because, in the final instance, they could only win by wearing down the British government.

Instead of going to the United States, Collins sent James O'Mara, one of the trustees of the Dáil, to help organise the bond-certificate drive. As the Irish Republic had not been officially recognised, it would have been illegal to sell bonds but with the help of Judge Daniel Cohalan of the New York Supreme Court, the law was circumvented by selling certificates entitling purchasers to buy bonds of a similar value once the Irish Republic was recognised.

De Valera's critics were not confined to a Clan na Gael clique, as has sometimes been suggested. Patrick MacCartan was an outspoken critic of Cohalan and Devoy, but he nevertheless complained that de Valera had been needlessly antagonising people by betraying 'an unconscious contempt' for their views. James O'Mara, the man sent out by Collins actually resigned over de Valera's high-handed actions.

'What on earth is wrong with Mr O'Mara?' Collins wrote to Boland.

'There always seems to be something depressing coming from the USA.'[13]

There was uneasiness in Dublin over the stance taken by de Valera in the *Westminster Gazette* interview. Fr O'Flanagan wrote to Collins complaining about the 'suspicion that we were prepared to desert our friends in a foolish attempt to placate our enemies.

'In the last resort,' O'Flanagan insisted, 'we must rely not upon the people who wish to make the world safe for the British Empire, but upon those who don't.'[14]

Within the cabinet, Brugha, Plunkett and Markievicz all 'showed marked hostility' to the interview, but Griffith – with backing from Collins – deftly limited the discussion and secured acceptance of the president's explanation. The cabinet also authorised de Valera to spend the money he requested on the American elections.

Devoy sought to drag Collins into the dispute by depicting him as the real Irish leader following his interview with Ackermann. 'Michael Collins Speaks for Ireland', Devoy proclaimed boldly in a *Gaelic American* editorial. The weekly newspaper also carried a large front-page photograph of Collins in uniform, with the caption: 'Ireland's Fighting Chief'. There was no doubt Devoy was hitting at de Valera, but Collins wanted nothing to do with it.[15]

'Every member of the Irish cabinet is in full accord with President de Valera's policy,' Collins wrote to Devoy on 30 September 1920. 'When he speaks to America, he speaks for all of us.'[16]

Collins went so far as to sever the IRB's connections with Clan na Gael a fortnight later. 'Let it be clearly understood,' he emphasised in a further letter to Devoy, 'that we all stand together, and that here at home every member of the cabinet has been an ardent supporter of the president against any and every group in America who have either not given him the co-operation which they should, or have set themselves definitely to thwart his actions.' Collins could not have been more forthright in his support of de Valera's position.

He clearly held de Valera in high esteem, and that affection extended to the president's family. Although the most wanted man in the country, Collins regularly visited de Valera's wife and children at their home in Greystones, County Wicklow. He brought Sinéad money and news from America, and he also played with the children. Sinéad de Valera sincerely appreciated his help. In later life she would go out of her way to tell members of the Collins family how much the visits had meant to her. She appreciated that he took the trouble to visit her personally, rather than sending messengers, as he could so easily have done.

'When Mother spoke of Michael Collins, which she often did,' Terry de Valera, her youngest son, later recalled, 'she did so with a feeling of real gratitude and affection and always acknowledged his daring and supreme courage.'[17]

In the summer of 1920 Collins arranged for her to visit the United States, but de Valera probably did not think this was one of his more helpful gestures. There were some ugly rumours circulating in the United States about de Valera's relationship with his secretary, Kathleen O'Connell, whom he met in the United States. They had been travelling together, and it was rumoured they were having an affair.

Years later de Valera told a stunned Dáil that there had been a smear campaign against him in the United States. 'It went on not merely from the platform and in private, but it was spoken from the pulpit; it came from the altar,' he complained. 'I myself was told by a lady in Chicago that a bishop told her that my wife had to go over to America in order to keep me straight there because I was associating with women.'[18]

De Valera had been in Ireland for less than two months since May 1918, so it seemed reasonable to assume he would welcome seeing his wife. 'The visit to America was one of the biggest mistakes I ever made,' Sinéad later wrote. 'It was a huge blunder for me to go to America. I derived neither profit nor pleasure from my visit.'[19]

De Valera had planned to stay in the United States for at least six months more until he heard that Collins had taken over as acting president following the arrest of Griffith. Upon his return de Valera lost no time in complaining about the way the IRA campaign was being conducted.

'Ye are going too fast,' he told Mulcahy on Christmas Eve. 'This odd shooting of a policeman here and there is having a very bad effect, from the propaganda point of view, on us in America. What we want is one good battle about once a month with about 500 men on each side.'[20]

Taking on the British in major battles was absurd in Collins' eyes. If he had learned nothing else from the Easter Rising, he had learned that Ireland was militarily incapable of beating the British in an all-out fight. De Valera was obviously going to have problems convincing Collins, so he proposed that the Big Fellow should go to the United States.

Collins flatly refused, but de Valera won cabinet approval for the idea. He outlined the reasons in a long letter to Collins on 18 January 1921. With a new American president due to take office on 4 March, de Valera argued there would be a whole 'new political situation in the United States'.[21] He wanted Collins to try to secure American support for Irish membership of the League of Nations in the event of United States joining the league. In putting forward a whole plethora of reasons for the proposed trip, de Valera seemed to be protesting a little too much. He stressed economic, financial, strategic and propaganda benefits. He wanted Collins to try to heal the Irish-American split, and he made a naked appeal to the Big Fellow's vanity.

'You probably do not appreciate, as I do, what your presence will mean there for the cause, if only you will not be too modest to exploit your fame, or notoriety if you prefer it, but I would suggest that it be mainly on the lines of how moderate and full of common sense you are,' de Valera wrote. As things stood there was a danger the British could inflict a lethal blow if they managed to arrest the whole rebel leadership. All the eggs would not be in one basket, however, once Collins went to America. 'Whatever *coup* the English may attempt, the line of succession is safe, and the future provided for,' he argued.[22]

Despite all the protestations and flattery, Collins thought de Valera was just trying to get him out of the way. He was indeed more moderate than was generally realised, but it was unlikely that anyone had ever before accused him of being overly modest.

'That long whore won't get rid of me as easy as that,' Collins said.[23]

The New Year had begun badly for Collins when the home of Eileen McGrane at 21 Dawson Street was raided on 1 January 1921. The British found a large cache of documents that she had been storing for him. Among the documents were the carbon copies of police reports typed by Broy. The documents included the book that Collins had taken from the G division archives of the telephone messages received during the Easter Rising.

Collins warned Broy the documents had been found and it would only be a matter of time before Broy would come under suspicion. 'Every vestige of political duty was immediately removed from the Brunswick St office to the Castle,' Broy wrote. British intelligence ceased to give any further confidential information to the DMP.

Jim McNamara, the other main police spy, was also compromised by the documents found at Eileen McGrane's place. He came under suspicion for having leaked the document to the IRA in relation to the accusation that American seamen were smuggling arms into Dublin. McNamara was summoned to the office of the DMP inspector-general and summarily dismissed from the force.

'Listen, Mac!' Neligan warned, 'don't go to your father's house tonight or any other night.'[24]

'You are lucky,' Collins told McNamara. Obviously the British did not have much on him, or they would not have let him go. But henceforth he went on the run with the IRA.[25]

Broy remained in contact with Collins and continued to work at the DMP, but 'the capture of the documents, having brought me under suspicion, had rendered me of very little future value to him, at least in the manner I had been in the past'.[26]

'I continued to meet Collins almost every night during this time and, of course, had to take extra precautions in doing so.' He found Collins 'very perturbed' about cabinet pressure both to ease off on the war that he had been waging against individuals and to get him to go to the United States.

The search for Collins was intensifying. Auxiliaries frequently burst into bars and other public places shouting, 'Where's Michael Collins. We know he's here!'

John Foley – a former secretary to the lord mayor of Dublin and well-known for his antipathy to Sinn Féin – was arrested while having lunch with a former high sheriff of Dublin, T.J. MacAvin in Jammet's restaurant on 10 January 1921.

'Come on Michael Collins, you've dodged us long enough,' the arresting officer said.[27]

Despite their protestations, Foley and MacAvin were taken to Dublin Castle, before they could convince the officer of his mistake. Republicans were highly amused by the incident, which was all the funnier because Foley did not look even remotely like Collins.

The following week some crown authorities again thought they had Collins when they arrested a barman in the Prince of Wales Hotel using the name of Corry. He turned out to be a Michael Collins all right. 'But,' *The Irish Times* noted, 'he is not the Michael Collins of IRA notoriety.'[28]

On 31 January the British raided Cullenswood House, because they had become suspicious of a number of seemingly unnecessary structural alterations that they had noticed during a recent raid. They therefore decided to inspect the alterations. They discovered the changes included false walls, false doors and a false wardrobe with a secret spring, which opened into a chamber that appeared to be a secret office. In one of the rooms secret doors and secret cupboards were found. There were nine exit doors giving access to adjacent fields. There was nobody on the premises, but in a room a supper had been laid.

The *Daily Sketch* reported that Collins had been shot off a white horse while trying to escape from Burgatia House on the outskirts of Roscarbery, County Cork on 2 February. About thirty-five men had seized the house with the aim of attacking a nearby police barracks that night, but the Black and Tans learned of their presence and surrounded the premises with some 100 men. The IRA nevertheless managed to break out without suffering any casualties. One volunteer, Billy Sullivan, rode out on a bay mare. Collins was not within a hundred miles of the place.

He was amused when IRA intelligence intercepted a coded message asking for confirmation from Cork about the reported shooting. 'Is there any truth that Michael Collins was killed at Burgatia?' Dublin Castle asked.[29]

'There is no information of the report *re* Michael Collins, but some believed he was wounded,' came the reply.

'We are hoping to hear further confirmation about poor Michael Collins,' the Big Fellow remarked facetiously in acknowledging the receipt of the two telegrams.[30]

There was a news agency report on 8 February that Collins had been killed in an engagement in Drimoleague, County Cork. Such reports added considerably to his notoriety, and for this, the British were largely responsible. Their frustrated forces sought to explain their failures by exaggerating the strength and the guile of their opponents, 'among whom,' Ormonde Winter (the chief of British intelligence) wrote, 'Michael Collins stands out pre-eminent.'[31]

Following the Burgatia incident, the Black and Tans sought to excuse their failure by claiming the IRA had a force of some 500 men in the house, and *The Irish Times* credulously reported it. While those who took part must have known better, they seemed to attribute the amazing escape to the guile of Collins. 'He combined the characteristics of a Robin Hood with those of an elusive Pimpernel,' Ormonde Winter wrote. 'His many narrow escapes, when he managed to elude almost certain arrest, shrouded him in a cloak of historical romance.'[32]

'The English papers have been giving me plenty of notoriety,' Collins wrote to his sister Lena. 'The white horse story was an exaggeration.' Others aspects of it may have been an exaggerated, but his white horse escape was pure fiction.[33]

Collins noted that the *Daily Sketch* described him as a 'super hater, dour, hard, no ray of humour [and] no trace of human feeling'.[34] While the characterisation was wide of the mark, it probably did reflect Dublin Castle's distorted perception and thus explained British difficulty in finding him. He was a very different type of person to the man they were looking for.

Certainly he could be serious and intent, but generally he had a breezy, affable manner. He went out of his way to be friendly with British troops or police. If he saw an area condoned off he would go over and talk with those on guard duty. 'There are several of these fellows I don't know yet,' he would say to colleagues.[35]

When stopped or searched himself, he would be cordial with the troops or auxiliaries, would smile at them and joke with them. They naturally welcomed his friendliness in the hostile atmosphere permeating Ireland.

'You're a good sort anyway,' one of them said to him one day. He liked that, it appealed to his sense of humour. Such friendliness was the last thing the British expected of Michael Collins.[36]

He liked to tell the story of talking to an auxiliary in a Grafton Street pub one day. 'That man Collins, I wish I could nail him,' Collins said.

'Don't worry,' replied the auxiliary. 'His days are numbered.'

Collins related what happened with a roar of laughter and held up a calendar.

'See here,' he said to O'Reilly, 'how many days have I got to live?'[37]

There were some loose ends in relation to Bloody Sunday that still needed to be cleared up. Collins learned that Corporal John Ryan, of British Army intelligence, had fingered Dick McKee and Peadar Clancy and he ordered the Squad to kill Ryan. Bill Stapleton asked for the job. 'I felt very keenly about the murder of Dick McKee,' Stapleton explained. 'I fought in 1916 and served subsequently with him in the 2nd Battalion. My request was granted and the second man instructed to accompany me was Eddie Byrne.' The intelligence officer pointed out Ryan in Hynes' public house at the corner of Old Gloucester Place and Corporation Street on 10.30 a.m. on the morning of 5 February 1921.[38]

'You are Ryan?' they asked.

'Yes, and what about it?'

'With that we shot him,' Stapleton recalled. 'We went back to the Squad dump, which was in a stable off North Great Charles St. near Mountjoy Square and that concluded the operation as far as we were concerned.'[39]

For their part the British charged ten men with murder in relation to the Bloody Sunday killings. Frank Teeling, who had been wounded and captured during the shoot-out as 22 Mount Street was tried along with three others who were not involved in the killing of Lieutenant H. Angliss (alias Paddy MacMahon). Teeling testified on behalf of those wrongly charged. Before a sentence could be pronounced on him, Teeling escaped from Kilmainham jail on 15 February, along with Simon Donnolly and Ernie O'Malley. They asked Paddy Moran to come with them. He had led the assassination team in the Gresham Hotel on Bloody Sunday morning, but he was being tried for the murder of Captain Peter Ames in Upper Mount Street.

'I'm not going,' Moran said when O'Malley tried to persuade him to escape with them. 'I won't let down the witnesses who gave evidence for me.'[40]

'Someone has to die for this,' O'Malley warned. 'Maybe Teeling or myself, but they'll hang you for certain if we get through.'

Following the escape from Kilmainham, Collins cycled out to meet O'Malley in his hiding place. The Big Fellow shook his hand for a long time.

'You're born to be shot,' Collins said. 'You can't be hanged! Why didn't Paddy Moran come with you?'

'I don't know,' O'Malley replied. 'He thought there was no case against him.'

'They'll hang him as a reprisal now,' Collins said. Moran was hanged on 13 March 1921.[41]

The formative intelligence network set up by Collins was seriously undermined. His best-placed spies had lost their effectiveness – Kavanagh was dead, McNamara had been sacked, and although Broy was trying to hold on in G division, he was under intense suspicion.

The head of the DMP questioned Broy about his handling of a sensitive report drawn up by a detective who watched Broy type it up. As a result Broy had not been able to make an extra carbon of that report, but he did give the file copy to one of Collins' people with the instruction that they should type up a copy and return the original to him without delay. Thus it was the re-typed copy that was found and Broy was quick to spot that it was typed on an elite typewriter with ten characters to the inch, as opposed to the typewriters at G division headquarters, which were all pica models with just eight characters to the inch. This was enough to raise doubts about Broy's guilt. 'I was in charge of the office from which the documents were taken and, consequently, was not likely to have given out the documents myself, as I would have been obviously the first to be blamed,' Broy argued.[42]

The man that he had to fear within the DMP was Detective Chief Inspector Joe Supple who was to prepare the case against him. He was a slightly built man with a goat face, according to Neligan. Supple began every day by attending mass in Mount Argus near his home, and McNamara suggested Collins warn Supple that if he took the case he should pick out his spot in Mount Jerome cemetery beside Mount Argus.

'By God,' Collins said, 'I'll get up there tonight!'[43]

Collins arranged for a man to deliver the warning without delay. 'I have a grave warning to give you!' the man told Supple. 'It concerns someone called Broy, of whom I know nothing. I am to tell you that if you go on with the case against him, you will be shot!'[44]

Collins enlisted the help of former Detective Sergeant Pat McCarthy, who had tried to play on both sides of the fence in the DMP for some time. His brother was active in Sinn Féin and he told Collins that Pat was not involved in political work but was merely dealing with the licensing of taxis. The Big Fellow promptly produced a report in which the detective sergeant provided details of the names, addresses and usual haunts of prominent Sinn Féiners. 'Ask him what has that to do with taxicabs?' Collins said.[45]

Pat McCarthy promptly resigned from the DMP and moved to London. Now Collins contacted him and, in order to deflect suspicion from Broy, asked him to flee to America as soon as secret transportation could be arranged. 'McCarthy agreed, and sent me word that, under no circumstances, would he make a statement to the British or come to Dublin,' Broy explained. 'When the Civil War was over, I had the pleasure of reinstating McCarthy in the Dublin Police and promoting him to inspector and later Superintendent.'[46]

Another valuable source of information, Sergeant Jerry Maher, came under suspicion at the county inspector's office in Kildare, and he quit the RIC, and was replaced by then-Sergeant Patrick Casey, who was already supplying Collins with information. He was able to continue until March, when he too came under suspicion and was transferred to Downpatrick.

David Neligan concluded he was wasting his time in the DMP, as the British secret service distrusted it. 'Now I was alone in the Castle,' he said. He therefore decided to try to get into British intelligence. He told Collins he wished to get out of Dublin Castle. 'It was useless staying there any longer,' he noted. 'The British secret service had taken over and we were completely in the dark. I told him I intended trying to join the British secret service, which I did in a few days.'

Major Stokes of the British secret service interviewed Neligan and told him he had been highly recommended. Neligan was promptly sworn into the service the same day, and he was assigned to the Blackrock, Dalkey and Kingstown area.

'Join the IRA by all means, if you can,' Major Stokes told him. 'We will be glad if you get in.' Stokes introduced him to a Captain Woolridge.

'When I told Collins the next day he was pleased,' Neligan noted. The Squad already knew Woolridge, but did not know Stokes. Neligan was not supposed to go into Dublin proper, so Collins agreed to come out to meet him in Keegan's Bar in Blackrock. 'I met plenty of the British secret service after this,' Neligan explained. 'They were scattered in various private houses about the city. These houses were all owned by loyalists and they were carefully screened by the British before the agents were allowed to go into them, a very wise precaution!'

'I was expected to make an intelligence report once a week,' Neligan continued. 'Collins often helped me to write these reports; in fact, he wrote them himself. Many a good laugh we had over them! He used to say in these reports that the IRA was in no way short of arms or ammunition; recruits were simply falling over each other; they had plenty of money; new columns were being formed to fight the British.'

Captain Woolridge complemented Neligan on his reports and said that he knew the IRA had plenty of ammunition, because they were deliberately feeding the republicans with booby-trapped ammunition so that the IRA would use it. 'We are dropping stuff here and there,' Woolridge explained. 'If they use them, they will get a shock.'

The doctored bullets were marked 'Z.Z.' Neligan passed on the information to Collins, who had a warning circulated.

16

'You'll Get None of My Men'

De Valera wished to get negotiations going as quickly as possible with the British. He actually wrote to Lloyd George in January suggesting secret talks. Maybe his proposal that Collins should go to the United States had something to do with Lloyd George's suggestion that Collins should leave Ireland for a while. A successful visit to the United States by Collins would have the advantage of putting further pressure on the British government, which was already worried about American opinion.

The president was astutely interpreting the situation when he suggested the IRA's campaign should be waged in a way that could be best exploited in America for propaganda purposes. He began to take a leaf out of Lloyd George's book – making conciliatory sounds in public, while privately advocating a militant policy.

In an interview with a French journalist, for instance, de Valera noted that the allies had supposedly been fighting for the right to self-determination for all peoples in the recent war. 'If England should concede that right,' he said, 'there would be no further difficulties, either with her or with the Ulster minority. If Ulster should claim autonomy, we would be willing to grant it.' Asked if he would accept Dominion status, he intimated such a settlement would be agreeable, seeing that even the leader of the British Conservative Party had publicly admitted that the Dominions had 'control of their whole destinies'.[1]

'Thus,' de Valera emphasised, 'the British Dominions had conceded to them all the rights which the Irish Republicans demand. It is obvious that if these rights were not denied us, we would not be engaged in the present struggle.' He went on to stress that Sinn Féin was not a radical organisation at all. 'We are thoroughly sane and reasonable people, not a coterie of political doctrinaires, or even party politicians, republican or other.'[2]

His moderate statements were viewed with alarm in some Sinn Féin quarters, where people felt he should be calling for recognition of the republican government. But he dismissed this.

'In public statements,' he maintained, 'our policy should be not to make it easy for Lloyd George by proclaiming that nothing but so and so will satisfy us. Our position should be simply that we are insisting on only one right, and that is the right of the people of this country to determine for themselves how they should be governed. That sounds moderate, but includes everything.'[3] Yet this was the issue on which he supposedly broke with Devoy and Cohalan.

It was widely understood that de Valera was offering to bargain on the extent of Irish freedom. As a propaganda ploy, it was certainly the impression he wished to give to the international press in order to force Britain to the conference table, but his efforts were being undermined by the unequivocal stand taken by Collins in his interview with Ackermann.

'Michael Collins is the soul of Ireland's fight for independence,' the *Boston American* declared. 'He has infinitely more sway in the country than President de Valera.'[4]

The seeds of another power struggle – this time between de Valera and Collins – were already being sown. Both men wanted power, but had differing motives.

Collins sought power to achieve national goals, to get things done. To him the trappings of power – office and title – were not important. But de Valera, brought up in loveless surroundings, essentially abandoned by his mother, had a driving need to demonstrate that he was somebody. Hence both power and position were vital to him.

During early 1921 Collins had several narrow escapes of which the British were unaware, such as when the auxiliaries raided 22 Mary Street, where he had his main finance office. They were primarily raiding another office in the building. When he casually walked down the stairs, they merely searched him and allowed him to leave the place.

One night he was staying at Susan Mason's house at 23 Brendan's Road when it was due to be raided, but the officer in charge of the raiding party mislaid his list in the course of a raid in Donnybrook. The officer had come across some love letters and was reading them when the woman to whom they had been sent entered the room and upbraided him for his ungentlemanly conduct. The embarrassed officer hurriedly stuffed the letters back into a drawer and inadvertently included his own list of houses to be raided that night. She found the list and passed it on to Batt O'Connor the next day, when Collins learned of his narrow escape.

He had another close call in Kirwin's Bar one night when it was raided. He was with Sergeant Maurice McCarthy of the RIC who had just come down from Belfast with the latest police codes. Everyone in the bar was being searched but when McCarthy produced his RIC identification, the officer in charge invited him and Collins to have a drink. Had they searched Collins they would have found the codes.

It was widely believed there was a reward of £10,000 for the capture of Collins, which was then as much as most Irish people could expect to earn in a lifetime. The Black and Tans, for instance, were considered well paid, but £10,000 amounted to more than they could earn in twenty-seven years, working seven days a week. As a result there was always the danger that someone might betray Collins for the money. The British arrested Christy Harte and offered him his freedom and a sizeable reward if he would telephone a certain number the next time Collins visited Vaughan's Hotel. Harte agreed, but promptly told Collins about the promise which he had no intention of keeping.

William Doran, the porter at the Wicklow Hotel, however, was apparently a different case. He was suspected of betraying some people, and Collins ordered the Squad to kill him. Doran had assisted Collins in the past and his widow thought British agents had killed her husband. She therefore appealed to the Sinn Féin regime for funds, as she had three small children. For her children's sake Collins ordered that she be given the money and not be told the true circumstances of her husband's death.

'The poor little devils need the money,' he said.

It was a humane response towards the family of a man whose death he had ordered, but he did not have the authority for such a gesture. It was the kind of thing that raised questions about his handling of finances.[5]

Brugha needled Collins relentlessly to provide the cabinet with a proper accounting of money allocated to purchase arms in Scotland. There was a discrepancy, which Collins was unable to resolve. In light of the pressure under which he was operating, together with the amount of money he had handled, the discrepancy was of little significance, other than as a whipping horse to attack his administrative credibility, if not his actually integrity.

Things got so bad that Mulcahy complained to de Valera about Brugha's attitude towards Collins.

'You know,' de Valera told him, 'I think Cathal is jealous of Mick. Isn't it a terrible thing to think that a man with the qualities that Cathal undoubtedly has would fall a victim to a dirty little vice like jealousy.'[6]

A small, sincere, resolute man, Brugha was dedicated to the cause with the zeal of a fanatic. While he and others worked unselfishly, he resented all the press attention given to Collins. Much as Mulcahy disliked Brugha's attitude, he never doubted his sincerity. 'He was naturally blunt and frank and was no more intending to intrigue than he was to diplomacy,' Mulcahy noted.[7]

A selfless, unassuming patriot, Brugha resented Collins for seeking personal glory and presuming too much. The Big Fellow was not content with his own legitimate ambit; he was always ready to take anything upon himself that he thought was for the good of the movement, even if meant meddling in the affairs of ministerial colleagues.

With his well-organised intelligence network, he was particularly well-placed to interfere. He knew more about what was happening throughout the movement than anyone, and he was able to exert considerable influence through an IRB clique of fellow Corkmen in key administrative positions. For instance, he managed to have himself replaced as adjutant general of the IRA by Gearóid O'Sullivan, and as director of organisation by Diarmuid O'Hegarty, who also became secretary to the government. Seán Ó Muirthile replaced Collins as secretary of the Supreme Council of the IRB, and Pádraig O'Keeffe was elected joint national secretary of Sinn Féin. Collins' influence with them was based largely on their recognition of his enormous organisational talents.

'A vast amount of stuff could be assembled associating his smiling buoyancy, his capacity for bearing tension, clearness of mind, perfectly controlled calm, and a devil-may-carishness,' wrote Mulcahy. 'His clarity of mind and his whole manner and demeanour, together with his power of concentration on the immediate matter in hand, gave him a great power over men.'[8]

Brugha so loathed the Big Fellow's personality, however, that he was apparently unable to see, much less appreciate, those qualities which so many admired. Maybe Collins' interference would have been more acceptable if he had not resented similar interference in his own areas. He seemed to think others should abide by certain rules, while he should be allowed to improvise as he went along.

'What the hell do you know about finance?' he snapped at Stack one day when the latter had the temerity to make some suggestion. 'I know more about finance, than you know about manners!' Stack replied.[9]

Though Collins and Brugha both belonged to the militant wing of the movement, there was a difference in their militancy. Brugha was 'a bit slow', according to de Valera, while Mulcahy described him as 'brave and as brainless as a bull'. Brugha basically reacted to events, whereas Collins provoked them.[10]

Collins had deliberately provoked the Black and Tan war to secure the support of the Irish people, but in the process he unleashed forces that he could not control and which would ultimately bring about his own death. Infuriated by the savagery of crown forces, Brugha wished to resurrect his old scheme to kill members of the British cabinet, but Collins realised that this kind of reaction would be to make the same mistake the British had made in Ireland; it would drive the British people into the arms of their militants. Hence Collins resolutely opposed Brugha's scheme.

'You'll get none of my men for that,' he declared.[11]

'That's all right, Mr Collins, I want none of your men. I'll get my own.'

Brugha called Seán MacEoin to Dublin and outlined the scheme to him. MacEoin agreed somewhat reluctantly to lead the attack.

'This is madness,' Collins thundered when MacEoin told him about the plan. 'Do you think that England has the makings of only one cabinet?' He suggested MacEoin consul the chief-of-staff.[12]

'I was appalled at the idea,' Mulcahy recalled.[13] He ordered MacEoin to go back to his command area and have nothing further to do with the proposed London project. On his way home by train on 3 March MacEoin was recognised and the auxiliaries arrested him at the railway station in Mullingar. He tried to run for it but was shot a number of times and seriously wounded. His capture was a serious blow, because he was one of the best IRA commanders and probably the most effective outside the Cork area.

'It is simply disastrous,' Collins wrote. 'Cork will be fighting alone now.'[14]

Collins wrote that he 'would almost prefer that the worst would have happened' than for MacEoin to have fallen into the hands of the enemy. He immediately set about planning MacEoin's escape as it was obvious the British intended to execute him as soon as he was fit enough to be tried and hanged.[15]

A rescue attempt had to be aborted when he was transferred from Mullingar to King George V Military Hospital in Dublin, and a number of different plans were considered to rescue him from the hospital. But he was moved to Mountjoy and the most audacious rescue attempt of all was carefully planned. This involved hijacking a British armoured car and sending it into Mountjoy with the aim of supposedly picking up MacEoin for questioning at Dublin Castle.

While working on this escape plan, Collins still continued to have the Squad target individuals.

The British brought Captain Cecil Lees back from the East in 1921 as they felt that he would be an excellent man for intelligence work in

Ireland. He joined the staff of Colonel Hill-Dillon with a reputation as an ace intelligence officer. Collins ordered that he should be killed as soon as possible, because he was reputed to use torture to extract information. Lees was staying in St Andrew's Hotel in Exchequer Street. He walked from there to work at Dublin Castle. As he left for work at 9.30 on the morning of 29 March, he was ambushed by Ned Bolster and Ned Byrne. 'He was accompanied by a lady, but we had no interest in her,' Ben Byrne recalled. 'We opened fire on Lees, and he fell mortally wounded.'[16] He was shot in the back and the back of his head. The bullet in his back exited through his chest. He was dead on arrival at hospital.

Collins demonstrated his reach five days later when Vincent Fouvargue from Ranelagh was killed on Ashford golf course in Middlesex, outside London. He had been in the IRA but offered his services to the British, according to Collins. He had been arrested by the British and had supposedly escaped from them one afternoon while being transferred. The truck in which he was being moved on 1 February supposedly came under fire and all the men chased the attackers, leaving Fourvargue to escape.

The story was 'too good to be true', both McNamara and Neligan told Collins. 'We thought it highly suspicious that this man should have escaped in broad daylight from an escort consisting of British intelligence officers who fired no shots,' according to Neligan. Reggie Dunne of the London IRA killed Fouvargue and left a note on the body: 'Let spies and traitors beware. IRA'.[17]

Meanwhile Collins' intelligence operations suffered another serious reversal with the discovery of his office at 5 Mespil Road, where most of his documents were stored. He had just left for the evening on 1 April, when the British raided the building, obviously acting on a tip. They found a considerable volume of material and staked out the office for his return next day. Patricia Hoey and her mother, who lived in the house, were held captive.

As they waited through the night, Hoey came up with a scheme to warn Collins. She had her mother pretend to become seriously ill and persuaded the British to allow her to summon a doctor. Alice Barry, the doctor who had put up Breen at her home while he was recuperating some months earlier, was summoned and told of the trap set for Collins. She managed to get word to Joe O'Reilly, and Collins and his staff were intercepted and warned the next morning.

'They waited for me all day Saturday,' Collins wrote to de Valera. 'The lady says they were so frightened they certainly would not have hit me in any case.'[18]

It was a touch of that raw vanity that some people found unbearable. The British had little to fear from Collins himself, as far as Brugha was concerned, because there was no evidence he ever fired a shot at any of them. While Collins had been in the GPO during Easter Week 1916, he would have had very little opportunity to fire at anyone then because crown forces had given the building a wide berth and had merely shelled it from afar. In view of the regularity with which people were stopped and searched in the streets of Dublin during the ensuing War of Independence, Collins did not normally carry any weapons, which really required a considerable amount of courage, especially after the fate suffered by his friends Dick McKee and Peadar Clancy.

Men like Tom Barry and Liam Deasy, who visited Dublin during the early spring, marvelled at the fearless way in which Collins moved about the city. Although they had both come up from the thick of the action in west Cork, they found Dublin unnerving.

Deasy and Gearóid O'Sullivan's brother, Tadgh, met Collins in Devlin's bar and joined him at a race meeting in Phoenix Park, with the place crawling with military and police. Yet Collins and his people showed no fear. 'Nothing would do him now but to bring us into the reserved stand where we stood shoulder to shoulder with the enemy,' Deasy noted.

'Good God!' Tadgh O'Sullivan exclaimed, 'these fellows are mad.'[19]

That night they adjourned to Vaughan's Hotel, and when someone warned Collins that it would be curfew time in twenty minutes, he was dismissive. 'To hell with curfew and them that enforce it,' he replied.[20]

'They seemed to have no fear of arrest, or if they had, they did not show it,' Barry wrote. 'Their lack of precautions was amazing and even made one angry.'

'One night at about nine o'clock,' Barry recalled, 'we ran into a hold up by about fifty Auxiliaries.' They were each searched. 'I was next to Collins and he put up such a fine act, joking and blasting in turn, that he had the whole search party of terrorists in good humour in a short time.' Needless to say they were not detained, but Barry was critical that Collins had not taken the precaution of sending a scout ahead.[21]

'Mick as usual guffawed and chaffed me about being a windy West Cork beggar,' Barry noted. 'Failing to see the joke, I told him crossly that it was quite true, I was a windy beggar, as I had a wholesome regard for my neck.'[22]

For months de Valera had been emphasising that the Irish side was prepared to negotiate a settlement with the British, but Collins told Carl Ackermann in early April that the IRA was going to continue the fight 'until we win'.[23]

'What are your terms of settlement?' Ackermann asked.

'Lloyd George has a chance of showing himself to be a great statesman by recognising the Irish Republic.'

'Do you mean a Republic within the British Commonwealth of Nations or outside?'

'I mean an Irish Republic.'

'Why are you so hopeful?'

'Because I know the strength of our forces and I know our position is infinitely stronger throughout the world,' Collins explained. 'The terror the British wanted to instil in this country has completely broken down. It is only a question of time until we shall have them cleared out.'

'So you are still opposed to compromise?'

'When I saw you before I told you that the same effort which would get us Dominion Home Rule would get us a Republic. I am still of that opinion, and we have never had so many peace moves as we have had since last autumn.'[24]

The British believed there was a power struggle going on in which de Valera was little more than a figurehead, crying in the wilderness for a negotiated settlement while Collins, the real leader, wanted to fight it out to the bitter end.

'De Valera and Michael Collins have quarrelled,' Lloyd George told his cabinet on 27 April. 'The latter will have a Republic and he carries a gun and he makes it impossible to negotiate. De Valera cannot come here and say he is willing to give up Irish independence, for if he did, he might be shot.'[25]

Dublin Castle had been predicting the IRA was on the verge of collapse before Christmas, but by April this collapse seemed no nearer. 'The tenacity of the IRA is extraordinary,' Tom Jones wrote to Bonar Law. 'Where was Michael Collins during the Great War? He would have been worth a dozen brass hats.'[26]

Bold statements from Collins undoubtedly contributed to the impression that the IRA was full of fight and thus undermined the credibility of Dublin Castle, but they also undermined de Valera's efforts to force the British to the conference table. From April 1921, the president later told his authorised biographers, 'Collins did not accept my view of things as he had done before and was inclined to give public expression to his own opinions even when they differed from mine.'[27]

De Valera and Brugha moved to whittle away at Collins' power base. The Squad was amalgamated with the active service unit of the Dublin brigade, and Collins was replaced by Stack as the designated substitute in the event of anything happening to the president.

Lloyd George wished to negotiate but he felt it would be pointless talking with de Valera, because Collins was the real leader, and he was afraid of the political repercussions among Conservatives if he talked with Collins. 'The question is whether I can see Michael Collins,' he said. 'No doubt he is the head and front of the movement. If I could see him, a settlement might be possible. The question is whether the British people would be willing for us to negotiate with the head of a band of murderers.'[28]

When the British cabinet discussed the possibility of a truce on 12 May, Lloyd George remarked that 'de Valera does not agree with the gun business', but Collins was uncompromising. Churchill, one of the most vocal proponents of the British terror, was now showing distinct signs of wavering. 'We are getting an odious reputation,' he said. It was 'poisoning' Britain's relations with the United States, so he was now in favour of a truce.[29]

But there was no point in having a truce without trying to negotiate a settlement, Austen Chamberlain, the newly elected leader of the Conservative Party, argued. He saw no point in this 'as long as de Valera is at the mercy of Michael Collins'.

'You can't make a truce without meeting with Michael Collins,' Lord FitzAlan declared. 'We can't have that.'[30]

The cabinet divided, with Churchill and four other Liberal Party ministers in favour of a truce, while Lloyd George sided with the Conservative majority. A fortnight later the British had to reconsider the Irish situation in the light of further developments.

On 14 May the plan to rescue MacEoin was implemented. Members of the Squad hijacked an armoured car escorting a lorry collecting meat at the abattoir on the North Circular Road for Portobello barracks. The crew of the armoured car, the lorry and the staff at the abattoir were held prisoners while Pat McCrae drove off in the Peerless armoured car. He picked up Charlie Dalton's brother Emmet, who was dressed in his old British officer's uniform along with Joe Leonard in another of Dalton's uniforms. Dalton waved an official-looking paper and they were allowed to drive into Mountjoy jail and the inner gates were opened for them. McCrae turned the armoured car and parked it so that the inner gates could not be closed. Dalton and Leonard jumped out of the car smartly and went to the office of Governor Charles Munroe. The plan had been for MacEoin to be there, but he had not been allowed to see the governor as there was a change of auxiliary guards at the prison that morning and they were being shown the prisoners.

Dalton produced a forged order to hand over MacEoin, but Munroe was suspicious and started to call Dublin Castle to verify the order. 'I sprang for the telephone and smashed it,' Leonard said. Dalton drew his gun and held up the governor and his staff while Leonard tied them up.[31] They then made a hasty retreat and managed to drive out of the prison amidst some shooting. Had MacEoin made it to the governor's office, they would probably have pulled off the most dramatic of escapes.

'The men worked glorious and gallantly, but they just failed to achieve complete triumph,' Collins wrote the next day. 'It was nobody's fault. There were no mistakes made. Things went on splendidly up to the last moment, and then there was a mishap. Our men fought their way out of the prison, and sustained only one slight casualty.'[32]

The differences between de Valera and Collins over the issue of major military confrontations were coming to a head. Oscar Traynor, the officer commanding the Dublin brigade, recalled a meeting at 40 Herbert Park attended by de Valera, Brugha, Stack, Collins, Traynor, Seán Russell and some others.

'Something in the nature of a big action in Dublin was necessary in order to bring public opinion abroad to bear on the question of Ireland's case,' de Valera argued. 'He felt that such an action in the capital city, which was as well known abroad as London or Paris, would be certain to succeed.' De Valera suggested that seizing the headquarters of the auxiliaries at Beggar's Bush barracks, 'would capture the imagination of those he had in mind, apart from the serious blow it would constitute to the enemy. As an alternative to this he suggested the destruction of the Custom House, which was the administrative heart of the British civil service machine in this country.'The Custom House was the headquarters of the inland revenue and various tax offices, the assay office, local government and the companies registration office. Traynor, as the officer commanding the Dublin brigade, was assigned the task of considering the alternative operations and reporting to the army council.

He had the help of the Big Fellow's intelligence people. 'Two weeks were spent on the investigation and examination of the possibilities of capturing Beggar's Bush,' Traynor noted. 'The experience of the men engaged on this work was such that they reported against such an operation. My activities were then turned to the alternative suggestion – the Custom House.'[33]

On 24 May, the eve of the attack on the Custom House, the British suffered an embarrassment when Brigadier General Frank Crozier, the recently resigned head of the auxiliaries, went public with a blistering attack on the conduct of some of his men and the Black and Tans generally. He said they had fired into the crowd in Croke Park on Bloody Sunday without provocation. The pressure on the British government might not have been as great if the crown forces were seen to be making progress, but the reverse had been evident, and things seemed even worse the next day with the attack on the Custom House, which was the largest single action in Dublin since the Easter Rising. Collins did not want any of his men to be involved, but he was overruled and members of the Squad were assigned to cover all entrances of the Custom House.

'I posted my twenty men at the various doors,' Paddy O'Daly noted. 'Their instructions were to allow nobody to leave the building once they went into position, but any civilian entering the building on business was to be admitted and then held prisoner so that the outside public would not be given the information that the building was held by the Volunteers.'[34]

'This was the only job allotted to the Squad,' he added. None of the staff at intelligence headquarters were involved. Collins gave strict orders 'that on no account were we to go near the Custom House, the reason being that he did not want to have everybody involved in it,' according to Dan McDonnell.[35]

Militarily the operation was a disaster. Over eighty of the men involved were arrested and five were killed. Paddy O'Daly, Joe Leonard and Vinny Byrne managed to escape, but most of the Squad were arrested, and Jim Slattery and Seán Doyle were both shot and wounded.

That evening Michael Collins viewed the Custom House for himself. Johnny Dunne and Joe Byrne of the Squad went with him. 'We walked down from the Engineer's Hall in Gardiner's Row and mingled with the people,' according to Byrne. 'Collins did not say anything but smiled when he saw the place was still burning, and then moved off. We went up Abbey Street, turned into O'Connell Street and to Parnell Street. Immediately on entering Parnell Street, Auxiliaries were holding up people and Collins was held up. I heard him abuse the Auxiliary.'

'How dare you!' Collins said. 'Do you know who I am? Give me your name and number. I'll deal with you later.'

'The Auxiliary apologised and Collins went on his way,' Byrne continued. 'Apparently the Auxiliary was so excited about the incident that he left us by also. We proceeded to Kirwan's public-house, Parnell Street, and Collins stood us two glasses of malt.' But Dan McDonnell observed that Collins 'was not too happy about the results'.[36]

Pressure on Collins was growing. Crown forces raided his office at 22 Mary Street just after lunch the next day and narrowly missed him. He had transferred his intelligence office there following the raid on Mespil Road and would normally have been there at the time, but had a foreboding during lunch with Gearóid O'Sullivan and decided not to return to the office that afternoon. 'I ought to have been there at that precise moment,' he wrote.[37]

The raiding party raced through the offices merely counting those present as they looked for Collins. Alice Lyons, his secretary, had her hat and coat on, so she promptly walked out of the place as the security forces were combing the building looking for the Big Fellow. Later all of the people in the building were interviewed and the officer in charge noted that one person was missing.

'I distinctly remember meeting a lady in the inner office when we first entered,' he said. 'Where is she now?'[38]

'That must be Mick Collins who escaped disguised as a lady,' someone suggested in an undertone.

'They depended too much on my punctuality,' Collins noted. Bob Conlon, his messenger boy, was arrested and taken to Dublin Castle.[39]

'They did not ill-treat him,' Collins explained with characteristic vanity, because they 'thought if they did that M.C. would murder them all.'[40] In fact, they actually did mistreat the boy, by using thumbscrews on him. And Collins found himself just one step ahead of crown forces in the following days.

'I may tell you the escape of Thursday was nothing to four or five escapes I have had since,' Collins wrote to de Valera on 1 June. 'They ran me very close for quite a good while on Sunday evening.'[41] He still tried to think of himself as not being on the run. 'He is on the run who feels he is on the run,' Collins wrote to Moya Llewelyn Davies in June. 'I have avoided that feeling.'[42]

The close calls were adding to his popular mystique, but his influence within the IRA was clearly on the wane. He had lost control of the Squad, whose remaining members were absorbed by the Dublin brigade.

Although the attack on the Custom House had been a military disaster, it was a propaganda coup and thus a political victory. The British government came under intense international pressure to alter its Irish policy.

The seventy-two police officers and soldiers killed that month seemed to make a mockery of Greenwood's predictions that the IRA was about to collapse. At first the British decided to declare martial law throughout the twenty-six counties and intensify the campaign. Collins learned that British forces were going to be trebled, and would intensify their searches and internment. 'All means of transport, from push bicycles up, will be commandeered, and allowed only on permit,' he warned de Valera.[43]

Before implementing this policy, however, Lloyd George was advised to make a genuine effort to negotiate a settlement. Otherwise, Jan C. Smuts, the South African premier, predicted irreparable damage would be done to relations within the British Commonwealth.

Smuts played an important role in persuading the British to initiate talks. It was decided to use the occasion of the opening of the new Northern Ireland Parliament by King George V on 22 June to foreshadow a more conciliatory approach. This process was nearly halted the same day, however, when de Valera was arrested by British soldiers. They possibly did not realise the government had ordered that he should be left alone. He was released the next morning, and asked to make himself available for a message from the British government. This was an invitation to talks in London with Lloyd George. The invitation set in motion the discussions that led to an agreed truce that was due to come into effect on 11 July 1921.

William Darling, who was serving as Major-General Tudor's secretary in Dublin Castle recalled a strange incident one night when he was sent out to collect a 'high official' following an accident in Newry. A police car was involved in a collision with the vehicle containing the official. When Darling arrived at the scene he found a group of men standing around with the official. They had been going from Belfast to Dublin, and they piled into Darling's car.

Collins got into the front with Darling and the driver. He could feel the gun that Darling was carrying. 'Are you carrying a gun?' Collins asked.[44]

'I am.'

He then guessed at Darling's name but was wrong, so he suggested a couple of other names. This time he was right.

'Do you know me?' Collins asked

'No,' Darling replied. 'I think I know your friends, but I don't know you.'

'I am Michael Collins.'

'Are you the Michael Collins whom the British police have made famous?'

'What do you mean by that?'

'A police force has a duty to apprehend criminals,' Darling explained. 'If they fail to apprehend criminals one defence is to say that the criminal whom they cannot apprehend is the most astute, remarkable, astonishing criminal in history, and so I say: "Are you Michael Collins whom the British police force have made famous?"'

Collins laughed at that. They talked on the way to Dublin and they were driven to 'an hotel in one of Dublin's squares'. They all went into the hotel. Collins chatted with Darling until the official was ready to leave.

'That was an astonishing thing meeting Michael Collins,' Darling remarked when they got into the car.

'What do you mean?' the official asked.[45]

He had not realised it was Collins. He rushed back into the hotel, but Collins was gone. Darling did not identify the official, but it was possibly Alfred Cope, who remains the most shadowy figure of the period.

Very shortly afterwards, just before the truce came into effect, Cope and Collins met. Tadhg Kennedy, who had worked for Collins in Dublin and was the officer in charge of intelligence in the Kerry No. 1 brigade of the IRA called to Vaughan's Hotel to meet Collins, who told him that a truce had been arranged. He invited Kennedy to sit in on a meeting that he was having with Cope.

'Mick again announced about the Truce.'[46] The Black and Tan War was over and they drank brandy and champagne to celebrate it.

Behind the scenes there were some ominous developments. De Valera selected four cabinet colleagues to accompany him to London — Griffith, Stack, Count George N. Plunkett and Robert Barton, as well as Erskine Childers, the acting minister for propaganda. On the evening that the truce Kathleen O'Connell noted that 'Collins called out this evening and spent several hours with the President'. He tried to insist on his own inclusion in the team going to London, but the president flatly refused to have him, saying that he feared the negotiations 'might end in a stalemate and that war might be resumed, so he saw no reason why photographers should, at this stage, be given too many opportunities of taking pictures of Collins'. They had an acrimonious meeting, with the Big Fellow refusing to accept the explanation because, for one thing, it could not be squared with de Valera's attempt to send him to the United States earlier in the year. 'Hot discussion,' Kathleen noted. 'President rather upset.'[47]

Having been already been demoted in favour of Stack, of all people, Collins was now being ignored for peripheral figures like Laurence O'Neill, the lord mayor of Dublin, and the Dáil deputy Robert Farnan, who had been invited along with his wife. In addition, two secretaries, Kathleen O'Connell and Lily O'Brennan were going.

'At this moment,' Michael Collins wrote after the truce came into effect on 11 July 1921, 'there is more ill-will within a victorious assembly than ever could be anywhere else except in the devil's assembly. It cannot be fought against. The issues and persons are mixed to such an extent as to make discernability an utter impossibility except for a few.' It was an ominous beginning to the peace negotiations, which are covered in another book, *I Signed My Death Warrant: Michael Collins and The Treaty.*[48]

Notes

Preface

1 Dáil Éireann, *Debate on the Treaty*, 20, 327.
2 *Ibid.*
3 *Ibid.*, 325.
4 Liam Collins to author, 19 Sept. 1990.
5 *Ibid.*

1 'Mind that Child'

1 Dwyer, *Big Fellow, Long Fellow*, 10.
2 *Ibid.*
3 Forester, *Lost Leader*, 7.
4 Dwyer, *Big Fellow, Long Fellow*, 11.
5 Hayden Talbot, *Michael Collins' Own Story*, 23.
6 *Ibid.*
7 Dwyer, *Big Fellow, Long Fellow*, 12.
8 *Ibid.*
9 Collins to Kevin O'Brien, 16 October 1916.
10 Rex Taylor, *Michael Collins*, 26–7.
11 *Ibid.*
12 Hannie Collins to Piaras Béaslaí, 25 Sept. 1923, Béaslaí Papers, MS 33,929 (19), NLI.
13 *Ibid.*
14 Talbot, *Michael Collins' Own Story*, 25.
15 Frank O'Connor, *The Big Fellow*, 20
16 *Ibid.*
17 Hannie Collins to Béaslaí, 25 Sept. 1923.

18 Collins, 'Evils of Undue Aggregation', Collins Papers, Marquette University [CPMU]
19 Collins, 'Letter to a friend who thinks the British Empire is expanding too rapidly, and his reply', CPMU.
20 *Ibid.*
21 *Ibid.*
22 *Ibid.*
23 Collins, 'Presence of Mind,' CPMU.
24 *Ibid.*
25 Collins, 'Nothing venture nothing have', 24 Apr. 1908, CPMU.
26 *Ibid.*
27 *Ibid.*
28 Collins, 'Contentedness of Mind,' 9 Oct. 1908, CPMU.
29 Collins, 'Charity and Its Abuses', 7 Nov. 1908, CPMU.
30 Béaslaí, *Michael Collins*, 1:19.
31 Collins, address on the Irish Famine, CPMU.
32 *Ibid.*
33 *Ibid.*
34 Rex Taylor, *Michael Collins*, 27.
35 Collins, 'Finland and Ireland', CPMU.
36 *Ibid.*
37 *Ibid.*

2 Collins and the GAA

1 Collins, *The Path to Freedom*, 122–23.
2 Frank O'Connor, *The Big Fellow*, 20.
3 Béaslaí, *Michael Collins*, 1:80.

4   Mrs Batt O'Connor, BMH WS 330.
5   Frank O'Connor, *The Big Fellow*, 37.
6   Béaslaí, *Michael Collins*, 1:304.
7   Collins, *The Path to Freedom*, 122.
8   *Ibid.*
9   Hart, *Mick*, 41.
10 *Ibid.*, 42.
11 Geraldine Club Minutes, 8 Jan. 1909, Béaslaí Papers, MS13329 (4), NLI
12 Geraldine Club Minutes, 21 July 1909, *Ibid.*
13 J. Harrison's report, 21 July 1909, Béaslaí Papers, MS13329, NLI (5)
14 Collins to Stack, 4 Nov. 1918, MS 5848, NLI.
15 Collins report of half-year ending December 1909, MS13329 (4). NLI.
16 Collins, report, Béaslaí papers, MS13329 (3), NLI.
17 Collins report of half-year ending December 1909, MS13329 (4). NLI.
18 *Ibid.*
19 Collins, Minutes of half-yearly general meeting of July 1910.
20 Collins, Minutes of Committee meeting, 18 Sept. 1910.
21 Rule 13.
22 Collins, report of meeting of 30 Mar. 1911.
23 Hart, *Mick*, 46–9.
24 *Ibid.*, 48.
25 Collins, Minutes of half-yearly meeting of 29 June 1912.
26 Taylor, *Michael Collins*, 31.
27 Collins to Seán Deasy, 5 January 1916.
28 Patrick Collins to Michael Collins, 8 March 1915, Béaslaí Papers, MS13329(2), NLI.
29 Hannie Collins, interview with David Adare FitzGerald, who kindly provided a tape.

3   Preparing for the Rebellion

1   Collins to Hannie Collins, 27 Jan. 1916, in Forester, *Michael Collins*, 34.
2   Good, *Enchanted by Dreams*, 18.
3   *Ibid.*, 18–19.
4   Ó Faoláin, *Constance Markievicz*, 144.
5   *Ibid.*
6   Comyn, *Irish at Law*, 64.
7   Alfred Cotton, BMH WS 184.
8   *Ibid.*
9   *Ibid.*
10 *Ibid.*
11 See Gavan Duffy, BMH WS 381. Gavan Duffy was a member of the Casement defence team at his trial.
12 Gavan Duffy, BMH WS 381.
13 Cotton, BMH WS 184, NAI.
14 Fr F.M. Ryan to George Gavan Duffy, 12 July 1916, *Irish Times*, 3 July 1998.
15 MacColl, *Roger Casement*, 166.
16 Fr Ryan interview, *Evening Mail*, 20 May 1916.
17 Tadhg Kennedy, BMH WS 135.
18 Fr Ryan interview, *Evening Mail*, 20 May 1916.
19 *Kerry Evening Post*, 22 Apr. 1916.
20 Christopher Andrews, *Secret Service*, 356.
21 Verbatim transcript of Casement's interrogation 23–25 Apr. 1916, article by Lord Kilbracken, *Irish Times*, 3 Jul. 1998.
22 *Ibid.*
23 Seán McGarry, BMH WS 368, NAI.

24   Brennan-Whitemore, *Dublin Burning*, 33.

25   Coffey, *Agony at Easter*, 4.

26   Dudley Edwards, *Patrick Pearse*, 277.

27   Caulfield, *Easter Rebellion*, 22.

4.   'We Lost, Didn't We!'

1   Brennan-Whitemore, *Dublin Burning*, 39.

2   *Ibid.*

3   *Ibid.*

4   *Ibid.*, 27.

5   Frank O'Connor, *The Big Fellow*, 28.

6   Coffey, *Agony at Easter*, 75.

7   *Ibid.*, 39

8   Dudley Edwards, *Patrick Pearse*, 291.

9   *Ibid.*

10   Coffey, *Agony at Easter*, 157.

11   FitzGerald, *Desmond's Rising*, 146.

12   *Ibid.*

13   Peadar Kearney, 'The Soldier's Song'.

14   Coffey, *Agony at Easter*, 154.

15   Pearse's address, 27 April, 1916, in Coffey, *Agony at Easter*, 171–2.

16   Pearse, *Political Writings*, 299.

17   *Ibid.*

18   Coffey, *Agony at Easter*, 76.

19   Taylor, *Michael Collins*, 31.

20   Collins to Kevin O'Brien, 6 Oct. 1916.

21   Dudley Edwards, *Patrick Pearse*, 245.

22   Collins to Kevin O'Brien, 6 Oct. 1916.

23   *Ibid.*; and 9 Nov. 1916.

24   Collins to Kevin O'Brien, 6 Oct. 1916 in Taylor, *Michael Collins*, 57–8.

25   *Ibid.*

26   Dudley Edwards, *Patrick Pearse*, 299.

27   Caulfield, *Easter Rebellion*, 320.

28   Coffey, *Agony at Easter*, 254–5.

29   *Ibid.*

30   Ryan, *Remembering Sion*, 207.

31   *Ibid.*

32   O'Broin, *W.E. Wylie*, 19–20.

33   Coffey, *Agony at Easter*, 260.

34   Ryan, *Remembering Sion*, 208.

35   Good, *Enchanted by Dreams*, 78.

36   O'Connor, *A Terrible Beauty*, 116.

5.   'In the End They'll Despair'

1   Joe Sweeney, interview, Griffiths and O'Grady, *Curious Journey*, 93.

2   Ryan, *Remembering Sion*, 211.

3   Collins to Hannie Collins, 16 May 1916.

4   Coogan, *Michael Collins*, 48.

5   *Ibid.*

6   *Ibid.*, 49.

7   Sweeney interview, Griffiths and O'Grady, *Curious Journey*, 93.

8   Ryan, *Remembering Sion*, 215.

9   Collins to Susan Killeen, 27 June 1916 in Coogan, *Michael Collins*, 50.

10   Collins to Hannie Collins, undated, (29 June 1916), in Forester, *Michael Collins*, 52.

11   Coogan, *Michael Collins*, 50.

12   *Ibid.*

13   O'Connor, *With Michael Collins*, 88.

14   J.I.C. Clarke, 'The Fighting Race,' in O'Connor, *A Book of Ireland*, 65–7.

15   Collins in autograph book at Frongoch, in Seán O'Mahony, *Frongoch*, 81.

16   Collins to Hannie Collins, 25 Aug. 1916.

17 Joe Sweeney, interview, Griffiths and O'Grady, *Curious Journey*, 95.

18 O'Connor, *With Michael Collins*, 90.

19 Brennan, *Allegiance*, 153.

20 Collins to Seán Deasy, 12 Sept. 1916.

21 O'Mahony, *Frongoch*, 19.

22 Collins to Susan Killeen, n.d., in Coogan, *Michael Collins*, 58.

23 Frank O'Connor, *The Big Fellow*, 37.

24 Collins to Jim Ryan, 23 Aug. 1916, P88/34, UCDA

25 Collins to Hannie Collins, 28 Oct. 1916.

26 *Ibid.*, 25 Aug. 1916.

27 Collins to Susan Killeen, 21 Sept. 1916, in Coogan, *Michael Collins*, 52.

28 Collins to Seán Deasy, 29 Sept. 1916.

29 *Ibid.*, n.d.

30 *Ibid.*, 12 Oct. 1916.

31 Letter from internees to T.M. Healy, 4 Oct. 1916 in *Gaelic American*, 2 Dec. 1916.

32 *Ibid.*

33 Collins to Hannie Collins, 25 Aug. 1916.

34 Collins to James Ryan, 2 Oct. 1916, P88/34, UCDA.

35 Collins to Hannie Collins, 28 Oct. 1916.

36 Richard Mulcahy, 'Conscription and the General Headquarters Staff,' *Capuchin Annual*, 1968, 386.

37 O'Mahony, *Frongoch*, 105.

38 *Ibid.*, 122.

39 *Gaelic American*, 16 Dec. 1916.

40 Béaslaí, *Michael Collins*, 1:114.

41 Collins to Seán Deasy, 22 Oct. 1916.

42 Cameron, *An Autobiography*, 161.

43 Collins to Seán Deasy, 8 Dec. 1916.

44 O'Mahony, *Frongoch*, 164; Joe O'Reilly notes, Béaslaí Papers, MS33929 (14), NLI.

45 Joe O'Reilly notes, *Ibid.*

46 O'Mahony, *Frongoch*, 164.

47 Joe O'Reilly notes, Béaslaí Papers, MS33929 (14), NLI.

6. 'Being Called Bad Names'

1 Collins to Hannie Collins, 29 Dec. 1916.

2 Rex Taylor, *Michael Collins*, 62.

3 Collins to Seán Deasy, n.d.

4 Collins to Hannie Collins, 24 Feb. 1917.

5 Collins to Seán Deasy, 19 Jan. 1917

6 Collins to Hannie Collins, 24 Feb. 1917.

7 *Ibid.*, 23 Jan. 1917.

8 Collins to Thomas Ashe, 24 Apr. 1917.

9 Ryan, *Remembering Sion*, 235.

10 *Ibid.*

11 Collins to Ashe, 24 Apr. 1917.

12 Sinn Féin election poster.

13 Brennan, *Allegiance*, 51–2.

14 *Ibid.*

15 Collins to Nora Ashe, 22 Aug. 1917.

16 Collins to Seán Deasy, 6 Sept. 1917.

17 Collins to Hannie Collins, 8 Oct. 1917.

18 De Valera's address to Ard Fheis, 25 Oct. 1917.

19 Mulcahy, 'Notes on Béaslaí's Michael Collins', MS 41.

20 Mulcahy, address, 29 Oct. 1963.

21 Collins to Hannie Collins, 10 Apr. 1917.

22 *Ibid.*

23 *Ibid.*, 20 Apr. 1918.

24 Dwyer, *De Valera's Darkest Hour*, 12.

25 *Ibid.*

26 Ned Broy, BMH WS 1,280.

27 Figgis, *Recollections of the Irish War*, 210.

28 *Ibid.*

29 Collins to Stack, 19 Aug. 1918.

30 *An t-Óglách*, 14 Oct. 1918.

31 O'Connor, *With Michael Collins*, 155.

32 Collins to de Lacy, 31 Aug. 1918.

33 *Ibid.*, 14 Sept. 1918.

34 Dwyer, *Big Fellow, Long Fellow*, 63.

35 *Ibid.*

36 Collins to Stack, 29 Aug. 1918.

7. 'All Ordinary Peaceful Means are Ended'

1 Collins to Stack, Nov. 1918.

2 *Ibid.*, 9 Dec. 1918.

3 Collins, election address, December 1918.

4 Barton, BMH WS 979.

5 Dwyer, *Big Fellow, Long Fellow*, 66.

6 For ester, *Michael Collins*, 97.

7 Collins to Stack, 15 Jan. 1919.

8 Breen, *My Fight for Irish Freedom*, 38–9.

9 *Ibid.*

10 Donie Murphy, *The Men of the South*, 57.

11 Macready, *Annals of an Active Life*, 434; *An t-Óglácht*, 31 Jan. 1919.

12 Patrick O'Donoghue, BMH WS 847.

13 *Ibid.*

14 Kelly, 'Escape of de Valera,' in *Sworn to be Free*, 35.

15 Collins to Stack, 9 Feb. 1919.

16 Liam McMahon, BMH WS 274.

17 *Ibid.*

18 Desmond Ryan, *Unique Dictator*, 100.

19 *Freeman's Journal*, 22 Mar. 1919.

20 Figgis, *Recollections of the Irish War*, 240.

21 *Ibid.*

22 *Ibid.*, 243.

23 *Ibid.*

24 Longford and O'Neill, *De Valera*, 90.

25 Coogan, *Michael Collins*, 104.

26 Patrick J. Berry, BMH WS 942.

27 Robert C. Barton, BMH WS 979.

28 *Ibid.*

29 Béaslaí, 'Twenty Got Away,' *Sworn to be Free*, 50.

30 Paddy O'Daly, BMH WS 220.

31 *Ibid.*

32 *Ibid.*

33 Frank O'Connor, *Big Fellow*, 63.

34 *Ibid.*

8. 'Too Many of the Bargaining Type'

1 O'Connor, *With Michael Collins*, 135.

2 O'Connor, *The Big Fellow*, 49.

3 *Ibid.*

4 Broy, BMH WS 1,280.

5 *Ibid.*

6 Coogan, *Michael Collins*, 106.

7 Mulcahy, address, 29 October 1963, Mulcahy Papers, UCDA.

8 Collins, *The Path to Freedom*, 69–70.

9 *Ibid.*

10   *Ibid.*

11   The file was later published in
     Stewart (ed.), *Michael Collins: The
     Secret File*, 40–41.

12   Broy, BMH WS 1,280.

13   Figgis, *Recollections of the Irish War*,
     247.

14   *Dáil Debates*, 1 (10 April 1919):
     46.

15   *Ibid.*, 67.

16   Broy, BMH WS 1,280, NAI.

17   De Valera speech, 11 Apr. 1919 in
     Dwyer, *De Valera's Darkest Hour*, 16.

18   *Dáil Debates*, 1 (11 April 1919),
     76.

19   Dwyer, *Big Fellow, Long Fellow*,
     78.

20   *Ibid.*

21   *Ibid.*, 79.

22   Béaslaí, *Michael Collins*, 2:297.

23   Collins to Stack, 11 May 1919.

24   Collins to Donal Hales, 16 May
     1919.

25   Ryan, *Remembering Sion*, 233.

26   Taylor, *Michael Collins*, 81.

27   Collins to Stack, 17 and 18 May
     1919.

28   Collins to Stack, 17 May 1919.

29   *Ibid.*, 18 May 1919.

30   *Ibid.*, 6 June 1919.

31   Collins to Boland, 19 July 1920.

32   Collins to Stack, 20 July 1920.

9.   'We Struck at Individuals'

1   Mrs Batt O'Connor, BMH WS
    330.

2   T.P. Coogan, *Michael Collins*, 117.

3   Jim Slattery, BMH WS 445.

4   Béaslaí, *Michael Collins*, 1:327.

5   *Ibid.*

6   *Ibid.*, 1:327–8.

7   Collins to de Valera, 25 Aug. 1919

     in Macardle, *The Irish Republic*,
     280–2.

8   De Valera to Collins, 6 Sept. 1919,
    in Béaslaí, *Michael Collins*, 1:353.

9   De Valera to Collins, 9 Sept 1919,
    in Béaslaí, *Michael Collins*, 1:
    353–4.

10   Collins to de Valera, 6 Oct. 1919,
     in Béaslaí, *Michael Collins*, 1:354.

11   Collins to de Valera 14 October
     1919, in Béaslaí, *Michael Collins*,
     356–7.

12   Collins to Hales, 11 Sept. 1919.

13   Collins to de Valera, 6 Oct. 1919.

14   Fisher to Lloyd George, 15 May
     1920 in McColgan, *British Policy
     and the Irish Administration*, 8.

15   Eibhlin Lawless, BMH WS 414.

16   *Ibid.*

17   Béaslaí, *Michael Collins*, 1:342.

18   Eibhlin Lawless, BMH WS 414.

19   Collins to Harry Boland, 13 Sept.
     1919, Ó Muirthile, 'Memoirs',
     MS, UCDA.

20   Forester, *Michael Collins*, 129.

21   Jim Slattery, BMH WS 445.

22   *Ibid.*

23   O'Daly, BMH WS 387.

24   Collins, *The Path to Freedom*,
     60–70.

25   *Ibid.*

26   O'Malley Notebook, UCD in
     Coogan, *Michael Collins*, 117.

27   Coogan, *Michael Collins*, 116.

28   *Ibid.*, 118.

29   Collins to Donal Hales, 11 Sept.
     1919.

30   H. Boland to Collins, in Ó Muirth-
     ile, MS, Mulcahy Papers, UCDA.

31   Sean Kavanagh interview, Grif-
     fiths and O'Grady, *Curious Journey*,
     137.

32   Breen, *My Fight*, 39.

33 *Ibid.*, 83.

34 Deasy, *Towards Ireland Free*, 80–1.

35 *Ibid.*

10 'Spies Beware'

1 Béaslaí, *Michael Collins*, 1:344.

2 *Ibid.*, 1:373–4.

3 Neligan, *Spy in the Castle*, 67.

4 Collins to Michael Ahern, Nov. 1919.

5 Report of Hurley's trial, *Irish Times*, 7 Feb. 1921.

6 James Slattery, BMH WS 445, NAI.

7 Broy, BMH WS 1285, NAI.

8 O'Connor, *With Michael Collins*, 147.

9 *Ibid.*

10 Report, 7 Dec. 1919, Eunan O'Halpin, 'British Intelligence in Ireland, 1914–21,' in Andrew and Dilks, *The Missing Dimension*, 71.

11 *Ibid.*

12 Quinlisk to MacMahon, 11 Nov. 1919, Béaslaí, *Michael Collins*, 1:393–402.

13 Collins to Hannie Collins, early Dec. 1919, in Forester, *Michael Collins*, 130.

14 French to Londonderry, 3 Jan. 1920, in Andrew, *Secret Service*, 364.

15 Mulcahy, 'Notes on Béaslaí's Michael Collins', MS, 1:127.

16 O'Connor, *With Michael Collins*, 158.

17 *Ibid.*, 159.

18 Collins to Art O'Brien, 20 Jan. 1920.

19 Forester, *Michael Collins*, 133.

20 Sgt W. Mulhern, report, 1 Jan. 1920, in Stewart, *Michael Collins*,
170–171.

21 J. Willard, report, 2 Jan. 1920, in *Ibid.*, 174.

22 H. O'Connor, note, 8 Jan. 1920, in *Ibid.*, 177.

23 H. O'Connor, note, 8 Jan. 1920, in *Ibid.*, 177.

24 Collins, letter to 'A Chara', 30 Dec. 1919, in *Ibid.*, 162–3.

25 Dolan, BMH WS 663, NAI.

26 O'Daly, BMH WS 387, NAI.

27 Dolan, BMH WS 663, NAI.

28 Andrew, *Secret Service*, 366.

11 'Well Shoot Him So'

1 Collins to Donal Hales, 25 Feb. 1920.

2 *Ibid.*, 15 Mar. 1920.

3 Ó Muirthile, 'Memoirs,' MS, 102.

4 *Ibid.*

5 *Ibid.*

6 *Cork Examiner*, 22 Feb. 1920.

7 *Ibid.*, 24 Feb. 1920.

8 O'Connor, *Big Fellow*, 92.

9 Lily Mernin, BMH WS 441.

10 Coogan, *Michael Collins*, 133.

11 Vinny Byrne, BMH WS 423.

12 *Ibid.*

13 James Slattery, BMH WS 445.

14 *Ibid.*, BMH WS 445.

15 *Gaelic American*, 18 Sept. 1920.

16 Collins to D. Hales, 15 Dec. 1920.

17 *Irish Times*, 19 Apr. 1920.

18 Collins to MacSwiney, 22 Mar. 1920, in Forester, *Michael Collins*, 135.

19 Collins to R.J. Cowman, 31 Mar. 1920, in Béaslaí, *Michael Collins*, 1:432.

20 Collins to D. Hales, 26 Mar. 1920.

21 *Irish Times*, 15 Apr. 1920

22 Paddy O'Daly, BMH WS 387.

23 James Slattery, BMH WS 445, NAI.

24 Inquest report, *Irish Times*, 22 Apr. 1920.

25 Paddy Daly, BMH WS 387.

26 *Ibid.*

27 Maurice Hankey, diary, 30 Apr. 1920, in Roskill, *Man of Secrets*, 2: 153.

28 MacSwiney address, Con Harrington, 'Arrest and Martyrdom of Terence MacSwiney', The Kerryman, *Rebel's Cork Fighting Story*, 87.

29 Hankey, diary, 23 May 1920, in Roskill, *Man of Secrets*, 2:153.

30 *Ibid.*

31 *Ibid.*

32 Jones, diary, 31 May 1920, *Whitehall Diary*, 3: 19–23.

33 *Ibid.*, 19–28.

34 *Ibid.*

35 Neligan, *Spy in the Castle*, 69.

36 Tadgh Kennedy, BMH WS 1,413.

37 *Ibid.*

38 *Ibid.*

39 Neligan, *Spy in the Castle*, 69.

40 Tadgh Kennedy, BMH WS 1,413.

41 Neligan, BMH WS 380.

42 Broy, BMH WS 1,280.

12 Settling Old Scores

1 Griffiths and O'Grady, *Curious Journey*, 79.

2 *Ibid.*

3 O'Daly, BMH WS 387.

4 Frank Thornton, BMH WS 618.

5 Con Casey, 'The Shooting of Divisional Commander Smyth, The Kerryman, *Rebel Cork's Fighting Story*, 78.

6 *Ibid.*

7 *Ibid.*

8 *Ibid.*

9 Mee, *Memoirs*, 131–2.

10 *Ibid.*, 133; see Smythe's account of the incident, *Irish Times*, 30 July 1920.

11 *Cork Examiner*, 27 July 1920.

12 James Slattery, BMH WS 445.

13 Crozier, *Ireland for Ever*, 218.

14 Seán Culhane, BMH WS 746.

15 McCorley, BMH WS 389.

16 *Ibid.*

17 Mulcahy, 'Notes on Béaslaí's Michael Collins', MS 2:22, Mulcahy Papers, UCDA.

18 *Ibid.*

19 Jones, *Diary*, 23 July 1920, *Whitehall Diary*, 3:28.

20 Wilson, diary, 1 Sept. 1920, in James Gleeson, *Bloody Sunday*, 110.

21 Collins to D. Hales, 13 Aug. 1920.

22 *Philadelphia Public Ledger*, 26 Aug. 1920.

23 *Ibid.*

24 Hankey, diary, 5 Oct. 1920, in Roskill, *Man of Secrets*, 2:196.

25 Jones, diary, 3 Nov. 1920, *Whitehall Diary*, 3:41.

26 Collins to Art O'Brien, 10 Oct. 1920.

27 Crozier, *Ireland for Ever*, 102.

28 Stove to King, 2 Mar. 1920, in Béaslaí, *Michael Collins*, 1:429.

29 *Ibid.*

30 Anonymous letter to MacCurtain, received 16 Mar. 1920.

31 Béaslaí, *Michael Collins*, 1:448.

32 *Ibid.*

33 O'Broin, *Michael Collins*, 57.

34 *Freeman's Journal*, 17 Sept.1920.

35 *Ibid.*

36 *Ibid.*

37 Collins to Griffith, 5 Oct. 1920.

38 *New York World*, 20 Oct.1920.

39 Sturgis, diary, 1 Sept. 1920, *The Last Days of Dublin Castle*, 32.

13 'I'll Report You to Michael Collins'

1 Neligan, *Spy in the Castle*, 107.
2 Broy, BMH WS 1,285.
3 Breen, *My Fight*, 142.
4 *Ibid.*
5 *Ibid.*, 152.
6 Neligan, *Spy in the Castle*, 130–1.
7 Neligan interview, Griffiths and O'Grady, *Curious Journey*, 186.
8 Vincent Byrne, BMH WS 423.
9 Joe Dolan, BMH WS 663.
10 David Neligan, BMH WS 380.
11 *Ibid.*
12 *Ibid.*
13 Neligan, *Spy in the Castle*, 132.
14 Neligan, BMH WS 380.
15 Béaslaí, *Michael Collins*, 2:59
16 Collins to Donal Hales, 18 Oct. 1920.
17 Mulcahy, 'Notes on Béaslaí's Michael Collins,' MS, 2:31.
18 Wilson, diary, 29 Sept. 1920, in Callwell, *Henry Wilson*, 2:263; Bennett, *Black and Tans*, 96.
19 Wilson diary, 14 Oct. 1920, in Callwell, *Henry Wilson*, 2:265.
20 Dwyer, *The Squad*, 145.
21 Wilson, diary, 13 Oct. 1920, in Callwell, *Henry Wilson*, 2:265.
22 *Manchester Guardian*, 3 Oct. 1920.
23 *Ibid.*
24 'Kevin Barry', Walton's, *Down By the Glenside*, 64.
25 For events in Tralee, see Dwyer, *Tans, Terror and Troubles*, 228–53.
26 *Ibid.*
27 See *New York Times*, 5 Nov. 1920.
28 *Irish Times*, 9 Nov. 1920.

29 Hankey, diary, 10 Nov. 1920, in Roskill, *Man of Secrets*.

14 'They Got What They Deserved'

1 Taylor, *Michael Collins*, 104.
2 *Ibid.*
3 Mulcahy, 'Notes on Béaslaí's Michael Collins', MS, 2:31.
4 Seán Kavanagh interview, Griffiths and O'Grady, *Curious Journey*, 174.
5 Collins to Kathleen MacCormack, 7 Apr. 1922.
6 Crozier, *Ireland for Ever*, 102.
7 Collins, notes in Taylor, *Michael Collins*, 106.
8 *Ibid.*
9 Andrews, *Dublin Made Me*, 153.
10 Hankey, diary, 25 Nov. 1920, in Roskill, *Man of Secrets.*
11 Gaughan, *Memoirs of Jeremiah Mee*, 189.
12 *Ibid.*
13 Mulcahy, 'Notes on Béaslaí's Michael Collins,' MS, 2: 51.
14 Kee, *Ireland*, 188.
15 Desmond Fitzgerald to D. O'Hegarty, 29 Nov. 1920.
16 O'Kelly, *Stepping Stones*, 13.
17 Seán Ó Muirthile, 'Memoirs', MS., 125, Mulcahy Papers.
18 Jones, diary, 1 Dec. 1920, *Whitehall Diary*, 41–2.
19 *Ibid.*, 43.
20 *Ibid.*
21 Sturgis, diary, 6 Dec. 1920, in *Last Days of Dublin Castle*, 87.
22 Collins to Clune, 6 Dec. 1920.
23 Collins to P. O'Keeffe, 6 Dec. 1920.
24 Collins to editor, *Irish Independent*, 7 Dec. 1920.

25 *Ibid.*
26 Art O'Brien to Collins, 9 Dec. 1920.
27 *The Times*, 11 Dec. 1920.
28 Collins to Griffith, 14 Dec. 1920.
29 Jones, *Whitehall Diary*, 3:41.
30 Collins to Griffith, 16 Dec. 1920.
31 Vinny Byrne, BMH WS 423.
32 Béaslaí, *Michael Collins*, 2:136.
33 Jones, *Whitehall Dairy*, 3:47.
34 *Irish Times*, 14 Dec. 1920.
35 Jones, *Whitehall Dairy*, 3:45.
36 Jones, diary, 20 Dec. 1920, *Whitehall Diary*, 3:46.
37 Collins to D. O'Hegarty, 9 Dec. 1920.
38 Béaslaí, *Michael Collins*, 2:173.
39 *Ibid.*

15 'He's No Big Fella to Me'

1   Longford, *Peace by Ordeal*, 81.
2   Mulcahy, 'Notes on Béaslaí's Michael Collins,' MS, 2: 23.
3   *Ibid.*, 2:36.
4   Younger, *Ireland's Civil War*, 95.
5   Barry interview, in Griffiths and O'Grady, *Curious Journey*, 169.
6   O'Connor, *My Father's Son*, 117–8.
7   *Ibid.*
8   Beasiaí, *Irish Independent*, 28 Aug. 1963.
9   O'Connor, *With Michael Collins*, 170–1.
10 *Ibid.*
11 *Ibid.*, 171.
12 Collins to Stack, 20 July 1919.
13 Collins to H. Boland, 19 Apr. 1920.
14 Flanagan to Collins, in Collins to Griffith, 16 Mar. 1920.
15 *Gaelic American*, 4 and 11 Sept. 1920.

16 Collins to Devoy, 30 Sept. 1920.
17 Terry de Valera, *A Memoir*, 138.
18 Dáil Éireann, *Parliamentary Debates*, 27 (22 Nov. 1928), 605–6.
19 Terry de Valera, *A Memoir*, 131.
20 Mulcahy, 'Notes on Béaslaí's Michael Collins,' MS, 2:61.
21 De Valera to Collins, 18 Jan. 1921.
22 *Ibid.*
23 O'Connor, *Big Fellow*, 134.
24 Neligan, *Spy in the Castle*, 130.
25 Béaslaí, *Michael Collins*, 2:161.
26 Broy, BMH WS 1,285.
27 Béaslaí, *Michael Collins*, 2:93.
28 *Irish Times*, 18 Jan. 1921.
29 Béaslaí, *Michael Collins*, 2:181.
30 *Ibid.*
31 Winter, *Winter's Tale*, 345.
32 *Ibid.*
33 Collins to Sr Mary Celestine Collins, 5 Mar. 1921.
34 *Ibid.*
35 O'Connor, *Big Fellow*, 105.
36 Mulcahy, 'Notes on Béaslaí's Michael Collins', MS, 2: 45; Béaslaí, *Michael Collins*, 2: 76.
37 Taylor, *Michael Collins*, 96.
38 William Stapelton, BMH WS 822.
39 *Ibid.*
40 Dwyer, *The Squad*, 212.
41 *Ibid.*
42 Broy, BMH WS 1,280.
43 Neligan, *Spy in the Castle*, 108.
44 *Ibid.*, 109.
45 *Ibid.*, 126.
46 Broy, BMH WS 1,280.

16 'You'll Get None of My Men'

1   *New York Evening World*, 27 Jan. 1921; see also *Gaelic-American*, 19 Feb. 1921.

2 De Valera's answers to *Manchester Guardian* questionnaire, *Gaelic American*, 26 Feb. 1921.

3 De Valera to Robert Brennan, 28 Apr. 1921.

4 *Boston American*, 29 Jan. 1921.

5 Longford, *Peace by Ordeal*, 45.

6 Mulcahy, 'Notes on Béaslaí's Michael Collins', 2:73.

7 *Ibid.*

8 *Ibid.*, 45, 56.

9 Colum, *Arthur Griffith*, 264.

10 De Valera to McGarrity, 27 Dec. 1921, MS 17,440, NLI; Mulcahy, *Richard Mulcahy (1886-1971)*

11 Colum, *Arthur Griffith*, 223.

12 Ó Broin, *Michael Collins*, 76.

13 Mulcahy, 'Notes on Béaslaí's Michael Collins', MS, 2: 84

14 Collins to Q. M. 2nd Cork Brigade, 7 Mar. 1921.

15 *Ibid.*

16 B.C. Byrne, BMH WS 631.

17 Neligan, BMH WS 380.

18 Béaslaí, *Michael Collins*, 2:212.

19 Liam Deasy, *Towards Ireland Free*, 256.

20 *Ibid.*, 257.

21 Barry, *Guerrilla Days in Ireland*, 164.

22 *Ibid.*

23 Collins replies, *Freeman's Journal*, 22 Apr. 1921.

24 *Ibid.*

25 Jones, *Whitehall Diary*, 3: 60.

26 Jones to Bonar Law, 24 Apr. 1921, *Whitehall Diary*, 3:55.

27 Longford and O'Neill, *De Valera*, 148.

28 Riddell, *Intimate Diary of the Peace Conference and After 1918–1923*, 288.

29 Jones, *Whitehall Diary*, 3: 68–69.

30 *Ibid.*, 70.

31 Joe Leonard, BMH WS 547.

32 Dwyer, *The Squad*, 240.

33 Oscar Traynor, BMH WS 340.

34 Paddy [O']Daly, BMH WS 387.

35 Dan McDonnell, BMH WS 486.

36 *Ibid.*

37 Collins to de Valera, 1 June 1921.

38 Dwyer, *The Squad*, 250.

39 Collins to de Valera, 1 June 1921.

40 *Ibid.*

41 *Ibid.*

42 Collins to Moya Llewelyn Davies, 24 June 1921.

43 Collins to de Valera, 16 June 1921.

44 Darling, *So It Looks to Me*, 211.

45 *Ibid.*, 212.

46 Tadhg Kennedy, BMH WS 1413.

47 Dwyer, *I Signed My Death Warrant*, 27–28.

48 *Ibid.*, 7.

Bibliography

NOTE: Much of the research for this book is based on letters written by Michael Collins, many of which were in private hands. I have had access to four separate private collections in the course of my research, including Collins' own personal papers. Other letters written by him relating to the period covered in this book can be found among the papers of colleagues deposited in the National Library of Ireland, State Paper Office in Dublin Castle, the archives of University College and Trinity College, Dublin, as well as the Marquette University.

Manuscript Sources

Robert Barton: Assorted Papers, Trinity College, Dublin.
Piaras Béaslaí: Papers, National Library of Ireland.
R. Erskine Childers: Papers and Diaries, Trinity College, Dublin.
Michael Collins: Papers, National Library of Ireland and private source.
Michael Collins: Papers, Marquette University, Milwaukee, Wisconsin, USA.
Dáil Éireann: Papers in the DE2 series, National Archives, Dublin.
John Devoy: Papers, National Library of Ireland.
Geroge Gavan Duffy: Papers, National Archives of Ireland.
Joseph McGarrity: Papers, National Library of Ireland.
Richard Mulcahy: Papers, University College Dublin Archives.
Art O'Brien: Papers, National Library of Ireland.
James O'Mara: Papers, National Library of Ireland.
Ernie O'Malley: Papers and Notebooks, University College Dublin Archives.
James Ryan: Papers, University College Dublin Archives.
Austin Stack: Papers, National Library of Ireland, and two private sources.

Bureau of Military History Witness Statements, *Irish Army Archives and National Archives:*

Maurice Ahern, 483.
Liam Archer, 819.
Robert Barton, 979.
Seán Beaumont, 709.
Patrick J. Berry, 942.
John C. Bolger, 1,745.
Eamonn Broy, 180, 1,285.

Bernard C. Byrne, 631.
Joseph Byrne, 461.
Vincent Byrne, 423.
Alfred Cotton, 184.
Seán Culhane, 746.
Charles Dalton, 434.
Emmet Dalton, 641.
Joe Dolan, 900.
James Doyle, 127.
Thomas Duffy, 1409.
George Fitzgerald, 684.
Christopher Fitzsimons, 581.
Thomas Fox, 365.
George Gavan Duffy, 381.
Christopher Harte, 2.
Joe Hyland, 644.
Patrick Kennedy, 499.
Tadhg Kennedy, 135, and 1,413.
Joe Lawless, 414.
Patrick Lawson, 667.
Joseph Leonard, 547.
Roger McCorley, 389.
Patrick McCrae, 413.
Seán McGarry, 368.
Michael McDonnell, 225.
Liam McMahon, 274.
Hugo MacNeill, 1,377.
Lily Mernin, 441.
David Neligan, 380.
Seán Nunan, 1,744.
Mrs Batt O'Connor, 330.
Major General P. (O')Daly, 220, 387.
Patrick O'Donoghue, 847.
Julia O'Donovan, 475.
P.S. O'Hegarty, 26.
Patrick O'Keeffe, 1,725.
James Slattery, 445.
William James Stapelton, 822.
Frank Saurin, 715.
Liam Tobin, 1,753.
Oscar Traynor, 340.
Frank Thornton, 615.
George White, 956.

Published Works

Andrew, Christopher, S*ecret service: The Making of the British Intelligence Community* (London, 1985)

Andrew, C.M. and Dilks, David N. (eds), *The Missing Dimension: Government and Intelligence Communities in the Twentieth Century* (London, 1984)

Andrews, C.S., *Dublin Made Me: Autobiography* (Dublin and Cork, 1979)

Barry, Tom, *Guerrilla Days in Ireland* (Tralee, 1962)

Béaslaí, Piaras, 'How it was Done - IRA Intelligence', in The Kerryman, *Dublin's Fighting Story, 1916-1921* (Tralee, n.d.)

____ *Michael Collins and the Making of the New Ireland*, 2 vols (Dublin, 1926)

____ 'Twenty Got Away', in The Kerryman, *Sworn to be Free*

Bennett, Richard, *The Black and Tans* (New York, 1959)

Brashier, Andrew and Kelly, John, *Harry Boland: A Man Divided* (Dublin, 2000)

Breen, Dan, *My Fight for Irish Freedom* (Dublin, 1950)

Brennan, Robert, *Allegiance* (Dublin, 1950)

Brennan-Whitmore, W.J., *Dublin Burning: The Easter Rising from Behind the Barricades* (Dublin, 1996)

____ *With the Irish in Frongoch* (Dublin, 1917)

Callwell, C.E., *Field Marshal Sir Henry Wilson: His Life and Diaries*, 2 vols (London, 1927)

Cameron, Sir Charles, *An Autobiography* (Dublin, 1920)

Carty, Xavier, *In Bloody Protest: The Tragedy of Patrick Pearse* (Dublin, 1978)

Casey, Con, 'The Shooting of Divisional Commander Smyth', in The Kerryman, *Rebel Cork's Fighting Story* (Tralee, n.d.)

Caulfield, Max, *The Easter Rebellion* (London, 1964)

Coffey, Thomas M., *Agony at Easter: The 1916 Rising* (London, 1969)

Collins, Michael, *Michael Collins: In His Own Words*, Francis Costello (ed.), (Dublin, 1997)

____ *The Path to Freedom* (Dublin, 1922)

Colum, Pádraig, *Arthur Griffith* (Dublin, 1959)

Comyn, James, *Irish at Law: A selection of famous and unusual cases* (London, 1981)

Connolly, Colm, *The Shadow of Béal na mBláth* (Radio Telefís Éireann, 1989)

Coogan, Tim Pat, *De Valera: Long Fellow, Long Shadow* (London, 1993)

____ *Michael Collins: A Biography* (London, 1990)

____ *1916: The Easter Rising* (London, 2001)

Costello, Francis, *Enduring the Most: The Life and Death of Terence MacSwiney* (Dingle, 1995)

Crozier, Frank, *Ireland for Ever* (London, 1932)

Dáil Éireann, *Official Report: Debate on the Treaty Between Great Britain and Ireland* (Dublin, 1922)

Dalton, Charles, *With the Dublin Brigade, 1917-1921* (London, 1929)

Darling, William Y., *So it looks to me* (London, n.d.)

De Valera, Terry, *A Memoir* (Dublin, 2006)

Deasy, Liam, *Towards Ireland Free: The West Cork Brigade in the War of Independence 1917-1921* (Dublin and Cork, 1973)

Doherty, Gabriel and Keogh, Dermot (eds), *Michael Collins and the Making of the Irish State* (Cork, 1998)

Dudley Edwards, Ruth, *Patrick Pearse: The Triumph of Failure* (London, 1977)

Dwyer, T. Ryle, *Big Fellow, Long Fellow: A Joint Biography of Michael Collins and Eamon de Valera* (Dublin, 1998)

_____ *De Valera's Darkest Hour: In Search of National Independence, 1919-1932* (Dublin and Cork, 1982)

_____ *'I Signed My Death Warrant': Michael Collins & The Treaty* (Cork, 2007)

_____ *Tans, Terror and Troubles: Kerry's Real Fighting Story, 1913-1923* (Cork, 2001)

_____ *The Squad and the intelligence operations of Michael Collins* (Cork, 2005)

Ebenezer, Lyn, *Frongoch and the Birth of the IRA* (Wales, 2006)

Figgis, Darrell, *Recollections of the Irish War* (London, 1927)

FitzGerald, Desmond, *Desmond's Rising: Memoirs 1913 to Easter 1916* (Dublin, 2008)

_____ *The Memoirs of Desmond FitzGerald* (London, 1968)

Fitzpatrick, David, *Harry Boland's Irish Revolution* (Cork, 2003)

Forester, Margery, *Michael Collins: The Lost Leader* (London, 1971)

Foy, Michael T., *Michael Collins' Intelligence War: The Struggle between the British and the IRA, 1919-1921* (Gloucestershire, 2006)

Gaughan, J. Anthony, *Austin Stack: Portrait of a Separatist* (Dublin, 1977)

_____ *The Memoirs of Constable Jeremiah Mee, RIC* (Dublin, 1975)

Gleeson, James, *Bloody Sunday* (London, 1962)

Good, Joe, *Enchanted by Dreams: The Journal of a Revolutionary* (Dingle, 1996)

Griffiths, Kenneth, and O'Grady, Timothy E., *Curious Journey: An Oral History of Ireland's Unfinished Revolution* (London, 1982)

Hart, Peter, *Mick: The Real Michael Collins* (London, 2005)

Jones, Thomas, *Whitehall Diary: Volume 3: Ireland, 1918-1925*, Keith Middlemass (ed.), (London, 1971)

Kee, Robert, *Ireland: A History* (London, 1981)

Kelly, Bill, 'Escape of de Valera', in The Kerryman, *Sworn to be Free* (Tralee, 1971)

Kerryman, The, *Dublin's Fighting Story, 1916-1921* (Tralee, n.d.)

_____ *Rebel Cork's Fighting Story: From 1916 to the Truce with Britain* (Tralee, n.d.)

_____ *Sworn to be Free: The Complete Book of IRA Jailbreaks, 1918-1921* (Tralee, 1971)

Longford, Earl of, and O'Neill, Thomas P., *De Valera* (London and Dublin, 1970)

McColgan, John, *British Policy and the Irish Administration 1920-22* (London, 1983)

McGarry, Seán, 'Michael Collins,' in The Kerryman, *Dublin's Fighting Story, 1916-1921* (Tralee, n.d.)

MacColl, R., *Roger Casement* (London, 1960)

MacDowell, Vincent, *Michael Collins and the Irish Republican Brotherhood* (Dublin, 1997)

MacEoin, UinSeánn (ed.), *Survivors*, (Dublin, 1980)

Mackay, James, *Michael Collins: A Life* (Edinburgh, 1996)

Macardle, Dorothy, *The Irish Republic* (London, 1968)

Macready, General Sir Nevil, *Annals of an Active Life*, 2 vols (London, 1924)

Maher, Jim, *Harry Boland: A Biography* (Cork, 1998)

Mulcahy, Richard, 'Conscription and the General Headquarters' Staff,' *The Capuchin Annual,* 1968

____ 'Chief of Staff, 1919', *The Capuchin Annual,* 1969

Mulcahy, Risteárd, *Richard Mulcahy (1886-1971): A Family Memoir* (Dublin, 1999)

Murphy, Donie, *Men of the South* (Midleton, 1991)

Neeson, Eoin, *The Life and Death of Michael Collins* (Cork, 1968)

Neligan, David, *The Spy in the Castle* (Dublin, 1968)

O'Broin, Leon, *Michael Collins* (Dublin, 1980)

O'Connor, Batt, *With Michael Collins in the Fight for Irish Independence* (London, 1929)

O'Connor, Frank, *A Book of Ireland* (London, 1959)

____ *My Father's Son* (London, 1968)

____ *The Big Fellow: Michael Collins and the Irish Revolution* (Dublin, 1965)

O'Connor, Ulick, *A Terrible Beauty* (London, 1975)

Ó Cuinneagáin, Míchael, *On the Arm of Time: Ireland 1916-22* (Donegal, 1992)

O'Donovan, Donal, *Kevin Barry and His Time* (Dublin, 1989)

Ó Faoláin, Seán, *Constance Markiewicz* (London, 1987)

O'Halpin, Eunan, 'British Intelligence in Ireland, 1914-21,' in Andrew and Dilks, *The Missing Dimension*

O'Kelly (Sceilg), J.J., *Stepping Stones* (Dublin, 1939)

O'Mahony, Seán, *Frongoch: University of Revolution* (Dublin, 1987)

O'Malley, Ernie, *On Another Man's Wound* (Dublin, 1936)

Osborne, Chrissy, *Michael Collins Himself* (Cork, 2003)

Pakenham, Frank, *Peace by Ordeal* (London, 1935)

Pearse, Padraic, *The Political Writings and Speeches of Patrick Pearse*, Desmond Ryan (ed.), (Dublin, 1966)

Riddell, Lord, *Lord Riddell's Intimate Diary of the Peace Conference and After 1918-1923* (London, 1933)

Roskill, Stephen, *Hankey: Man of Secrets*, 2 vols (London, 1970-74)

Ryan, Desmond, *Remembering Sion* (London, 1934)

____ *Unique Dictator: A Study of Eamon de Valera* (London, 1936)

Ryan, Meda, *Tom Barry: IRA Freedom Fighter* (Cork, 2003)

Stapleton, William J., 'Michael Collins' Squad', in *The Capuchin Annual,* 1969, 368-377

Steward, A.T.Q. (ed.), *Michael Collins: The Secret File* (Belfast, 1997)

Street, C.J.C., *Administration in Ireland, 1920* (London, 1921)

_____ *Ireland in 1921* (London, 1922)

Sturgis, Frank, *The Last Days of Dublin Castle: The Diaries of Mark Sturgis*, Michael Hopkinson (ed.) (Dublin, 1999)

Talbot, Hayden, *Michael Collins' Own Story as told to Hayden Talbot* (London, 1923)

Taylor, Rex, *Michael Collins* (London, 1958)

Townsend, Charles, *Easter 1916: The Irish Rebellion* (London, 2005)

_____ *The British Campaign in Ireland, 1919-21: The Development of Political and Military Policies* (London, 1975)

_____ 'The Irish Republican Army and the Development of Guerilla Warfare, 1916-1921', *English Historical Review*, 94: 318-345

Valiulis, Maryann Gialanella, *Portrait of a Revolutionary: General Richard Mulcahy and the Founding of the Irish Free State* (Dublin, 1992)

Winter, Ormonde, *Winter's Tale* (London, 1955)

Index